# The Great
# Empires
# of Asia

# The Great Empires of Asia

EDITED BY JIM MASSELOS
FOREWORD BY JONATHAN FENBY

WITH 27 ILLUSTRATIONS

**Note on spellings and transliterations**
There is no single agreed system for transliterating into the Western
alphabet names, titles and terms from the different cultures and
languages represented in this book. Each culture has separate traditions
for the most 'correct' way in which words should be transliterated from
Arabic and other scripts. However, to avoid any potential confusion
to the non-specialist reader, in this volume we have adopted a single
system of spellings and have generally used the versions of names
and titles that will be most familiar to Western readers.

*On the cover:* Map of Unidentified Islands off the Southern Anatolian
Coast, by Ottoman admiral and geographer Piri Reis (1465–1555).
Photo: The Walters Art Museum, Baltimore.

First published in the United Kingdom in 2010 by
Thames & Hudson Ltd, 181A High Holborn, London WC1V 7QX

This compact paperback edition first published in 2018

*The Great Empires of Asia* © 2010 and 2018
Thames & Hudson Ltd, London
Foreword © 2018 Jonathan Fenby

British Library Cataloguing-in-Publication Data
A catalogue record for this book is available from the British Library

ISBN 978-0-500-29442-0

Printed and bound in the UK by CPI (UK) Ltd

To find out about all our publications, please visit
**www.thamesandhudson.com**. There you can subscribe
to our e-newsletter, browse or download our current catalogue,
and buy any titles that are in print.

# CONTENTS

# The Legacy of Empire

JONATHAN FENBY

T he empires of Asia spanned 5,000 miles from the Pacific to the Balkans, marking the history of the planet for over a thousand years as they established realms that brought together a multiplicity of ethnic groups, cultures and religions. They were founded and led by some of the most extraordinary figures the world has seen: Chinggis Khan, the emperors of China claiming to hold the Mandate of Heaven, the Ottoman Sultans and the great Mughal emperor Akbar. They created capitals with architecture and cultural treasures to underline the awesome nature of their rule: the monuments of the Mughals, the Forbidden City of Beijing, the grandiose Suleimaniye mosque and Topkapı Palace in Constantinople/ Istanbul, the great edifices of Angkor and the mosques of Isfahan.

At the outset and often well beyond, military prowess was a constant theme as they fought to expand – and then defend – their vast territories. But rulers also had to develop systems of governance and bureaucracy to buttress their control while strengthening the economy of their domains and fostering trade that provided earnings for their subjects, tax revenue and links with other states. Their impact as they established themselves and then turned their conquered lands into imperial states is laid out in the seven chapters of this book, whose distinguished authors bring out the achievements and failings, similarities and differences, innovations and diversities that left an indelible print on history.

With the exception of Japan's expansion after the Meiji Restoration, these empires were notable for their longevity. They lasted for several centuries or, in the case of China, for more than two millennia. The political, economic and cultural legacies they left have shaped lands from the Pacific to the Mediterranean to this day, providing a powerful backdrop to the evolution of the 21st-century world.

Unlike later European colonies separated from the seat of power by thousands of miles of sea, these Asian empires were primarily land-based – so there was a direct geographical connection between the central capital and the further frontiers, with a melding of populations, customs and cultures along the route. That is not to say that maritime trade was irrelevant: with territories stretching round the Mediterranean and the Black Sea, the Ottomans had a formidable fleet, while Ming emperor Yongle sent admiral Zheng He on voyages through the seas of Asia and East Africa with a flotilla of huge ships to overawe local rulers and bring back treasure.

But the European model of using sea power for long-range conquest was not the way Asian empires operated. Rather, they followed a pattern in which the creators of empire established a base by defeating rival clans in local wars before expanding either to defend the homeland or in search of fresh territory. For the most far-flung empire of all, the Mongols, this process led from conflict on the steppes of north Asia to the throne of China, undertaking conquests as far west as the Black Sea and Ukraine, and reorganizing the nomad tribes into a nation that could field a million-strong army. At the end of this Asian saga, Japan played out in a relatively short time but on a huge scale the 'imperial syndrome' by which 'the enlargement of territory or influence was required to confirm the new political order, which then needed to defend new, contested boundaries.' This thirst for expansion and the strains it caused often came to spell the end of empires, even if the strength of the edifice constructed in the years of glory could stave off collapse for a long time.

While the empires and their rulers reigned supreme, with structures designed to buttress their authority, there was usually a degree of decentralization in such enormous territories. Conquered lands had to be made into entities that could contribute to the overall strength and prosperity of the empire. Far away in their capitals or out on military campaigns, sovereigns needed to ensure not only stability throughout their realms, but also supplies of food and goods for their troops and subjects. Smooth transport was essential to foster trade within and across imperial frontiers, and to guarantee the flow of tax revenue which commerce yielded. The construction of palaces and religious edifices required the mobilization of large labour forces from conquered lands – even more so the Great Wall of China under the Ming or the canals and reservoirs of the Khmer.

So, once they had brought new regions under control, the rulers had every interest in melding coercive rule with a degree of conciliation. Governance systems needed to draw on the best and brightest of their subjects. Commanding territory that stretched from Afghanistan to South India, the Mughal emperor Akbar pursued a policy of incorporating defeated princes into the administrative system while allowing them to remain as active heads of their ancestral lands; he proclaimed 'peace to all' and allowed freedom of worship. His overarching vision led the official historian to depict him as a semi-divine, enlightened father to his subjects.

The Ottoman empire, pre-dating the Mughals but outlasting them, can be seen as a set of concentric circles with core zones close to the centre, more remote frontier provinces and, even further away, loosely attached vassal or client states. The longevity of the emperors in Constantinople/Istanbul from 1281 to 1922 can be attributed, writes Gábor Ágoston, to their 'flexibility, pragmatism and relative tolerance for centuries over peoples who followed multiple religions and spoke languages as diverse as Turkic, Greek, Kurdish, Slavic, Hungarian, Albanian and Arabic.'

Once they had imposed themselves, empires generally offered a system of law and order and a bureaucracy that connected with the subjects, even if corruption and incompetence took hold when central control began to dissolve. It also offered tempting career prospects for ambitious young men if they joined the imperial service either as civil servants or as elite bodyguards and shock troops. For artists, architects and city planners, imperial capitals and courts provided a rich seedbed for achievement and innovation as the different chapters of this book make strikingly evident

– from the grandeur of the Taj Mahal and the monuments of Angkor to the finesse of Ottoman miniatures, the silk paintings of the Ming and the lines of Japanese prints. Safavid rulers of the sixteenth century presided over an extraordinary fusion of artistic achievement in painting, carpets, manuscripts, textiles, metalwork, book-binding and poetry, using resources from conquered lands to celebrate the greater glory of Persia.

Still, like all empires, the system rested, in the end, on top-down rule backed by seemingly invincible armies and the threat of savage retribution to any who opposed. Akbar might practice tolerance but his empire rested on the military conquests of his more warlike predecessors. As the founder of the biggest empire of them all, Chinggis Khan set the tone, blending harsh reality and a supranatural aura. After one victory he warned, 'I am the punishment of God' – if the defeated Muslims had not committed great sins, he added, 'God would not have sent a punishment'. On his death bed he told his sons and soldiers to continue a war against rebels in China until 'maimed and tamed, they are no more'.

Neither the original leaders nor their progeny harboured any doubt about the imperial mission; conquest was seen as a natural undertaking for the strong, and territories acquired by warfare were the personal possessions of the dominant clan. Power could be built in many ways, from the near-accidental to the carefully plotted process that led to the proclamation of the Khmer Jayavarman II as the Universal Monarch. But, however they achieved power, occupants of the throne could follow their whims as they wished whatever the results. Even if internal balances were built into the system, the basis of the empires was an assumption of autocratic authority. To challenge the emperor's will was treason.

Such patriarchal systems were prone to internal rivalries once the founder had died, the glue of personal power proving a source of fragility as well as a strength. Relatives, favourites, wives and concubines undermined effective rule, especially when the dynastic cycle ran into military defeat, economic strain or natural catastrophes that seriously weakened the original power base. Obsessions, too, led rulers down counterproductive paths. The later Ming period saw several spells when the emperor was a minor, withdrew from supervision of government, or surrendered authority to court eunuchs. A century after Akbar, a patron of the arts notably open to foreign influences, the Mughal Aurangzeb pursued sharia-driven policies, which, combined with his insistence on fighting southern rebels, significantly strained the fabric of the empire. Military failures led to a long period when the Ottomans 'reigned rather than ruled', as Ágoston puts it, while the Persian Shia Safavid empire suffered from growing factional rivalries and financial demands of senior court officials, on top of multiple military threats, before Isfahan fell to the Afghans in 1722.

The crushing defeat in 1945 of Japan, the last of the seven empires covered in this book, appeared to spell the end of Asian geopolitical power. The Ottomans had been succeeded by the Republic of Turkey in 1923, their empire splintered following defeat in the First World War. The final Chinese imperial dynasty, the Qing, gave up the throne in 1912 after a long decline. The British deposed the last Mughal ruler of India in 1858. Earlier empires – the Khmer, Mongols and Safavids – lived on in national memories but were no longer functioning regimes. After the most destructive of conflicts, the globe was dominated by the struggle between the United States and the Soviet Union, with an array of associated states on either side. When the Communist bloc collapsed around 1990, some prophesied the end of history and the West appeared to carry all before it.

Three decades later, things look very different, above all for Asia. China has become the second largest economy on earth and is playing an ever-growing international role as its leader, Xi Jinping, declares that it is time to move to the centre of the global stage. Japan ranks as the third biggest world economy and its government shows every sign of moving beyond the severely limited external and military role set out in its constitution of 1945. India is positioned to become a major power, the world's largest democracy led by a forceful government and with a population likely to exceed China's before long. South-east Asia is a vibrant region of ambitious nations. As in the days of the Safavid empire, Iran is asserting itself in counterpoint to Sunni nations – and the United States. Turkey has found a new nationalist confidence under a leader whose style harks back to the Ottomans. As growth rates have soared, forecasts roll out that the 21st century will belong to Asia, where supply chains bind economies together and new technology races ahead in ways unseen in the West.

Much of this is due to specifically 21st-century factors, but a distinct imperial legacy is still apparent. Size, population and economic weight are all vital; equally, Asian leaders' individual force of personality evokes the days of empire. For all his invocations of Marxism, Xi Jinping strikes a decidedly imperial pose, a new iteration of the Mandate of Heaven. Japan's ruling class have family ties to the era of expansion, an emperor still sits on the Chrysanthemum Throne, and its government made a major effort to mark the 150th anniversary of the Meiji restoration in 2018. India's dominant BJP party looks back to an era of national greatness (even if the rulers then were Muslim rather than Hindu). In Turkey, the evocation of its great era grow steadily more evident.

As global fragmentation rather than unchallenged Western supremacy has become the norm, the world seems set to return to a time that, in many ways, resembles the centuries in which the empires that fill this book rose and prospered. There are, of course, huge differences; yet the parallels are there. The past is not another country, but an integral, indeed often essential, part of the current narrative for leaders who seek to mould history to serve their current designs. So, while the accounts of Asian empires in this book are fascinating and authoritative in themselves, taken together they also lay down a basis for better understanding the world of today. Apart from anything else, they demonstrate the complexities of building and maintaining a great international presence, the unplanned elements in that process – and how empires can take on a self-fulfilling dynamic until excessive expansion and lack of a solid base points to disintegration.

**Jonathan Fenby** is author of *The Penguin History of Modern China* and edited and contributed to *The Seventy Wonders of China*.

# The Distinctiveness of Asian Empires

JIM MASSELOS

There have been many empires in Asia. Some of the greatest flourished during the last thousand years, holding sway over vast tracts of land and enormous populations, long before European powers began to move into the region two or three hundred years ago. These Asian empires were, of course, by no means the only imperial states on the planet in these centuries, but they were dominant world forces, some of them occupying and absorbing parts of Europe. This book presents empire as an Asian experience and as an Asian enterprise. It is about Asia as a stage for grand empire, not what the continent later became when subsumed within European imperial formations. For much of the past thousand years, and particularly up to and around the 1600s, Asian kingdoms dominated the world's political geography and it was Asian empires that constantly challenged the states of Europe, rather than the reverse. The following chapters collectively explore how this happened and provide fascinating insights into the characters, events and influences that shaped the great empires of Asia.

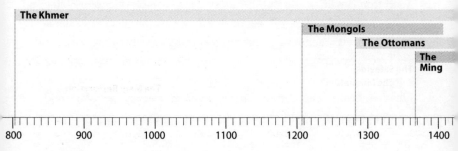

The Khmer

The Mongols

The Ottomans

The Ming

800        900        1000        1100        1200        1300        1400

Given the size of Asia and its multiplicity of cultures, religions and societies, it is natural that Asian empires should be highly diverse. In Asia, as elsewhere, each empire was a centre of power with its own focus and ethos. Only once in Asia's history did a single power, the Mongols, rule the greater part of the continent. The Mongol Empire fractured in less than two centuries and, even at its height, major regions such as Japan and much of South and South-East Asia did not fall under its sway. However, when the Mongol Empire atomized, it left a legacy probably as profound as that of the ancient Roman Empire or the British Empire in our own times. The seven chapters that follow show how, in different ways and at different periods, other empires emerged. The Ottomans from their Turkish home-land and the Safavids in Persia carved out their own spaces and in India the Mughals established a new sovereignty. The Yuan (a Mongol dynasty) were replaced in China by a native dynasty, the Ming – a good example of regional drives against external absorption. The Ming, in turn, were to be displaced by the Qing from Manchuria, who enlarged their empire even further, but it is the Ming on whom we focus in this volume. South-East Asia, meanwhile, remained unaffected by these upheavals, maintaining its own religious dynamic, its own rulers and governance and its own imperial structures. A bird's eye view reveals how a pattern of polycentric power, of separate co-existing kingdoms and empires in different parts of Asia, was asserted in the aftermath of the Mongol Empire's dissolution. So, indeed, were centralist structures of governance and a centrist ruling ethos within the individual empires.

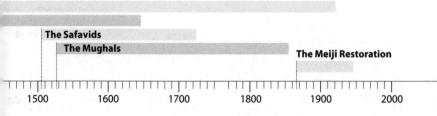

**The Safavids**

**The Mughals**

**The Meiji Restoration**

| | | | | | |
|---|---|---|---|---|---|
| 1500 | 1600 | 1700 | 1800 | 1900 | 2000 |

This, then, is what the contributors to this book collectively explore: locations and forms of power, underlying ideational structures and the profound contributions to culture and civilization made by these Asian states in the process of acquiring, and maintaining, imperial sway. Other examples of empires might have been chosen, and the same issues might also be profitably examined in relation to non-Asian states – but that is outside the scope of this book. The seven empires discussed here provide a sufficiently broad canvas to examine an imperial model for states of the time, and certainly its adaptability and acceptability throughout the Asian, and perhaps Euro-Asian, land mass. Evidently, there was no single over-arching Asian identity, nor a single Asian people, nor even a stereotypical 'Asian-ness' of the type so favoured by 19th-century European Orientalism. There were, however, encounters predicated on difference. The Ottomans bridged three continents in ways that went far beyond the geographic, with a concomitant range of cultural interactions, though their position depended largely upon assuring their Asian bases. In another sense, the Japanese under the Meiji Restoration did something comparable. Their bridge was their encounter with the new Western technologies of war and statecraft, which the Japanese adopted and used to conquer an area of land and sea in east Asia of unprecedented size. Such examples, in all their variability, give insight into how empires and imperial dynasties operated in times when an imperial structure was the dominant mode of governance and the working model to which all great leaders – more or less successfully – aspired.

## Elements of Empire

The seven chapters sweep across Asia, creating a vivid panorama of the regions of the continent and of the dominant empires. Each writer surveys an empire and its region. Each tells a different story in terms of an empire's rise and fall, the society and culture it expressed and the nature of its state organization. Despite the distinctiveness of the seven empires, there were overall similarities and links between them: the drive of individual leaders; innovative military technologies or strategies; the fashioning or refashioning of bureaucracies; the incorporation of subject populations; and the ethos and culture of the imperial state. The chapters articulate the differences between the seven empires, while collectively pointing to similarities and commonalities in these very different phenomena.

Together, such similarities help pinpoint the distinctive qualities of the Asian empires of the time. All were centralized around an emperor and his bureaucracy. Unlike his 19th-century European counterparts, whose power was considerably restricted by the rise of parliamentary democracy, he could be almost untrammelled in his exercise of power (though in some situations his bureaucrats did limit his actions). Each Asian emperor's dominance of the military assured his own personal position within the empire and protected his domains against external enemies. Inevitably, armies were critical to imperial survival: most of the empires were land-based, spreading over extensive contiguous territories. One exception was the Ottoman Empire, which of necessity had a powerful naval presence in the Mediterranean. Another was Japan, which in the late 19th and early 20th centuries built up a modern Western-style navy that enabled it to cross the sea and enter nearby Asian territories as a colonial power. The Chinese under the Ming dynasty also built navies, though after a time they withdrew from state seafaring enterprises. Generally, however, Asian empires (unlike their later European equivalents) were not physically separated from their home territory by the sea. They were characterized by their control of enormously extended and widespread land-based territories.

Any empire, by definition, has a big and diverse population, but the Asian empires controlled the world's largest populations in terms of size and included peoples of great ethnic and religious diversity. The empires were, perforce, multi-cultural and they were surprisingly accommodating in their treatment of their conquered ethnicities, nationalities and communities. The initial drive which led to the creation of these empires may have come largely from the energy of specific social groups – clans, tribes, and the like – but as empires stabilized they increasingly incorporated social diversities into their military and administrative structures of governance. In a very real sense the conquered peoples, or at least some of them, became part of the ruling establishments in most of these empires. A contradiction of empire was that what began with ferocious military campaigns, rampant cruelty, mass killings and destruction had an aftermath in which differences were accommodated and brought within the imperial body. Of course, without their subject populations the empires could not have functioned; the imperial economy and prosperity certainly depended on them. Peasants provided food and revenue, and also served as soldiers in the armies; merchants worked the trade routes, ensuring the interchange of goods and helping maintain contact between the various empires and kingdoms in Asia. The empires were not isolated entities, but were interconnected by trade, diplomacy and religion. Trade provided linkages, the means of transmission, at all sorts of levels, of both ideas and material goods. Conversely, empires also interacted with one another in conflicts over ambitions, objectives and interests that could, and did, end in wars and carnage.

Asian emperors amassed legendary wealth. Some of these riches were lavished on grand displays of ostentatious extravagance, and some went to develop and beautify the cities that were central to the empire – after all, the largest cities in the world at that time were in Asia. Enormous sums were spent on making the empire a hub of culture, sophistication and civilization. Prosperity provided the wherewithal to patronize the arts and sciences and to encourage intellectual and creative endeavours. Apart from all their other achievements, these Asian empires were renowned as centres of culture and civilization. An Asian style of empire was manifested in the grand buildings, the superb arts and crafts, the philosophical and religious speculation and the science and technology of the time. Each empire in itself was a superb artefact, a distinct – and distinctive – achievement, whatever the negative outcomes of unbridled power and military conquest.

## Emperors and Empires

The book begins with the largest land-based empire ever, that of the Mongols. At its height, as Timothy May reminds us, the empire stretched from the Sea of Japan to the Carpathian Mountains in Europe. There has been nothing like it, before or since: no empire has managed to conquer, much less rule, a domain as vast as that of the Mongols. That this explosion, this creation of a mighty new empire, happened over a single generation adds to the singularity of the achievement. Responsible for this feat of empire-building was one man, a minor tribal leader on the steppes who in 1206 CE became the mighty monarch known as Chinggis Khan. The title means 'Firm (or Fierce or Resolute) Ruler', and it was the quality of his charismatic leadership, his military genius and his insistent drive that gave him command over most of the Euro-Asian land mass and took him to the position of virtual world conqueror.

Chinggis Khan's achievement is not at all diminished by the fact that the empire as an entity lasted only a relatively short time before it disintegrated into constituent fragments through succession disputes. The impact of the Mongol Empire continued for centuries afterwards. Parts of it survived as viable entities for varying periods. Qubilai (Kubla) Khan, for instance, though nominally Khan of the empire, established himself as ruler of China and so founded the Yuan dynasty, which lasted until it was overthrown by the Ming in 1368. Elsewhere, over a century after Chinggis Khan's reign, Timur (Tamerlane) also made spectacular conquering sweeps, but his domains likewise atomized after his death. In the aftermath of the great Mongol Empire, successor states – small emirates and larger kingdoms – appeared across the Asian land mass, until many coalesced or were coerced into new state formations. These too were established or sustained through the actions of exceptional leaders. In the first few centuries of the millennium it would seem that a necessary pre-condition for the making of empire was the rise of a strong and brilliant ruler, though none managed to approach Chinggis Khan's extraordinary achievement.

Once an imperium was established by conquest, other factors and qualities were usually required to sustain and nurture the complex and varied entity that military successes had brought into being. Almost as important as the leader who established the empire were his successor monarchs. If they were lacking in the requisite abilities to govern and sustain their territories, then the empire could weaken or ultimately fail to survive as a potent entity.

The initial Indian conquests that established the Mughal dynasty were achieved in 1526 by the emperor Babur, a descendant of both Timur and Chinggis Khan. A minor princeling, he moved with his finely honed army from Central Asia down onto the dusty and often searingly hot plains of northern India. Here, his victories laid the basis of the Mughal Empire, while he continued to dream longingly of the walled gardens and moderate climes he had left behind and to which he never returned. It was left to his grandson, Akbar, to set up a lasting structure of governance and suitable policies for the new territories, though he also continued to expand his territories. In the process, as Catherine Asher shows us, he managed to create a wondrous artefact of an empire. He is often called Akbar 'The Great' in appreciation of his distinctive abilities, though the phrase is a tautology: the name Akbar itself means 'great'. In his regnal name he had already decided on his place in history. The qualities of the founding emperor might be critical, but the abilities of his successors were no less so.

The situation in the Ottoman Empire, centred on Turkey, was a little different. There, it was a succession of capable Ottoman rulers who managed to establish themselves on the Mongol periphery and then to withstand subsequent Mongol threats. At the same time they steadily built up an empire of their own by conquering neighbouring emirates. It was Sultan Mehmed II's conquest of Constantinople (Istanbul) in 1453 that won him the title of 'Conqueror' and set the seal on an empire that, as Gábor Ágoston reminds us, at its height straddled most of western Asia and North Africa, and made significant inroads into Europe. By the time of Suleiman I 'The Magnificent' (r.1520–66), the empire covered some

2.3 million square kilometres (888,035 square miles) of territory and had reached the pinnacles of artistic and cultural achievement that were commonly part of the collateral of empire creation.

The story in Persia was similar. There it was Ismail, the head of a militant Shia religious order, who through conquest won Persia (modern Iran). He declared himself Shah, or Ruler, of the new state and laid the basis for the Safavid rule of the region. Sussan Babaie shows how, between 1501 and 1722, the Safavids transformed Persia from a feudal to an early modern world economy and created an empire famed for its artistic and other achievements.

On the other side of Asia, in China, another great leader established a lasting empire. Zhu Yuanzhang led attacks against the ruling Yuan (Mongol) dynasty and, having defeated them, returned China to native Chinese rule. He declared himself emperor in 1368, assuming the regnal name of Hongwu, and became the founder of the Ming dynasty. He was followed by a succession of rulers, some of whom were capable, some not. As J.A.G. Roberts points out, for 276 years the Ming ruled a population larger than that of Europe at the time. In the process, like other post-Mongol empires, they reached new levels of culture and trail-blazing scientific achievement, the extent of which is still being comprehended.

In South-East Asia, where the Cambodian region was constantly under challenge from forces coming from what are now Thailand to the west and Vietnam to the east, it was a succession of monarchs who managed to build up and defend a kingdom centred around Angkor. Among them, as Helen Ibbitson Jessup outlines, was King Jayavarman VII, a relatively late ruler, who from the end of the 12th century focused the synergies of the region into building many of the glorious structures that abound in Angkor and elsewhere.

## Maintaining Empire

In such times an individual's ambition, and capacity to realize it, were essential in making an empire, but of course each would-be emperor also had to have military ability and required a formidable and well-organized army. This is true of more recent empires as well as earlier ones. Japan's invasions of mainland eastern Asia from the late 19th century were made possible by Japanese superiority in weaponry, military organization and discipline, much of it derived from Western examples and suppliers. Much earlier, at the other end of our time spectrum, Chinggis Khan's armies drew on Mongol nomadic pastoral communities who were mobile and accustomed to defending themselves. They had the advantage of fast horses able to conquer the enormous spread of the Asian steppes and, since the steppes were free of significant geographical barriers, to speed along what was virtually an early super-highway. As his territories expanded, Chinggis Khan needed to remove competing tribal and clan loyalties from his imperial military force and to provide a place for newly subjugated peoples within the state as well as the army. Timothy May shows how his restructuring of the military away from purely ethnic groupings, by using a 'decimal system' of organization, broke down clan loyalties and promoted a sense of unity in the new empire. Similarly, the pattern of civil governance that Chinggis Khan established gave conquered populations their own place and enabled them to be absorbed, to some extent, within the new imperial formation. The result was that clan, tribal, ethnic and regional identities were at least in part subsumed within the wider entity of empire.

The initial momentum in the making of empire came, more often than not, from the military expansion of specific, ethnically cohesive groups and depended upon their aggressive militant drive. However, an empire's subsequent success required, in part, the merging of such groups into new entities and the incorporation of at least some of the newly conquered. The military structure of the Ottoman Empire as it expanded illustrates the point. Between the 15th and 17th centuries, Gábor Ágoston considers the Ottoman army to have been one of the best-organized in the Euro-Asia land mass. The army had a tiered structure, ranging from the outer reaches of provincial forces deriving from military fiefdoms, through other intermediate stages, to the elite military corps at the centre known as the Janissaries. It was a structure that was both adaptive and resilient in terms of its personnel and methods. Crucially, it was able to absorb the new technologies of warfare that were coming onto the battlefield at this period, technologies incorporating the use of gunpowder in cannons, muskets and other forms of early firearms. Military organization and an adaptability to new military technology went hand-in-hand, not only in the winning of an empire, but also in protecting the gains of conquest and ensuring the empire's stability and continuance.

The civil governance of the Ottoman Empire was equally well organized. It was adjusted to suit the historical exigencies of particular territories and their mixed demographics. The actual structure of the administration varied according to the distance from the central control of the sultan. Core areas were administered somewhat differently from the peripheries. Regional and local administrative divisions were run by military commanders as well as by bureaucrats, who also operated a secretariat from Istanbul and maintained an archive that, over the centuries, became the collective memory of the empire. In addition, Christian and Jewish religious leaders were used as intermediaries between their communities and the imperial government, thus reducing, though by no means eliminating, the tensions that flowed from social and religious differences.

Other empires likewise developed structures of governance that transmuted conquered territories into functioning domains of the state. In India, Akbar used his warrior nobles as administrators of regions and provinces, but moved them around so that they could not set down roots and establish hereditary bases of their own. He also built up alliances with subsidiary Rajasthani princes and brought talented Hindus into his central administration. The effect was to create a civil organization for empire that went beyond the local and the limited, and beyond specific ethnic formation, and was able to accommodate the diversities of population within it. Catherine Asher contrasts this situation with Ottoman and Safavid practices, in which non-Muslims who had been captured in war or acquired through a levy system were taken, converted to Islam and then trained so that they gave their allegiance only to the ruler. Japan, at the end of the millennium, tried to use education to inculcate notions of the new empire it was establishing in China and Korea and adopted more draconian methods. As Elise Kurashige Tipton points out, in the case of Korea the imperial government implemented industrialization and intensified assimilation policies in the name of imperialization.

Some four centuries earlier, the Chinese return to imperial power through the Ming dynasty involved the restoration of the old examination system. As J.A.G. Roberts notes, this system became once again the main avenue into the civil service and the pool from which the centralized power of the emperor drew its most senior officials. In theory it was a system that drew on talent rather than privileged position or inherited wealth, but it was also a means whereby Confucian values, respect for authority among them, were inculcated and promoted.

Whatever the values underpinning the bureaucratic structure of the empires, one of its prime duties was the ordering of land ownership throughout the domains. The primary objective was to ensure continued income to the empire from land tax and land revenue (maintaining stability in agriculture for the peasant and landholder was a useful by-product). A major activity of the bureaucracy was determining the amounts to be raised from the land and its produce, and running a tax-collection structure. Moneys raised from the land funded state activities, maintaining imperial status and presence with all due pomp and grandeur. As empires stabilized, their bureaucracies confronted the issue in various ways, sometimes taking advantage of pre-existing revenue collection customs and sometimes implementing land reforms. In Cambodia, the Khmer faced an added complexity, the need to ensure the water supply for an economy based on rice-growing. In consequence, the Khmer monarchs ran what may be termed a hydraulic economy. It was one in which they controlled the waterways and ran a (mostly) efficient water system, which ensured prosperity both for their subjects and for themselves.

## Advancing Empire

Within the empires, the collateral benefits of prosperity and stability were periods of extraordinary creativity – massive building programmes, the creation of much fine art, the writing of books, scientific discourse and debate, and technological advance. Some of the world's greatest and finest art and architecture were created in these empires at their height. It was the Ming who erected the Great Wall of China as we see it today, though it has precedents back to the 200s BCE. It was built for strategic defence needs (the protection of China from attack from Mongol threats from the north and north-west) rather than for the glory of the emperor, but it remains one of the world's most famous and visible structures. It was a Mughal emperor in India, Shah Jahan, who erected the Taj Mahal as the tomb for his beloved wife and thereby created a monument whose beauty and perfection has made it forever afterwards a cliché for romantic love. In Cambodia, the major temples and structures built by Khmer rulers at Angkor and elsewhere combined the ethos of Mahayana Buddhism with regional notions of kingship to achieve a grandeur that still reverberates in world imagination. In Persia, the great mosques and structures of Isfahan have an equally potent impact, as do the splendid Ottoman buildings of Istanbul. Such monuments have multiple readings. They were expressions of imperial grandeur and of imperial taste and connoisseurship, and they were assertions of the empire's wealth and resources. For us, looking back at them across the centuries, they are also statements of the ethos of the empire, the underlying values and religious belief patterns of those who ruled.

So it was with other arts and sciences. Long lists of Asian imperial achievements in literature, art, scientific advances and metaphysical and religious debate could be compiled. Empires patronized creativity and could be instrumental in creating new forms and styles. Painting in Persia and India illustrates the point. Emperor Akbar in India encouraged the painters in his royal atelier to re-work and blend prevailing painting styles from within and outside his domains into a distinctively new form,

Mughal painting. It was first evident in the groundbreaking Hamza Nama series of paintings, which detailed the picaresque adventures of the eponymous Hamza. In Persia, painting reached unsurpassed heights in the series of illustrations for a core literary epic, the Shahnama or Book of Kings, commissioned by Shah Ismail I, the founder of the Safavid dynasty, for his son Prince Tahmasb. Like the grand buildings, such paintings fulfilled multiple purposes. They asserted the connoisseurship of the ruler and the wealth of the empire in patronizing such costly enterprises. Some paintings illustrated formative epics and popular tales, and some were records of the environment and the territories over which the emperor ruled. Others were histories of the dynasty and blatant assertions of its supremacy, such as Mughal paintings that depict the emperor seated with his line of ancestors stretching back to Timur, or standing on top of a globe of the world. Like the common title of 'King of Kings' that monarchs frequently assumed, the paintings asserted superiority and supremacy – and the core values of the kingdom.

Each empire at its height was, as the chapters in this volume clearly show, a universe of creativity and advancement in terms of the fine and decorative arts, and in knowledge and learning. However, that creativity and intellectual endeavour was not indulged purely for its own sake. It also served the needs of the imperial ruler and of the state over which he ruled in varying degrees of absolutism. These Asian empires were themselves wondrous creations in the years of their flowering, even if over time they were to wilt and wither, and be cut down and replaced by other states and other powers. The effects of their flourishing were nevertheless long-lasting, and their impacts did not easily or quickly dissipate.

# CHAPTER ONE
# Central Asia: The Mongols 1206–1405
TIMOTHY MAY

The Mongol Empire arose in the steppes of Mongolia in the 13th century and went on to change the map of the world forever. It became one of the most important empires in Asia and, indeed, the world. Stretching from the Sea of Japan to the Carpathian Mountains, it was – and remains – the largest contiguous empire in history. However, the Mongol Empire's significance does not lie in size alone: its impact on history, and the institutions it established, truly made it great.

## The Rise of Chinggis Khan

The forging of the Mongol Empire was an arduous process that began in the crucible of the Mongolian steppes. The first stage was the conquest and unification of the various Mongolian and Turkic tribes of Mongolia. Temujin (1162–1227) was initially a minor leader on the steppes, but his abilities and charisma slowly gained him a following. He became a *nokhor* (companion or vassal) to Toghril (d.1203/1204), Khan of the Kereits, the dominant tribe of central Mongolia. While he was still in the service of Toghril, Temujin's obvious talents made him a major leader among the Mongol tribes. Eventually, Temujin's increase in power and the jealousy it evoked among Toghril's other supporters caused Temujin and Toghril to part ways and ultimately clash in battle. Their quarrel came to a head in 1203, with Temujin emerging as the victor.

By 1206 Temujin had unified the tribes of Mongolia into a single supra-tribe known as the *Khamag Mongol Ulus*, which translates awkwardly as 'the All Mongol State'. Temujin reorganized the social structure

**KEY DATES**

by dissolving old tribal lines and regrouping them into an army based on a decimal system (units of 10, 100 and 1000). His purpose was to forge a single identity for the nomads, one that transcended old tribal loyalties. This process eventually created the Mongolian nation. Furthermore, Temujin instilled a strong sense of discipline into the army. Although he had defeated all of his rivals by 1204, it was not until 1206 that Temujin's

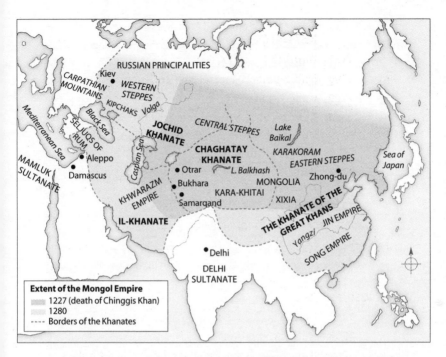

Map showing the extent of the Mongol Empire created by Chinggis Khan, and the four khanates into which the empire divided after the death of his grandson Mongke.

followers recognized him as the sole authority in Mongolia by granting him the title of Chinggis Khan, meaning Firm, Fierce or Resolute Ruler.[1] (The spelling 'Genghis Khan', once common in the English-speaking world, is incorrect.)[2]

The Mongols quickly expanded beyond Mongolia, conquering the Tangut, a Tibetan people who ruled the kingdom of Xixia (the modern Ningxia and Gansu provinces of China) by 1209. Then in 1211 Chinggis Khan invaded the Jin Empire (1125–1234) of northern China.[3] Initially, there is little indication that Chinggis Khan sought an empire beyond Mongolia. In many ways his creation of empire was accidental: his original intention was to eliminate threats from states that had traditionally interfered in the politics and economies of the steppes. This quickly changed. The Mongol campaigns began as raids, but as their successes grew the Mongols began to retain the territory they plundered after resistance ceased. Although the Mongols won stunning victories and conquered most of the Jin Empire by 1215, Jin resistance to the Mongols continued until 1234, seven years after the death of Chinggis Khan.

Mongol expansion into Central Asia began in 1209 as the Mongols pursued tribal leaders who opposed Chinggis Khan's rise to power in Mongolia and thus constituted a threat to his authority at home. With their victories, the Mongols gained new territory. Several smaller polities, such as the Uighurs of the Tarim Basin, sought the protection of Chinggis Khan as vassals. Ultimately, the Mongols found themselves with a large empire, now bordering not only the Chinese states but also the Islamic world in Central Asia, including the Khwarazmian Empire, which spanned portions of Central Asia, Afghanistan and Iran.[4]

At first, Chinggis Khan sought a peaceful commercial relationship with the Khwarazmian state. This abruptly changed when the governor of Otrar, a Khwarazmian border town, massacred a Mongol-sponsored caravan. After diplomatic means failed to resolve the issue, Chinggis Khan left a token force in northern China and marched against the Khwarazmians in 1218.

After capturing Otrar, Chinggis Khan divided his army and struck the Khwarazmian Empire at several points. With the large Khwarazmian army spread across the empire in an attempt to defend its cities, Muhammad Khwarazmshah II could not compete with the more mobile Mongol forces in the field. The Muslim population saw their defeat not simply as a military conquest, but as a signal that God had forsaken them. Indeed, the Mongols cultivated this idea. After capturing Bukhara, Chinggis Khan ascended the pulpit in the Friday mosque and announced:

O people, know that you have committed great sins, and that the great ones among you have committed these sins. If you ask me what proof I have for these words, I say it is because I am the punishment of God. If you had not committed great sins, God would not have sent a punishment like me upon you.[5]

Muhammad II watched his cities fall one by one, until finally he fled with a Mongol force in pursuit. He successfully eluded them and escaped to an island in the Caspian Sea, where he died in 1220/21 from dysentery. His son, Jalal al-Din (d.1230) attempted to rally the empire in Afghanistan, but Chinggis Khan defeated him near the Indus River in 1221, forcing Jalal al-Din to flee to India.

The Khwarazmian Empire was now ripe for annexation, but Chinggis Khan kept only the territory north of the Amu Darya, wisely not over-extending his army. He then returned to Mongolia in order to deal with a rebellion that had broken out in Xixia. After resting his army, he invaded Xixia in 1227 and besieged the capital of Zhongxing. During the siege, Chinggis Khan died (possibly from injuries sustained from a fall from his horse while hunting), but he ordered his sons and army to continue the war against Xixia. Indeed, even as he lay ill in his bed, Chinggis Khan instructed them,

While I take my meals you must talk about the killing and the destruction of the Tang'ut and say, 'Maimed and tamed, they are no more'.[6]

The army that Chinggis Khan organized and led was the key to Mongol expansion. It fought and operated in a fashion that other medieval armies did not or could not replicate. In essence it operated very much as a modern army does, over multiple fronts and in several autonomous corps, but in a coordinated effort. Also, the Mongols embraced the concept of total war. The only result that mattered was the defeat of enemies by any means, including ruses and trickery. The famous traveller Marco Polo observed,

In truth they are stout and valiant soldiers, and inured to war.
And you perceive that it is just when the enemy sees them run, and imagines that he gained the battle, that he has in reality lost it, for the [Mongols] wheel round in a moment when they judge the right time has come. And after this fashion they have won many a fight.[7]

## The Empire after Chinggis Khan

Ogodei (d.1240/41), Chinggis Khan's second son, ascended the throne in 1230 and quickly resumed operations against the Jin Empire, successfully conquering it in 1234. Chinggis Khan had announced previously that he had been sent as the scourge of God, but Ogodei promoted the idea that Heaven (Tengri the sky god) had declared that the Mongols were destined to rule the world. Before invading a region, Mongol envoys delivered correspondence indicating that, as Heaven had decreed that the Mongols were to rule the earth, a prince should come to the Mongol court and offer his submission. The Mongols viewed any refusal as an act of rebellion not only against the Mongols, but also against the will of Heaven. This process was aided by a multi-ethnic bureaucracy staffed not only by Mongols, but largely by the educated elites from such sedentary conquered populations as the Chinese, Persians and Uighurs. Thus the letters could be translated and delivered in triplicate, each in a different language, so that there was a high probability that someone at the other court could read them.

Ogodei pursued his purpose of world domination by sending armies out to multiple fronts. While Ogodei led his army against the Jin, another army conquered Iran, Armenia and Georgia under the command of Chormaqan (d.1240). Meanwhile, a massive force under the leadership of Prince Batu (fl.1227–55) and Subedei (1176–1248), the renowned Mongol general, marched west, conquering the Russian principalities and the Pontic and Caspian steppes before invading Hungary and Poland. While they did not seek to control Hungary and Poland, the Mongols left both areas devastated before departing, possibly owing to Ogodei's death in 1241.

Ogodei's son, Guyuk (r.1246–48), came to the throne in 1246 after a lengthy debate over the succession. In the interim, Guyuk's mother, Toregene (d.1246), served as regent. Once in power, Guyuk accomplished little in terms of conquest as he died in 1248. His wife Oghul-Qaimish (d.1250) served as regent but ignored the process of electing a new khan. Her inattention led to a coup in which Mongke (r.1250–59) seized power with the backing of most of the Chinggisid princes in 1250. During his reign, the Mongol armies were once again on the march. He and his brother Qubilai (d.1294) led armies into the territory of China's Southern Song (1126–1279) south of the Yangzi River, while Hulegu (d.1265), another brother, led an army into the Middle East.

In 1256 Hulegu's forces successfully destroyed the Ismailis, a Shia[8] group also known as the Assassins, in northern Iran. The Persian chronicler Juvaini, who also worked in the Mongol bureaucracy, revelled in the demise of the much-feared Ismailis, who used assassination to intimidate and extend their influence in parts of the Middle East. Juvaini wrote:

> So was the world cleansed which had been polluted by their evil. Wayfarers now ply to and fro without fear or dread or the inconvenience of paying a toll and pray for the fortune of the happy King who uprooted their foundations and left no trace of any one of them.[9]

Hulegu then moved against the Abbasid Caliphate in Baghdad. The Caliph, nominally the titular leader of Sunni Islam, refused to capitulate but did little to defend the city. The Mongols sacked Baghdad and executed the Caliph, ending the position of Caliph among the Sunnis in 1258. Hulegu's armies invaded Syria, successfully capturing Aleppo and Damascus. Hulegu, however, withdrew the bulk of his army in 1259/60 after receiving news that Mongke had died during the war against the Song. Meanwhile, the Mamluk Sultanate of Egypt struck the Mongol garrisons in Syria, defeating them at Ayn Jalut in 1260. As the Mongol Empire spiralled into civil war after the death of Mongke, Hulegu never recovered the Syrian conquests. Instead, civil war with the Mongols in the Pontic and Caspian steppes (the so-called Golden Horde) and those in Central Asia occupied much of his attention.

There was no clear principle of succession, other than being descended from Chinggis Khan, so warfare between rival claimants was frequent. Civil war erupted after Mongke's death as two of his brothers vied for the throne. Qubilai eventually defeated Ariq Boke in 1264, but the damage to the territorial integrity of the empire was great. While the other princes nominally accepted Qubilai as the Khan of the empire, his influence dwindled outside Mongolia and China. Qubilai and his successors, known as the Yuan dynasty (1279–1368), found their closest allies in Hulegu and his successors. Hulegu's kingdom, known as the Il-Khanate of Persia, dominated Iran, Iraq, modern Turkey, Armenia, Azerbaijan and Georgia. Central Asia was ruled by the Chaghatayids, the descendants of Chaghatay, Chinggis Khan's third son, although often they were the puppets of Qaidu, a descendent of Ogodei and rival of Qubilai Khan. Meanwhile in Russia and the Pontic and Caspian steppes, descendants of Jochi, Chinggis Khan's first son, held power. Their state is often referred to as the Golden Horde.

Other regions found independence with the collapse of the Mongol Empire, such as Korea. Korea, however, had to walk a fine line afterwards – showing respect to the Ming dynasty (which replaced the Mongols in China), but also proper respect to the Northern Yuan, as the Mongols were known in Mongolia, Inner Mongolia and parts of Manchuria (that is, areas bordering Korea). Many scholars think that the Mongol invasions greatly contributed to the rise of a Korean national and cultural consciousness in the wake of the massive devastation wrought by the Mongols.

## The Army of the Empire

The rapid and destructive conquests of the Mongols often obscure what truly made the Mongol Empire an impressive state. It is one thing to conquer, but quite another to rule the conquered lands, particularly when the conquered are more numerous and, in many areas, much more advanced. The Mongols successfully created an empire by incorporating territory only gradually, and installing a military government to rule before control was relinquished to a civil authority. They did not over-extend themselves: their conquering armies often strayed far beyond the territory that they actually annexed into the empire.

The army was the primary institution of the Mongol Empire. Indeed, after securing his position in Mongolia in 1206, Chinggis Khan immedi-ately reorganized his nomadic warriors into an army whose feats remain unparalleled today. As part of this reorganization, Chinggis Khan trans-formed the steppe tribes into a pre-modern version of a military-industrial society. He dispersed enemy tribes among loyal tribes to ensure that his former enemies could never oppose him again. In addition, all groups were divided along decimal lines. The primary unit of organization, not only for the military but for the empire as well, became the *mingan*, or unit of one thousand. These were then divided into a corresponding number of *jaghun* (hundreds) and *arban* (tens). As the empire increased in territory and population, the *mingan* was replaced by the *tumen* (ten thousand) as the primary unit for government and military purposes.

The importance of the *mingan* extended beyond the army, as the households that belonged to these units not only produced the warriors who filled them, but also supplied their equipment. Thus a *mingan* was not just a thousand warriors, but a thousand households. In order to provide stability to the system, as well as to meld the normally fissiparous tribes into a single entity – the Mongols – Chinggis Khan decreed that no one could move to a different unit. Thus, he erased the tribal divisions that had kept Mongolia in an incessant state of war. He also appointed the commanders, who then selected their junior officers based on talent rather than kinship. Officers could also be removed from their posts. Indeed, Chinggis Khan once said:

Let any officer who cannot keep order in his own squad be branded a criminal along with his wife and children, and let another be chosen as officer from his squad and companies of a hundred, a thousand, and ten thousand likewise.[10]

Chinggis Khan did not invent this decimal system. The same form of military organization had been used by the Khitans, who dominated much of Mongolia during their reign as the Liao dynasty (907–1125) of northern China, and by the Kereit tribe that ruled central Mongolia during Chinggis Khan's rise to power. Chinggis Khan, however, was an innovator in using the system to organize wider society.

Additionally, Chinggis Khan devised the *keshik*, or bodyguard. This became a training ground not only for his generals, but also for governors of the empire. Divided into dayguards, nightguards and quiverbearers, the *keshik* guarded the khan. A commander, or *noyan*, from the *keshik* outranked a non-*keshik* commander by one rank. Thus a commander of a *mingan* in the *keshik* held the same rank as a commander of a tumen outside the *keshik*. The *keshik* started off as a few hundred fighters, but it eventually expanded to ten thousand men, with a thousand of them accompanying the khan into battle.

The *keshik* was more than just a bodyguard. It was also the khan's household staff, performing duties from tending his flocks to serving food to advising. Vassals and generals sent their sons to join the *keshik*, where they became hostages. This practice served two functions. It ensured the good behaviour of the officer or vassal, but also the son would be trained in Mongol warfare and administration. His loyalty to the khan was tested and so he could be sent to replace his father if necessary. Thus the generals and the governors were all men the khan knew personally.

Light cavalry composed most of the Mongol army. Indeed, initially, the entire army consisted of lightly-armoured horse-archers, but as they expanded the Mongols incorporated other military units into their forces. This included heavy cavalry and siege engineers. Rather than attempting

to make these units fight as horse-archers, the Mongols allowed ‸
to maintain their own fighting styles. Thus those who had traditionally
fought as heavy cavalry continued to do so. However, some groups, such
as the Russians, did abandon their old methods and adopt Mongolian
combat forms, both in tactics and accoutrements. The Mongols acquired
siege engineers by conscripting those with engineering abilities from
conquered populations, but some also joined as volunteers. At first, the
Mongols had little use for infantry, but later they used foot-soldiers extensively in regions ill-suited for cavalry warfare, such as southern China with
its mountainous terrain and rice-paddies.

While the *mingans* were never dissolved, new formations could be
created. These forces were known as the *tamma*. The *tammachin*, or those
who served in a *tamma*, played a pivotal role in the expansion of the
empire as they were stationed on the borders. Their purpose was expressly
to maintain control of the region, and extend Mongol control and influence into neighbouring territories. When the main army marched for a
new round of conquests, the *tammachin* often served as the vanguard.

As we have seen, the Mongol army steadily grew by incorporating
conquered groups into the military. This process was crucial not only to
increase the size of the Mongol army, but also to drain a potential source
of rebellion by placing conquered fighters on the front lines. It also gave
the new conscripts a vested interest in the empire. The most important
additions to the Mongol army were Turkic nomads, who lived a lifestyle
similar to the nomadic Mongols and dominated ethnically from the Altai
Mountains to the Carpathians. Indeed, in many cases the Mongol army
was a Turkic army commanded by Mongols.

As the empire grew, so did the resources and manpower available to
the Mongol war machine. At the time of the ascension of Chinggis Khan
to the throne in 1206, the Mongol army numbered approximately 95,000
men. By 1260, the Mongol Empire stretched from the Sea of Japan to
the Mediterranean Sea and Carpathian Mountains and could mobilize
approximately a million men under arms.

conception is that Mongols came out of the steppes as
ians who quickly conquered far more advanced civili-
the management of the government in the hands of the
conquest. essence, Chinese bureaucrats still did their job in China, and
local rulers throughout the empire stayed in power as long as they did not
cause the Mongols any trouble. There is some truth to this, but it ignores
the complexity of Mongol rule. The method of rule was not consistent
throughout the empire, but was malleable for each region. With an empire
of approximately 36,260,000 square km (14 million square miles), an area
roughly the size of the African continent, the Mongols had to adjust their
governing styles to a vast array of geographical, cultural and linguistic vari-
ations. Simply put, one style of governance would never work for the entire
empire. Some consistency existed at the upper levels of the government,
but at the local level, the Mongols preferred simply to use what worked.
This did not mean that Mongol rule was perfect or free of corruption;
indeed, at times it could be oppressive. When evaluating their government,
however, it is important to keep in mind that the Mongol khans simply
viewed the empire as their property. The ultimate purpose of the empire
was to provide for the khans and their family, and not for their subjects.

Indeed, because of this, the Mongols were actually very involved in the
administration of the empire. Before the Mongols expanded beyond the
Mongolian plateau, considerable effort was spent in organizing the new
state. When Chinggis Khan reorganized the nomadic structure of the early
empire in 1206 by placing everyone in units of one thousand (*mingan*),
it was not simply for military purposes but also to organize taxation.
Furthermore, although Chinggis Khan was illiterate, he promoted literacy
among the Mongolian nobility, particularly the princes, as he recognized
the need for writing in the administration of the empire. This led to the
creation of a secretariat that recorded its activities in a vertical script
introduced by Chinggis Khan's decree. The script is still used in China's
Inner Mongolia Autonomous region today and is also taught in Mongolia

(which switched to a Cyrillic script in the 20th century under the influence of the Soviet Union).

Ultimately, however, Mongol government officers originated from two sources: the imperial clan (the lineage of Chinggis Khan) and the *keshik* (the khan's bodyguard). The imperial clan viewed the Mongol Empire as its joint property. Thus all members had representatives to watch over their interests throughout the imperial administrative apparatus. The *keshik* served not only as a bodyguard, but also as a training centre for generals and provincial governors, or *jarghuchi*. Few governors of large territories came from outside the keshik.

While these two institutions formed the imperial upper echelons, at lower levels it was the abilities of other groups that kept the empire functioning. The Mongols always sought pragmatic solutions, and looked for talented individuals to serve in their government. As the Mongols conquered territories, they appropriated many of the ruling structures and personnel of the conquered. This is how men such as Yelu Qu Cai (1189–1243 and formerly of the Jin Empire), and Mahmud Yalavach (d.1262) and his son, Masud Beg (both formerly of the Khwarazmian and possibly Kara-Khitan Empires), as well as countless others, joined their service. The Mongol khans always respected and recognized the need for talented administrators. Furthermore, when local rulers submitted peacefully they often maintained their rule as Mongol vassals, so that in administrative terms very little changed for the region at the local level. This has led many commentators to believe that the Mongol conquerors relied on native administrators actually to run their empire.

It is true that the majority of government personnel were non-Mongols, but a sizeable number were Mongols. Indeed, the chief judge (*yeke jarghuchi*) was Chinggis Khan's adopted brother, Shiqi Qutuqtu. Still, the non-Mongols were not necessarily locals: the empire contained many ethnicities and cultures. The famous Venetian, Marco Polo, is an excellent example. Although in his writings he portrays himself as a major figure within the government of Qubilai Khan, in reality he was a minor official.

Nonetheless, he was an Italian serving a Mongolian ruler in China, where he worked alongside Turks, Persians, Arabs and some Chinese. A large part of his travels was on government business. It was not unusual to have Arabs serving in Russia or Persians in China. The Mongols used qualified people wherever they were needed. Still, they did prefer not to tinker too much with systems that worked well. Hence, when the great minister and governor of northern China, Yelu Qu Cai, demonstrated how much wealth the region could produce to Ogodei Khan, the Mongols kept his system in place. In China, because of their distrust of the Chinese population, the Mongols preferred to use 'Westerners' (that is, anyone born west of China) and non-Chinese like Jurchen (from Manchuria) and Khitans (a proto-Mongolian people who were then mainly centred on the Liao River in China and just north of Korea).

Marco Polo gained employment because of this preference, although his claims of high rank can be dismissed. Generally speaking, the *shi*, traditional Confucian bureaucrats of China, were left out of the administration. This was partly due to the Mongols' disregard of the Confucian system and distrust of the *shi*, but also partly to the *shi* themselves. The *shi* often refused to serve because the Mongols did not value the Confucian system of governance, and also limited the administrative positions that the *shi* could hold. Many *shi* retired to a life of scholarly or artistic work.

Although the civil administration of the empire remained a secondary institution behind the military, they did work together. As the Mongols conquered territories, military governors known as *tammachi* ruled the new lands. The *tammachi* held the job of securing and controlling a recently conquered area. The quality of the *tammachi* varied greatly. Some ruled justly; some were rapacious. The various populations that came under their jurisdiction were not always unanimous in their opinions of their new ruler. For instance, Chormaqan, who ruled much of Persia, Georgia, Armenia and Azerbaijan in the 1230s, was thought by the Armenian population to be a fair and moderate governor, whereas many of the Muslim subjects considered him a thug.

Gradually, as new conquests went forward, the military governors were replaced by civil governors called jarghuci, aided by civil administrators known by three terms: *darughachi*, *basqaq* and *shahna*. The variance in terms reflects the origins of the words. *Darughachi* is a Mongolian word while *basqaq* and *shahna* are Turkic and Persian respectively. The officials performed the same duties, but were called by the local title. These officials, who governed localities, had a few soldiers at their command, but as the *tammachi* pacified the region and then moved to the new frontier, there was less need for military support. The *darughachi* was accompanied by secretaries and other officials to integrate conquered regions into the empire. Local rulers were often given the title of *darughachi* as well.

Personnel who served in these positions also reflected the cosmopolitan nature of the empire. The *tammachi* was always a Mongol, although his troops varied greatly, whereas the *darughachi* could be a Mongol or someone else. Most of those who ruled the largest areas, however, invariably came from the *keshik* or bodyguard of the khan.

As the Mongols conquered new territories, they took measures to establish an effective government. After achieving a modicum of security and stability, the Mongols conducted a census. From this, they determined how many men were present, what kind of occupations existed, and how much tribute and tax a region could provide. The *darughachi* (whether Mongol, transplant or local ruler) was then expected to collect the tribute or supply men upon request.

Although the Mongols maintained many local rulers in their positions, it was not because they were dependent on them. Indeed, the Mongols kept tabs on the local rulers through the use of their postal system, known as the *yam*. In practice it worked in a manner very similar to the Pony Express of the American Old West era. Yet there were significant differences. Rather than the letters and messages of the general public, only government information passed along the *yam*. Yet the postal riders were not the only ones who used it. In addition to the messengers, others could use its resources, but only those who possessed a *geregen* or *paiza*, translated loosely as a 'passport'. These passports could be of various levels: wood, bronze, silver and finally gold. The more valuable the material, the more important the person. Messengers switched horses at the various stations and by virtue of the passport they carried could requisition food and/or animals from the populace. During periods of corruption, many abused the yam system, and it became quite oppressive to populations near the post stations because of the vast privileges granted to the riders.

Although the government of the Mongol Empire was flexible and efficient when managed properly, corruption penetrated easily because of its very flexibility, and the population could be heavily exploited. Nonetheless, through the yam system, information (including reports on local rulers) reached the khan in a matter of days rather than months.

## The Rule of Law

Anyone who disobeyed the commands of the khan risked death, but even the khan had limits to his power. The Mongol Empire was governed by a rule of law known as the *Yasa*. The *Yasa* was not the law for the entire population of the empire, but rather was applied to the nomadic population. In general, the sedentary population maintained their own traditions and customary law as long as it did not conflict with the *Yasa*. This law code was a combination of steppe nomadic tradition and imperial decree, and was strongly influenced by the *biligs* or maxims of Chinggis Khan. Its creation has been attributed to Chinggis Khan, but the primary shaper in the foundations of the *Yasa* was the man who compiled and executed the law, Chinggis Khan's adopted brother, Shiqi Qutuqtu. As with most laws, custom and tradition set the foundation, with the intention of protecting the stability of society and punishing those who transgressed social norms. The imperial decrees formed the other basis of law, though these had to conform to existing thoughts on jurisprudence in the context of tradition (though this could be ignored when necessary). To complicate the matter, an individual decree or order from the khan was also known as a *yasa*, a word that entered the Persian language as a decree, but was also a synonym for capital punishment – which gives some indication of the contents of many *yasas*.

A greater influence on the shaping of imperial decrees, however, were the *biligs*. Technically, the *biligs* or maxims of Chinggis Khan were not laws. Rather, the Mongol elite considered them examples of proper and virtuous behaviour, and abiding by them could influence laws and decisions within the court. An example is this maxim concerning the recognition of appropriate military leaders:

> There is no warrior like [Yesugei] Bahadur, and no one else possesses the skills he had, but he did not suffer from hardship and was not affected by hunger or thirst. He thought his liege men could tolerate hardship as well as he could, but they couldn't. A man is worthy of leadership who knows what hunger and thirst are and who can judge the condition of others thereby, who can go at a measured pace and not allow the soldiers to get hungry and thirsty or the horses to get worn out.[11]

Thus Chinggis Khan demonstrated that simply being the best warrior did not automatically make one a great war leader.

Not abiding by the *biligs* did not equate to transgressing the law of the land, but it could be used as evidence against a person, demonstrating their lack of character. Although there are plenty of examples of *biligs* in the primary sources, there is no surviving example of the Yasa, if indeed a written copy of it ever existed. As it was primarily applied to the steppe nomads and based on their own well-understood customs, it is likely that no one saw a need to write the *Yasa* down. Non-Mongols, even some court officials, did not always understand the difference between the Yasa and the *biligs*. This is partly because Chinggis Khan was so revered that almost any of his sayings could appear to be sacred law, at least from the perspective of an outsider. A good example of this occurred during the regency of Toregene and the election of her son Guyuk to the throne.

When discussing Guyuk's enthronement, Juvaini, a Persian who worked in the court of Hulegu, expressed his disapproval of Toregene's reign and perhaps also of Guyuk's behaviour. Juvaini first states that although Guyuk had arrived for the *quriltai*, or congress where a new khan was chosen, the business of state was still in Toregene's hands and 'Guyuk did not intervene therein to enforce yasa or custom nor did he dispute with her about these matters.'[12] Juvaini indicates that Toregene had veered from the laws and customs established by Chinggis Khan and Ogodei and ruled instead according to her desire. As the new khan, Guyuk could have reversed this, but he chose not to at that time. Within a few months, however, Guyuk became estranged from his mother. Although there is no conclusive evidence, the cause of the breach may have been her abandonment of the *Yasa* and disregard of the *biligs*.

Nonetheless, *yasas* remained in use in the 14th century, well after the Mongol Empire had split into four khanates in 1265. As time passed it is clear that the *Yasa* of Chinggis Khan was still respected and upheld, but it largely lost its cohesion, if indeed it ever had any. By and large, laws and traditions attributed to Chinggis Khan became the backbone of custom throughout the steppe world until the 17th century. Their importance remained evident even after the Mongols converted to Islam. Many Mongols resisted the switch to the sharia (Islamic law), or used it in conjunction with the *Yasa*.

## Decline and Dissolution

Ever since Edward Gibbon penned his *Decline and Fall of the Roman Empire*, historians and students of history have tried to pinpoint defining moments and reasons for the collapse of an empire. The Mongol Empire, however, tends to resist being neatly categorized with a start and end date, as do most states if carefully considered. It is not possible to pinpoint the demise of the Mongol Empire, as offshoots continued on for centuries in various permutations. Indeed, the last Chinggisid ruler was removed from his throne in Khiva by the Bolsheviks in 1920. What is notable about the end of the empire is that the decline of the Mongols occurred not owing to internal corruption or outside invasion, but rather because of sibling rivalry as sons fought for power, thus undermining one of Chinggis Khan's most important ideas – the maintenance of stability.

As so often, the foundations for the end of the empire were laid at the very beginning. Although Chinggis Khan continually sought to provide and maintain stability in his empire by rewarding loyalty and eliminating opposing lines of leadership, his focus on the *altan uruk* or 'Golden Family' (that is, the family of Chinggis Khan) completely undermined the process. During the unification of Mongolia, Chinggis Khan eradicated all other tribal ruling elites, leaving the steppes with a single royal family and thus only one familial avenue to the throne. While theoretically any Chinggisid had a claim to the throne, in reality only the senior lines descended from the sons of Börte, Chinggis Khan's first wife, had primacy. Nonetheless, this produced a very large and self-important royal family.

If any date can be identified as the beginning of the end, the death of the fourth khan, Mongke, in 1259/60 might be the most logical. Mongke, a grandson of Chinggis Khan, came to the throne in a coup in 1250. Perhaps the greatest of the Mongol rulers as an administrator, he eliminated much of the corruption that had entered the empire's government after Ogodei's death in 1240/41. Under Mongke's efficient rule, the Mongol Empire could mobilize immense forces; it possessed an army of at least a million men supported by the resources of the entire empire. Now there was no need to avoid over-extending the army. The administrative reforms of Mongke allowed the Mongols to unleash a juggernaut. Rather than raiding and creating a buffer between their frontier and the next state, the Mongols simply eliminated those who defied their authority one by one. In the Middle East, the Ismailis of Iran, also known as the Assassins, were destroyed in 1256 and Baghdad fell before the armies of Mongke's brother, Hulegu, in 1258. In 1259, Mongol armies entered Syria and quickly took Damascus and Aleppo. By 1260, it appeared that Egypt and the remaining Crusader states were next. But then fate took a hand, as shown by events in China.

In addition to the Middle East, Mongke and his brother Qubilai invaded the Song Empire of southern China. This was a difficult campaign because of the mountainous terrain and the extensive rice paddies, both of which hindered the Mongol cavalry. Nonetheless, the Mongols made progress, albeit slowly, until 1259, when Mongke died. Like so many warriors of the Middle Ages, he died either from an arrow wound or dysentery. The sources vary considerably.

Ironically, the death of the man who led the Mongol Empire to its most powerful period also aided its decline. Unfortunately, Mongke had not declared a successor before embarking on campaign. His regent and youngest brother, Ariq Boke, attempted to set himself up in power in Mongolia with the backing of several commanders and princes who might be considered conservative or, more precisely, pro-steppe. Meanwhile, Qubilai did the same in China with the support of those with ties and interests connected to the sedentary world. To the west, Hulegu also considered throwing his hat into the ring; however, he suffered from a number of setbacks.

Owing to the lack of sufficient pasture in Syria, Hulegu kept the bulk of his army in the Mughan steppes of Azerbaijan. Seeing an opportune time to make a pre-emptive strike while Hulegu's gaze was averted eastward, the Mamluks, former slave-soldiers of the descendants of Saladin, invaded. The Mongol forces in Syria were driven out after a defeat at Ayn Jalut in 1260. To Hulegu this appeared to be a minor setback, as the Mongols had lost battles before, but always avenged their defeats. This time, however, would be different. The defeat inspired resistance by others in Syria. In addition, Hulegu had to defend his lands from invasion by his cousin Berke, the ruler of what became known as the Golden Horde.

Berke's invasion was principally to gain territory that he felt belonged to his family, the Jochids (that is, the family of Jochi, the eldest son of Chinggis Khan). As a Muslim, Berke also claimed that he was avenging the Caliph as he was horrified by Hulegu's execution of the Muslim leader. While Berke's indignation may have been genuine, the avenging of the

Caliph's death as justification for the invasion is somewhat dubious. Berke may have been sincere in his religion, which he adopted in his youth, but his followers were by and large not Muslims, and it is doubtful that they would have followed him solely for this reason. The revenge factor was really a propaganda device to gain the support of Muslims outside his own realm, whether subjects in Hulegu's domain or outside, such as the Mamluks of Syria and Egypt.

The territorial claim, on the other hand, carried great importance as it was this issue that would lead to the fracturing of the Mongol Empire into four parts. Jochi, the father of Berke, was possibly not Chinggis Khan's own child. Jochi's mother had been kidnapped before his birth, and only recovered by Chinggis Khan several months later. Although Jochi's lineage did not matter to Chinggis Khan, it was a source of ongoing tension and conflict between Chinggis Khan's sons. The Mongols also divided their territory among their sons, with the youngest keeping the ancestral pastures. While this provided an inheritance for all of the heirs, it also kept them separated. Jochi was promised territory as far west as the Mongol horses' hooves trod, which included the Middle East. This territory, however, had never been officially given to the Jochids, although they maintained representatives in the region.

Thus the Il-Khanate (the kingdom of Hulegu and his successors) and the Golden Horde, as the Jochid territory is often called, became embroiled in almost continuous war for a century. In addition, a civil war between Ariq Boke and Qubilai raged until 1264. This war allowed the other Mongol princes to assert their independence, as it was not clear, at first, who would win. Even after Qubilai Khan won the war, his authority over the other khanates consisted of little more than token recognition, and even this gradually diminished with his successors.

This decline in the authority and power of the khan was due in large part to Qubilai's method of ascension to power. In selecting the khan, a *quriltai*, or assembly of all the Mongol princes and major commanders, was traditionally held to discuss the eligible candidates. To be considered one had to be descended from Chinggis Khan; as stated previously, there were numerous candidates in theory, but only a handful of contenders in reality. Still, as Chinggis Khan had possessed at least half a dozen wives and numerous concubines (and his sons likewise), he had numerous descendants. Indeed, one DNA study indicates that perhaps sixteen million people today are descended from him.[13] Qubilai, like Ariq-Boke, did not convene a complete *quriltai* and thus was never officially recognized by many of the princes.

In the end, the four khanates went their own way. The Khanate of the Great Khan, which dominated East Asia, fell in 1368 to the Ming dynasty. Yet the Mongols had established China as a sea power, built the Grand Canal that connected northern and southern China, and also reunited China for the first time in three hundred years. Also, they facilitated the spread of a wide variety of Chinese influences westward, while bringing in western (that is, western Asian) influences to China.

The Il-Khanate, located in modern Iran, Iraq, Turkey and the Caucasus and part of Afghanistan, was the shortest-lived. It fell, curiously, in a rare moment of stability in 1335 simply because of a lack of male heirs. However, the impact of the Il-Khanate was enormous. Because of the Mongol invasion of West Asia, a Turkic tribe fled into Anatolia, or modern Turkey. These Turks took advantage of the power vacuum and established the Ottoman Empire, which lasted until the end of World War I. In addition, the Mongols of the Il-Khanate also patronized a wide number of religious sects, including the Safaviyye Sufi order, which eventually established the Safavid Empire in Azerbaijan and Iran. It is because of this Safavid state that Iran favours Shia Islam. Curiously enough, the Safavid Empire more or less mirrored the borders of the Il-Khanate.

The third Khanate, the Golden Horde (more properly known as the Jochid or Kipchak Khanate) dominated the Pontic and Caspian steppes and the lands that make up modern Kazakhstan, Russia, Ukraine and Belarus. It eventually disintegrated for a variety of reasons in the late 1400s. However, the Golden Horde gave rise to a number of Central Asian nations including the Uzbeks, Kazakhs, Crimean and Kazan Tatars and even a powerful successor state in Moscow, which led to the rise of the Russian Empire.

In Central Asia, the Chaghatayid Khanate gradually fragmented into oblivion but allowed a Turkic ruler named Timur (sometimes known as Tamerlane) to emerge. Timur, who greatly contributed to the demise of the Golden Horde and also set back the Ottomans for a number of years, lacked one crucial element: he was not a descendant of Chinggis Khan. Thus, he always kept a Chinggisid puppet on the throne to legitimize his rule.

The rise of the Mongol Empire was unexpected, its decline and dissolution equally so. Nonetheless, the empire's impact continues to shape the world today. It is this lasting legacy that has made the Mongol Empire truly great.

## The Greatness of the Mongol Empire

What would the world be like today if the Mongol Empire had held together longer? Trade had prospered greatly under the Mongols. Indeed, the khans had their own 'personal shoppers' who sought out the best goods from caravans before they even arrived at their capitals. A key to the expansion of trade was the security that the Mongols provided for the trade routes. Travellers and caravans were much less likely to be plundered by bandits. In addition, since the Mongols ruled an area that stretched from the Carpathians to Korea, merchants passing through the empire had to pay far fewer taxes and tariffs than previously. Certainly, many Mongol commanders expected a payment, although at times it is not clear if this was graft or an official sales tax of sorts, known as the tamgha. Nonetheless, even with the occasional officer on the take, the security of the trade routes improved tremendously and the cost of goods decreased significantly. Even after the empire began to fracture, commerce continued to flourish.

Nonetheless, the continued balkanization of the empire did lead ultimately to a collapse of the trade routes. As the Mongol Empire splintered into a myriad of increasingly small states, the trade routes became less secure. Various Chinggisid and non-Chinggisid princes, vying for dominance, pillaged caravans for short-term gain. A few more powerful figures, such as Timur, resisted plundering merchants. Timur did his utmost to redefine the trade routes by sacking and destroying key cities such as Sarai and New Sarai in the Golden Horde. In doing so, he ensured that more trade went to his own domain, particularly his capital of Samarqand. After Timur's death in 1405, with declining security and a single empire no longer dominating the trade routes along the Silk Road, tariffs increased and the price of goods went up once more. In Western Europe, the days of relatively inexpensive spices and eastern luxuries disappeared. The increase in prices drove some Europeans to seek new trade routes, eventually leading to Columbus's journey in 1492.

Another remarkable aspect of the Mongol Empire was its policy of religious toleration in an era of religious strife across much of Eurasia. Indeed, in 1218 when the Mongols invaded the Buddhist-dominated state of Kara-Khitai (in what is now Kazakhstan and Kirghizstan) Jebe, the Mongol general in charge of the operation, ended Buddhist persecution of Muslims. His actions prompted one Muslim commentator to write that Jebe:

> ... caused a herald to proclaim in the town that each should abide by his own religion and follow his own creed. Then we knew the existence of this people to be one of the mercies of the Lord and one of the bounties of divine grace.[15]

All sects were welcome to practise as they desired, and clergy of all faiths received respect and, generally, exemption from taxes. The sole requirement was to say prayers for the Mongol rulers – viewed, from the Mongolian perspective, as celestial insurance. Mongol rulers, queens and other elites patronized various religions, but rarely exclusively. Indeed, many of the Mongolian queens were Nestorian Christians, believing that

Jesus was a human imbued with the Holy Spirit, but they were known to provide funds not only for the construction of churches, of any Christian denomination, but also for Buddhist temples and Muslim mosques.

Yet it would be inappropriate to praise the Mongols for their pre-Enlightenment consciousness. As many of the Mongols followed their native shamanistic practices, they did not quite conceive of a spiritual life in the same manner that Christians, Muslims, Buddhists and others did. Much of their rationale for religious toleration stemmed from the basic insistence on imperial stability. The Mongols realized that religious strife could lead to increased violence and insecurity, so they took steps to prevent it.

However, as the empire fragmented, individual rulers and courts gradually gravitated to the religion of their subjects or allies until they became Muslims or Buddhists. This greatly facilitated the spread of both Islam and Buddhism. Although several among the Mongol elite had been Christian in the early empire, the number of Christians in Asia diminished as the Mongols focused their attention on the majority religion in each area. Whether some of the initial conversions were sincere or motivated by other reasons hardly matters. Within a few generations, the Mongols viewed themselves as belonging to their adopted religion and, correspondingly, favoured it above others. Thus ended a period of remarkable religious toleration.

The Mongol Empire remains the largest contiguous empire ever to have existed. While the very word Mongol still conjures images of sweeping destruction and mayhem, it is quite clear that factors beyond the military made the Mongol Empire truly great. A more recent trend in the 21st century has been for historians to reassess the long-term impact of the Mongol Empire with a focus on trade, religion and the exchange of ideas. Nonetheless, while the Mongols came to view their domination as ordained from heaven, even Chinggis Khan appears to have been amazed by his success. He realized that only through unity, always fleeting among the nations of the steppe, and an adherence to the principles upon which the empire was founded could the empire remain strong. It is recorded that he once said:

> If the rulers, who come after the present one, and the grandees, bagaturs, and noyans, who surround them do not in all things obey the [Yasa], the work of the government will be jeopardized and discontinued. Then they will be glad to find a second Chingis [sic] Khan, but they will find none.[16]

Indeed, within two generations, the empire had split into four and it continued to spiral into ever smaller units. While many attempted to walk in the footsteps of Chinggis Khan, no leader has come close to his accomplishments.

## CHAPTER TWO

# China: The Ming  1368–1644

## J. A. G. ROBERTS

The Ming dynasty (*ming* means 'brightness') was the last native Chinese dynasty to rule China. It overthrew the Yuan, or Mongol, dynasty in 1368 and was in turn overthrown by the Qing, or Manchu, dynasty from Manchuria in 1644.

The Ming period has been described as 'one of the great eras of orderly government and social stability in human history.'[1] For 276 years a population far greater than that of Europe enjoyed long periods of peace. The economy expanded, a dynamic urban culture developed and scholarship and art reached new levels of achievement. The period began with territorial expansion and ambitious maritime expeditions, but then turned to a defensivity marked by the construction of the Great Wall. Ming rule developed absolutist tendencies, which inhibited further political development. From about the middle of the 16th century a succession of ineffectual emperors, court intrigues, internal disorder and external threats were the characteristics of a long period of decline and fall.

### The Establishment of the Ming Dynasty

The dynasty came to power by overthrowing the Mongol Yuan dynasty that conquered north China early in the 13th century and the rest of China in 1279. Zhu Yuanzhang, who was to become the first Ming emperor, was born in 1328 in Nanjing province. This region had been badly affected by the silting up of the Grand Canal, and was also an area where the White

**KEY DATES**

| | |
|---|---|
| **1368** | The Ming dynasty is established in China |
| **1370** | The examination system is reintroduced |
| **1398** | Hongwu, the first Ming emperor, dies |
| **1405** | Zheng He sails on his first great voyage |
| **1407** | The Yongle encyclopaedia is published |
| **1421** | The Ming capital is moved from Nanjing to Beijing |
| **1449** | The Tumu incident: the Ming switch to a defensive strategy |
| **c.1500** | Rise of commercial printing in China |
| **1514** | First Portuguese ship reaches China |
| **1531** | 'Single Whip' tax reform is initiated in China |
| **1550s** | Construction of the Ming Great Wall begins |
| **1590s** | *Journey to the West [Monkey]* appears in print |
| **1593** | The Bencao Gangmu (the Compendium of *Materia Medica*) is published |
| **1601** | Matteo Ricci resides in Beijing |
| **1602–4** | European mania for Chinese porcelain begins |
| **1628** | Rebellions break out in north China |
| **1644** | The Ming dynasty is overthrown by the Manchus |

Lotus sect, a Buddhist sect that anticipated the coming of a future Buddha, was very strong. From about 1340 White Lotus adherents, calling themselves the Red Turbans, turned to violence and Zhu Yuanzhang, whose parents had died of famine in 1344, was caught up in this movement. When in 1351 Toghto, the last effective Yuan leader, conscripted thousands of men to dredge the Grand Canal and re-route the Yellow River, a major Red Turban rebellion broke out. Zhu Yuanzhang joined one of the rebel bands, recruited men from his local region, and married the daughter of

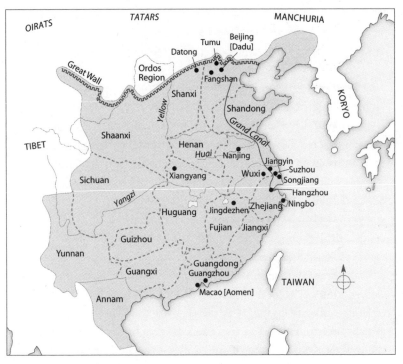

Map showing the Ming Empire.

the leader of the band. His military ability led to his emergence as a major leader; one of his most famous battles was a naval engagement fought on the vast Poyang Lake. Unlike other Red Turban leaders, Zhu was willing to take advice from Confucian scholars. In 1356 he captured Nanjing and established a civil administration, severing his links with the Red Turban leadership. He proceeded cautiously and it was only in 1368, after the death of his main rivals, that he declared himself emperor and assumed the reign title of Hongwu. He sent an expedition north and forced the Yuan court to flee from its capital of Dadu, then in 1372 despatched a large force into Mongolia to prevent further Mongol incursions. The south western province of Sichuan, which had been occupied by a branch of the Red

Turbans, was recaptured, the Korean state of Koryo, which had fallen under Mongol control, was forced to recognize the new dynasty, and in 1379 Tibet acknowledged the legitimacy of the new regime.

## The Reign of Hongwu, 1368–98

Hongwu declared that his intention was to restore the ideal society of Han civilization, which had been despoiled by Mongol rule. He claimed to be restoring the practices of the Tang (618–907) and Song (960–1279) dynasties, but he retained features of government introduced by the Mongols. Notable examples of this were a military system headed by a hereditary officer class and a political system that continued the Yuan form of central government. Hongwu's government was headed by two chancellors, who conducted all routine business; a bureau of military affairs, which supervised the armed forces; and the censorate, which watched over the work of officials. Away from the capital, branch secretariats administered areas that were the forerunners of the modern provinces of China. Hu Weiyong, one of Hongwu's earliest supporters, played a major role in the development of civil government and he was given the post of chancellor. However, the influence Hu Weiyong acquired over the bureaucracy led to him being accused of disloyalty and, in 1380, Hongwu turned against him. He was executed and 15,000 others accused of supporting him were purged. The post of chancellor was abolished, the military commission was fragmented, and Hongwu became his own chief minister.

Hongwu was a hard-working and conscientious ruler. He oversaw the promulgation of a new legal code, promoted resettlement schemes and encouraged textile production and trade. Two of his actions were particularly memorable. One was the revival of the examination system, which, for much of the Yuan period, had been in abeyance. Success in the state examinations once again became the main avenue for entry into the civil service, which comprised about 15,000 officials. Of the successful candidates only a few hundred gained the highest award, the title of *jinshi*. When in 1397 Hongwu discovered that not a single northerner had passed the *jinshi* examination, he introduced a system of quotas to ensure the representation of various groups among the examination candidates.

Hongwu's other major reform concerned the land tax system. In 1370 he had ordered that every family in the country should have a certificate recording its status and occupation. These records were consolidated into the 'Yellow Books' of registers. He also commissioned a cadastral survey, producing a detailed record of land-holdings that became known as 'fish-scale books' because the charts resembled the scales of fishes. Rural families were organized in a system known as the *lijia*, groupings of 110 households, which were held jointly responsible for the payment of taxes and the performance of labour services.

A description of the actions taken by the early Ming government raises the question: was this the work of a state? Did the Ming government exercise powers that were not available to European states until the 16th century? The administrative system imposed by Hongwu, which has been described as 'powerful, well articulated, ambitious to penetrate social life'[3] would seem to be characteristic of a state. There are other examples of government activity that provide evidence of the state's ability to intervene in society: the control of publishing and the stocking of libraries with approved books; the regulation of Buddhist institutions and clerics; and the monopoly of the means of violence. Moreover these systems, these controls, were imposed on a continental scale. On this evidence the use of the term 'state' would appear appropriate. However, a Ming emperor was not an absolute monarch, because he had to follow constitutional precedents. State intervention required the co-operation of the gentry – those leading families whose sons had succeeded in the examination system and who had supplied members of the bureaucracy. The gentry, in turn, were well aware of the need to take account of the interests of the communities within which they lived. The Ming was a state with considerable powers to govern and intervene, but it was also a state that competed with local elites over the control of resources and had to accept that it could not alter social practices such as kinship rules.[4]

Hongwu died in 1398 and was buried on the slopes of Zijinshan, on the outskirts of Nanjing, where his body still lies. His posthumous reputation has been mixed. On the one hand he has been praised for his role in expelling the Mongols and admired for his determined efforts at state-building. On the other hand, he has been criticised for the despotic nature of his rule and the violence of his purges. One redeeming feature of his personality may be recorded. He was deeply attached to his consort, the Empress Ma, who until her death in 1382 may have exercised a moderating influence on Hongwu's suspicious and vengeful character.

## The Reign of Yongle, 1403–24

Hongwu was succeeded by his grandson, who was soon deposed by his uncle the Prince of Yan, the commander of the northern frontier army. The prince, to be known as the Yongle emperor, justified his action by claiming that his predecessor was ineffectual and depraved. However, throughout his reign he remained vulnerable to the charge of being a usurper.

Yongle's reign is remembered for two major initiatives, the first of which was the decision to move the capital from Nanjing in the south to Beijing in the north, which had become his power base. He decided to move soon after his accession, and chose Dadu, the location of the Yuan imperial court, as the site of his new capital. A palace of 9,000 rooms was designed, with its main buildings facing south and the whole complex arranged on a north-south axis. In 1406 the collection of materials for its construction began. Vast quantities of the hardwood *nanmu* tree were transported 1,500 kilometres (about 930 miles) from Sichuan province. Huge slabs of marble, one of which weighed about 180 tons, were quarried at Fangshan and dragged to the site in winter, over surfaces of ice. The labour was provided by a million convicts and conscripts, and by 100,000 craftsmen. At the same time the Grand Canal was restored and extended to ensure the food supply to Beijing. The Forbidden City was completed by 1420 and the following year the emperor and his entourage moved into their new capital.[5]

Yongle's second major initiative was the pursuit of an ambitious foreign policy. At the beginning of his reign the main military threat came from inner Asia. In 1404 the Mongol ruler Timur (Tamerlane) set out to conquer China, but died en route in the following year. In Mongolia the Tatar and Oirat tribes continued to present a danger. Yongle led five expeditions against them, employed tactics of divide and rule and inflicted a severe defeat on the Oirat. The emperor died in the course of his last campaign, leaving the Chinese frontier still insecure.

Between 1405 and 1421 Yongle commissioned six major maritime expeditions. The motives for his despatching these expeditions are not clear. Perhaps he was searching for his dethroned nephew, who was rumoured to have survived his deposition and to have fled abroad. More probably the expeditions were intended to search for treasure and to promote the reputation and recognition of the emperor.

The expeditions sailed under the command of Zheng He, a Muslim from Yunnan, who had become a trusted adviser to the emperor. The first expedition, which set out in July 1405 and which comprised 62 large vessels, 255 smaller ones and crews of 27,870 men, visited Java, Melaka, Sri Lanka and Calicut in south-west India. Ambassadors from these places accompanied the fleet when it returned to Nanjing and presented tribute. Two years later a second expedition returned to Calicut and invested the local ruler with Chinese titles and gifts, a memorial being erected to commemorate this event. On the third expedition, which retraced the previous route, the king of Sri Lanka tried to plunder the fleet. He was defeated and taken as a prisoner to Nanjing. The fourth expedition, which set out in 1413, was even larger. Its sixty-three great ships were up to 80 metres (262 feet) long, far bigger than the typical Spanish three-master of the time, which barely measured 30 metres (98 feet) in length. This expedition sailed on past Calicut and reached Hormuz on the Persian Gulf, and ships from the expedition reached Aden and sailed down the east coast of Africa as far as Malindi in present-day Kenya. Members of this expedition reached Mecca and recorded of its inhabitants:

They speak the A-la-pi language. The law of the country prohibits wine-drinking. The customs of the people are pacific and admirable. There are no poverty-stricken families. They all observe the precepts of their religion, and law-breakers are few. It is in truth a most happy country.[6]

In 1417 Zheng He's fleet revisited the African coast and brought back a spectacular cargo of tribute and exotic animals, including the first giraffes seen in China. The last voyage headed by Zheng He was on a smaller scale and had as its main task the return to their homes of foreign ambassadors who had for long resided in China. Ships from this expedition reached Jiddah, but there is no evidence to support claims that they also reached the Americas or Australia.

After Yongle's death in 1424 a seventh expedition returned to the Persian Gulf, but this was to be the last of the great voyages. On a tablet he erected in Fujian province Zheng He summarized what he had achieved:

We have traversed more than one hundred thousand *li* [a *li* is approximately one-third of a mile] of immense waterspaces and have beheld in the ocean huge waves rising sky high, and we have set eyes on barbarian regions far away hidden in a blue transparency of light vapours, while our sails, loftily unfurled like clouds day and night, continued their course [as rapidly as] a star, traversing those savage waves as if we were treading a public thoroughfare.[7]

But by now the expeditionary programme had been abandoned. For two decades China had displayed its maritime power and expanded its tribute system. The 'treasure ships' had brought back wealth to China, but it is doubtful whether the voyages made a profit, and after Yongle's death any political advantage they had gained was no longer apparent. Before the end of the century China's lead in geographical knowledge and commercial enterprise was being overhauled rapidly by the Portuguese.[8]

## Military Defeat and the Great Wall

Yongle's death marked the end of the expansionary stage of the Ming period. In 1449 the Tumu incident, 'the greatest military fiasco of Ming times',[9] forced the dynasty onto the defensive, a posture which it was to maintain until it fell two centuries later.

The incident had its origins in Ming attempts to control the steppe transition zone, that is, the intermediate zone between the steppes and settled regions. The key area was the Ordos region, north of Shaanxi province and south of the Yellow River. If China controlled this area, it could exert influence on the steppes, but if it lost control there the security of China was at risk. Hongwu had recognized the importance of the Ordos region and accordingly established a string of garrisons in the area. However, Yongle, although he had campaigned vigorously in the region, withdrew the outer frontier garrisons, thereby surrendering control of the zone.

In the 1440s the Oirat tribes, the Western Mongols, were united by a new leader, Esen. The Oirat had enrolled as tributaries of the Ming early in the dynasty and this gave them the right to present tribute at the Chinese court. However, they were dissatisfied with the terms of this relationship and took offence when the very large tribute mission of 1448 was treated contemptuously by Wang Zhen, the chief eunuch. The following year Esen led a large force aiming at Datong, a key garrison town on the northern frontier. When news of this threat reached the Chinese court, Wang Zhen urged the Zhengtong emperor (r.1435–49; 1457–64), who was only twenty-two years old, to counter-attack. Notwithstanding warnings from military leaders who knew the dangers of campaigning against the Mongols, a force of half a million men was assembled hastily with the emperor at its head. Despite heavy rain and the defeat of supporting units, for sixteen days this force attempted to pursue the Mongols. Wang Zhen then called off the expedition. The army retreated and fell straight into the trap prepared by Esen at Tumu. The Chinese army was surrounded and the emperor was captured.

Such was the panic in Beijing when news of the emperor's capture was received that it was suggested that the court should abandon the capital. However, Yu Qian, the minister for war, took charge. The emperor's younger brother was placed on the throne and some order was restored. Fortunately for the dynasty, Esen's leadership of the Mongols soon faltered. In 1450 the former emperor relinquished his claim to the throne and returned to Beijing, but the presence of two emperors in the capital caused constant intrigue. In 1457, in a coup d'état, the former emperor was restored to the throne and Yu Qian was sentenced to death. His reputation as a defender of China's spirit was to be preserved in a memorial temple in Beijing and for many years students taking the metropolitan examinations would visit Yu Qian's shrine to invoke his spirit.[10]

The Tumu incident marked the point when the Ming dynasty, like other Chinese dynasties previously, abandoned control of the steppe transition zone and elected to pursue a defensive strategy towards the inhabitants of the steppes, a strategy marked in particular by the construction of the Great Wall. This was not the first defensive wall to be built in that area. The First Emperor (r.221–210 BCE) had ordered the construction of walls to protect the northern frontiers of his empire, consolidating earlier defences.

Through the 1470s the comparative cost and advantages of campaigning and the construction and garrisoning of walls was debated. The chief proponent of a wall strategy, Yu Zijun, who had been put in charge of the Ordos, built 965 km (600 miles) of walls sealing off the region. The value of this barrier was demonstrated in 1482 when a large band of Mongol raiders was trapped against the wall and suffered a severe defeat. Nevertheless it was not until the 1550s, when a new Mongol leader, Altan Khan, posed a major threat to the Ming, that the construction of the Great Wall began. Over the next fifty years, proceeding largely from west to east, walls were constructed with forts and signalling towers to warn of attacks. Whereas in the past defensive structures had been built out of pounded earth by local people, the new wall was built of brick and stone. To support the construction, brick kilns and quarries were developed and transportation routes opened up. It was said that the work that one man might have done in a month using earth as a building material now required a hundred men to complete in stone.[11]

## Ming Absolutism

The political character of the Ming period is often referred to as 'Ming absolutism'. Hongwu's decision to abolish the post of chancellor and to carry out the duties of chief minister himself ensured that no part of central government enjoyed any degree of autonomy. Provincial governments were under strict supervision and towns and cities did not secure the liberties enjoyed by some places in the West. Although China had developed a sophisticated judicial system, the courts could not challenge the exercise of imperial power. The absolutist framework was supported by systems of surveillance. Hongwu used secret agents and a body known as the Embroidered Guards to denounce those suspected of disloyalty. He treated corrupt officials with notorious harshness. On one occasion an official who had been found guilty of accepting a bribe was decapitated, his head spiked on a pole and his body flayed and stuffed with straw.

The Xuande emperor (r.1426–35) reorganized the operation of the censorate, the agency that supervised the workings of government. During his reign 240 officials were demoted, 659 officials were impeached and 251 memorials were submitted to the emperor offering him counsel and remonstrance. It was a long-established, although fragile, convention that officials had a duty to remonstrate with the emperor if they felt he was failing to perform his role appropriately. The most famous instance of a remonstrance occurred in 1565, when Hai Jui, an official who had a reputation as an unflinching critic of wrongdoing, submitted a memorial impeaching the emperor himself. For this he was imprisoned and only released when the emperor died. His celebrated protest was to be remembered during the Cultural Revolution, when a play entitled *Hai Jui Dismissed from Office* was denounced as a covert attack on Mao Zedong.

Another aspect of Ming rule associated with absolutism was the role played by court eunuchs. Eunuchs had no independent basis of power and so were the most reliable of agents to preserve imperial absolutism. Hongwu, aware that eunuchs had meddled in the politics of previous dynasties, ordered the erection of an iron tablet with the inscription:

> Eunuchs are forbidden to interfere with government affairs. Those who attempt to do so will be subjected to capital imprisonment.[12]

Nevertheless, eunuchs were appointed to control the secret police and under the Xuande emperor a palace eunuch school was established and eunuchs became the emperor's personal secretaries. Under Hongwu there had been only a few hundred court eunuchs. By the end of the 15th century their numbers had grown to about 10,000 and by the end of the Ming period to approximately 100,000. One reason for this increase was to serve the Ming royal family, which by 1604 was estimated to number over 80,000. Another was the indispensable role eunuchs played in the performance of court rituals and the transmission of official documents, a role which led them to be described as 'the cogs and grease of the Ming despotic machinery'.[13]

Some eunuchs gained such influence at court that they have been described as 'eunuch dictators'.[14] The role of Wang Zhen, who precipitated the Tumu crisis, has already been noted. The most infamous of the eunuch dictators was Wei Zhongxian, who rose to power under the Tianqi emperor (r.1621–27). The emperor showered him with gifts and allowed him to instigate a reign of terror.

## The Economy under the Ming

The Ming Empire comprised China proper, the fifteen provinces where Han Chinese were the dominant population, but excluded Tibet, Xinjiang, Manchuria and Inner Mongolia. Although the vast majority of the inhabitants were Han Chinese, there were also many minority groups, especially in the south west of the country. In 1368 the population of China was approximately 65 million. By 1644 it had risen to about 150 million. At the beginning of the Ming period approximately 400 million *mou* of land (a *mou* is about one seventh of an acre) was under cultivation and by the time the dynasty had fallen this area had increased to about 500 million *mou*. This increase was in part a result of internal migration to the province of Yunnan and Guizhou and the opening of arable land in those areas. More land under cultivation and greater agricultural productivity enabled the food supply at least to keep up with population growth.

An agricultural revolution had already occurred under the Song: new crops had been introduced (including fast-ripening Champa rice, which enabled double cropping); irrigation had been extended; and a free market in land had been introduced. Through the three centuries of Ming rule there were no dramatic advances in agricultural technology but many incremental improvements. There was also the introduction in the late Ming period of plants from the New World, notably sweet potatoes, peanuts and maize. By then cotton was planted on some of the best land in the lower Yangzi region and a major cotton industry had developed. The key economic development was the transition, in regions where climate and communications favoured improvement, from a subsistence economy to one of specialized production for the market.

The Ming period saw a remarkable expansion of internal and external trade. The number and size of towns and cities grew rapidly and the volume of inland trade grew continually. China was importing substantial quantities of raw materials, in particular spices and hardwood from South-East Asia, and was the world's largest exporter of manufactured goods. Silk was exported in vast quantities to Nagasaki and to Manila, where it was sold on to Spain. Jingdezhen, in Jiangxi, produced a million pieces of porcelain a year for export. Jingdezhen porcelain was manufactured in many shapes and glazes, but the most famous of its wares were pieces decorated in blue underglaze and polychrome enamels. Some of its output was for the imperial court, which set rigorous quality standards. Porcelain to be exported to the Muslim world was decorated with flowers and abstract patterns, while that for Europe carried Christian motifs and coats of arms. A 16th-century description of Jingdezhen stated:

> Tens of thousands of pestles shake the ground with their noise.
> The heavens are alive with the glare from the fires, so that one cannot sleep at night. The place has been called in jest 'The Town of Year-Round Thunder and Lightning'.[15]

In the late 16th century Portuguese traders began purchasing blue and white porcelain, known as Kraak porcelain after the Portuguese carracks in which it was transported. In 1602 and 1604, two Portuguese carracks were captured by the Dutch and their cargoes, over 200,000 items of porcelain, were auctioned in Amsterdam, setting off a European mania for Chinese porcelain.

China's exports of porcelain and silk were paid for in vast quantities of silver: almost all the silver produced in the mines of South America and Japan between 1570 and 1620 ended up in China. It has been commented that 'Ming China – not London or Seville – was the economic centre of the world in 1600, its global importance analogous to Britain in 1850 or to the United States today'.[16]

It has often been remarked that the Ming period was a period of technological stagnation and as a result China failed to make the transition to an industrial revolution. Various explanations have been put forward for why this occurred. One suggestion is that bureaucratic conservatism among officials inhibited technological progress, another that capital investment was inadequate or that markets were restricted, and a third that improvements in transportation and marketing continually corrected and relieved any bottlenecks in supply.

For one historian, however, Ming China was not a period of stagnation. Francesca Bray argued in her book *Technology and Society in Ming China*[17] that the spread of improved techniques and machinery, and most importantly a major development in transport technologies and facilities, allowed the economy to continue to expand until the 18th century. One example she used to support her view concerned the paper industry and the development of printing. Under the Song paper had been produced in large quantities for government use. Under the Ming the rapid increase in commercial printing led to the development of a paper-manufacturing industry. In Jiangxi one district had 30 paper mills, each with 1,000–2,000 workers. Moveable type had been invented in the mid-11th century, but the problem of using thousands of characters meant that woodblock printing continued to be used and was particularly suitable for small commercial runs of prints. From about 1500 commercial printing began to expand rapidly. Publications included agricultural treatises, among them the *Nongshu* (The Book on Agriculture), written under the Song by Wang Zhen, which appeared in a commercial edition in 1530. Other agricultural treatises provided illustrations and directions for the use of agricultural machinery such as the square-pallet chain-pump, which could be used both to irrigate and to drain land. In the *Tiangong kaiwu* (The Exploitation of the Works of Nature), Song Yingxing (1587–1666) explained the operation of machines such as the draw loom, on which figured cloth could be woven. By the 1550s many books were illustrated with high-quality pictures, diagrams and maps. These books were relatively cheap and some families had libraries amounting to several hundred titles.[18]

The Ming government played only a minor role in the regulation of this economy. Its most important concerns were raising revenue and regulating the currency. The two main sources of government revenue were the land tax, which at the start of the Ming period included labour services, and the salt monopoly. As a punishment for supporting his main rival to the throne, Hongwu had imposed punitive tax assessments on the lower Yangzi prefectures of Suzhou and Songjiang. He had attempted reforms of the land tax, in particular by introducing a tax quota system whereby wealthy families were made responsible for the collection of grain taxes in their area. In practice these reforms were too ambitious for the technological capacity of the Ming state. Moreover, they were based on a mistaken assumption that the level of taxation was too burdensome. This was true in the lower Yangzi provinces, but in general the level was too light to finance the tasks the government should have performed. The shortfall was exacerbated by farming families moving to escape the tax burden. From 1528 onwards the Ming government treasury was constantly in deficit. Starting from 1531 a series of measures, known as the 'Single Whip reform', were introduced. The key change was the amalgamation of the land tax and the labour service requirement into a single payment, which had to be made in silver. The reform was first introduced in the south, and gradually extended to other parts of the empire. It has been described as the beginning of a modern land tax system, but in practice it fell far short of that description. The payment of tax in kind and the performance in labour services continued in some areas and the land tax system became more rather than less complicated.

The Ming government's record with regard to the currency was also mixed. A paper currency had first been issued under the Song but over-issue of notes towards the end of the Yuan period had led to inflation and a silver shortage. In the early Ming measures were introduced to enforce the use of paper money, but this currency was not convertible and it depreciated rapidly. By 1450 the issue of notes was suspended, and so China, the first country in the world to issue a paper currency, was forced to switch to a bimetallic system using copper and silver, with one tael, or ounce, of silver being equal to one thousand copper cash.

## Ming Society

An aristocratic elite had completely disappeared by the Southern Song period and under the Ming only the royal family enjoyed privileges based on birth. The true elite of the age was the gentry or literati. The term 'gentry' is used to translate the Chinese term *shenshi*, meaning 'officials and scholars'. Formal entry into this group was determined by the imperial examination system, which served as a means of recruiting officials to fill governmental posts. This system, which can be traced back to the earlier

Han dynasty (206 BCE – CE 9), had been established fully under the Song. The Mongols had mistrusted Chinese officials and for most of the Yuan period the examination system was suspended. Hongwu, although he treated officials with scant respect, recognized the importance of reintroducing the examination system as a means of recruiting talented men to office. The first round of the new examinations began in 1370, with candidates being required to demonstrate their knowledge of the Confucian classics and their skill in archery. Over the next century the organization and content of the examinations was formalized. Examinations were held at three levels, the lowest being the preliminary examinations in the district town. Successful candidates could proceed to the examinations held every two to three years in the prefectural city. If they passed these they received the *xiucai* or 'cultivated talent' degree, which exempted them from labour service and corporal punishment. They could then sit the second-level examinations, held every three years in the provincial capitals. Many thousands of men attended on these occasions, but only about one in two hundred gained the coveted *juren* or 'recommended man' degree which made the holder eligible for appointment to a government post. The third and highest level was that of the metropolitan examinations held every three years in Beijing. Successful candidates became *jinshi*, 'presented scholars', their final test being prescribed by the emperor himself. Those who had become *jinshi*, and at any one time there might be about 2,000–4,000 in the empire, provided the pool from which senior officials were selected.

This extraordinary system, unparalleled in any other great empire, provided a pool of highly educated men to staff the civil service. The syllabus, with its emphasis on detailed knowledge of the Confucian classics, carried a heavy dose of indoctrination. The examinations tested a limited range of skills, and this range became even narrower after 1487 when the famous 'eight-legged essay' ruling was adopted. Essays had to be written under eight main headings, be no more than seven hundred characters long and make much use of balance and antithesis.

Did this unique system offer a career open to talent? A classic study in 1967[20] analysed the background of the 14,562 men who obtained the *jinshi* between 1371 and 1904 according to whether or not their families had produced degree-holders in the three previous generations. In the early Ming 57.6 per cent of *jinshi* came from families without degree holders, and in the later Ming that figure remained as high as 49.4 per cent. Only under the Qing did the figure fall to below 40 per cent. The study concluded that this was evidence of an unparalleled instance of upward social mobility in a major society prior to the industrial revolution.[21] Since this study was published, further research has demonstrated how important it was for examination candidates to come from a family which was prosperous enough to bear the cost of prolonged study, and this prosperity was often associated with land ownership. A family that succeeded in getting one of its members into the bureaucracy would benefit very substantially in material terms. Sons of the highest officials might be appointed to posts without having to pass the examinations. From time to time, when short of funds, the government might sell titles and positions to wealthy families.

The gentry and their families, who in the later Ming period numbered perhaps half a million persons, also played an essential role in local affairs. They assisted district magistrates, the lowest official appointees, in the administration of their district. They performed many of the functions which elsewhere might have been the responsibility of local government, for example by raising funds for public works such as irrigation schemes, and by supervising their construction. They set an example in the building and use of Confucian temples, where they displayed the moral injunctions that Hongwu had issued in 1397:

Be filial, be respectful to elders and ancestors, teach your children, peacefully pursue your livelihood.[22]

For the gentry the promotion of education was of particular importance. At the beginning of Hongwu's reign, in 'a move nothing short of extraordinary in the fourteenth-century world',[23] the emperor had mandated that every county and prefecture in the empire should have an advanced school, and that in every village there should be a 'community school', an elementary school to educate every boy. In the Ming period at least 9,000 of these schools were established. Such an action might be interpreted as evidence of the formidable power of the central government. However, by the late Ming the initiative relating to community schools had passed to the local elite. This partnership between central government and gentry, based in part on common interests, but also marked by the pursuit of the competing interests of both sides, was central to the balance of power under the Ming.[24]

Much of what has been written about the position of women in Ming society is derived from how they were represented in male writings. In dynastic histories and local gazetteers, the emphasis is on women who epitomized female virtue, most obviously in terms of chastity and fidelity to their husbands' memory if widowed. Outstanding examples of a widow's chastity might be rewarded with an imperial commendation or by the erection of a memorial arch. The remarriage of widows was deplored and cases of widows who committed suicide were extolled. Footbinding, a practice that had spread in Song times, was now widespread. Only occasionally was this view of the appropriate role of women in society challenged. The heterodox writer Li Zhi (1527–1602) argued that women were the intellectual equals of men and should have access to education. Although Confucianism praised female chastity, courtesan culture thrived in the late Ming period and plays that depicted romances between talented scholars and devoted courtesans were popular. The famous courtesan Liu Rushi became the concubine of the official and scholar Qian Qianyi (1582–1664). Together they composed poems and compiled books.

## Philosophy, Art and Literature in the Ming Period

In the Song period a Confucian revival had led to the development of a number of schools of thought, one of which was known as the School of

Principle. Its ideas were synthesized by the philosopher Zhu Xi, whose commentaries on the Confucian classics became the interpretation all examination candidates were required to accept. In the Ming period Neo-Confucianism remained the dominant school of thought, but another philosophical school, known as the School of the Mind, which emphasized innate knowledge and the unity of thought and action, was developed by Wang Yangming (1472–1529), who had also had a distinguished career as an official and a soldier. His emphasis on intuitive moral sense was later to be influential in Japan, where he is known as Oyomei.

During the Ming period remarkable compendia of knowledge were produced. In 1407 the *Yongle Dadian* (the Yongle Encyclopedia), a collection in 12,000 volumes of materials relating to the government, history and geography of China, was completed. Another remarkable publication was the *Bencao Gangmu* (the Compendium of *Materia Medica*), which identified and arranged in a logical sequence nearly 1,900 substances of potential medical value. Its author, Li Shizhen (1518–93), had read all the available literature on the subject and had collected many of the materials that were illustrated in the work. He included descriptions of smallpox inoculation and the use of drugs such as ephedrine, derived from the plant *Ephedra sinica* and used in the treatment of asthma and bronchitis. In addition he listed some 8,000 prescriptions.

In the visual arts the most important activity was in the field of landscape painting. One school of painting was associated with scholarly amateurs. A notable representative of this school was Wen Zhengming (1470–1559), a poet and calligrapher from Suzhou, whose landscapes illustrate the austere quality of literati art. Dong Qichang (1555–1636), well known for his calligraphy and poetry, expounded the aesthetic ideals that informed such painting. For him, the scholar painter did not seek to capture outward reality, but aspired to express through his art the inner reality of his own character.[26] Wen Zhengming is also remembered for his part in the development of the Humble Administrator's Garden in Suzhou, which to this day illustrates the ideal world of the Ming aesthetic.

The development of urban society and the advances in the publishing industry also encouraged the emergence of popular literature. Three famous novels, *The Romance of the Three Kingdoms, Water Margin and Journey to the West* (otherwise known as *Monkey*) all of which had previously circulated in handwritten form, now came out in print. The notorious novel *Jin Ping Mei*, also known as the *Golden Lotus*, was published in 1610. It combines a lively picture of social change in late Ming China with graphic descriptions of sexual activity. It has been described as the first true Chinese novel. Feng Menglong (1574–1646), a failed examination candidate who lived in Suzhou, popularized the *huaben*, the vernacular short story, in his *Stories Old and New*. Many of these stories portrayed women engaged in a variety of roles, as entertainer, virago, predator and recluse. Among the poets of the time, Yuan Hongdao (1568–1610) and his two brothers are remembered for their expression of genuine emotion deriving from personal experience.

The leading playwright of the late Ming was Tang Xianzu (1550–1616). His most famous play, *Mudan ting* (The Peony Pavilion), tells the story of two young lovers who first meet in their dreams. The play was set to music in the form known as *kunqu*, one of the oldest surviving forms of Chinese opera. The court maintained troupes of hundreds of actors who gave daily performances of operas.

## Contacts with the West

After the fall of the Yuan dynasty, overland travel from Europe ceased to be practical and the Ming dynasty, when the oceanic voyages had been discontinued, no longer sought out foreign contacts. Instead it fell to the Portuguese to establish a maritime route to China. The first Portuguese ship reached there in 1514 and three years later Tomé Pires, who had been appointed Portuguese ambassador, arrived at Guangzhou and was eventually permitted to travel to Beijing. By the 1550s Portugal had established a trading station at Aomen (Macao). In 1636 Captain John Weddell commanded the first English expedition to China. Its purpose was to challenge the Portuguese near-monopoly of Chinese trade with the West. On board one of the ships was the traveller Peter Mundy, who wrote a lively account of his experiences, which he illustrated with sketches of daily life. He recorded a list of 'China's Excellencies' that read:

> This countrie May bee said to excell in these particulars – Antiquity, largenesse, Ritchenesse, healthynesse, Plentifullnesse. For Arts and manner of governmentt I thinck noe Kingdome in the Worlde Comparable to it, Considered altogether.[27]

In 1552 Francis Xavier, who had begun the Jesuit mission in Japan, died on an island off the south China coast. His failure to obtain permission to preach in China was seen as a challenge to proselytising Christians. In 1577 Father Alessandro Valignano arrived at Aomen and twenty-five years later Matteo Ricci reached Beijing and was allowed to reside there permanently. Ricci's knowledge of the Chinese classics gained him acceptance at court. Among the services he performed there was the production of a map of the world, showing China at its centre, which was published in a Ming encyclopaedia of 1607. Ricci died in 1610, but the Jesuit mission continued, and twenty-one Jesuits left Europe for China in 1618. They brought with them a variety of skills as astronomers, mathematicians and engineers and they were accepted at court. Other Christian missionaries, notably Dominican and Franciscan friars, settled in the coastal provinces.

## The Decline and Fall of the Ming Dynasty

In 1644 the Ming dynasty was overthrown by an internal rebellion, and the rebels were then routed by a Manchu invasion.

Traditional Chinese historiography explained the fall of the Ming by reference to a dynastic cycle. According to that view, dynasties were founded by able and virtuous rulers but their successors failed to maintain the moral standards required. If they ignored warnings about their behaviour, which took the form of portents, the mandate of heaven was transferred to the founder of a new dynasty. Some modern historians have suggested that the concept of a dynastic cycle has some validity, but it is the product of economic and administrative rather than moral factors. The ruler of a new dynasty eliminated his rivals, established an effective government, levied moderate taxes and secured the frontiers. Under later rulers the costs of government rose, powerful families began to evade taxation, and the frontiers became over-extended. In time, officials became corrupt, public works were neglected and the burden of tax borne by the peasants increased. Finally the peasants rose in rebellion and overthrew the dynasty.

If the concept of the dynastic cycle were applied to the Ming, it would be noted that in the later Ming period there were several occasions when the emperor was a minor, or when he had surrendered effective control to eunuchs. The Jiajing emperor (r.1522–66) withdrew from the active supervision of the government for long periods. A notable example of eunuch control occurred in the reign of the incompetent Tianqi emperor (1621–27), which saw the rise of the eunuch dictator Wei Zhongxian.

Another explanation of the fall of the dynasty concerns the response of the elite to social and economic changes in the late Ming period. It has been noted that by the early 16th century Hongwu's ideal society, in which owner-cultivators worked within a subsistence economy, had been subverted by the growth of a wealthy land-based gentry.[29] The gentry found that the competition for examination success had increased and the risks associated with an official career had multiplied. So they changed their orientation from a 'state-centered vision of gentry life', with its emphasis on engagement with worldly affairs, in favour of embracing Buddhism, which implied withdrawal from public life.[30]

The relationship between the state and the gentry was also damaged by a Confucian revival, which gave rise to factional disputes at court. In the late 16th century private academies were established, where scholars and ex-officials bemoaned the decline of Confucian standards and the political immorality of the court. The most famous of these was the Donglin academy based near Wuxi in the Yangzi delta. It was alleged that Donglin had 'set in motion the collapse of the very dynasty they had thought they were rescuing'.[31]

In the late Ming period, and in particular between 1626 and 1640, China experienced unusually severe weather marked by low temperatures, drought and floods. By then the economy was being supported by the inflow of silver to pay for Chinese exports. A European trade depression in the 1620s, and the interruption of trade with the Philippines and Japan in the 1640s, reduced the inflow of silver, damaged the silk industry and drove up the price of grain. However, the sharpest phase in the decline in the influx of silver occurred in the 1650s, after the dynasty had fallen.[32]

The immediate cause of the fall of the dynasty was a peasant rebellion. It has been calculated that the incidence of rebellions and banditry was far higher in the second half of the Ming dynastic period than in the first.[33] These incidents were not a response to social change, because they were more common in the less commercialized parts of the country, nor were they a response to the grosser examples of misgovernment, because the rise in incidents of violence was gradual and incremental. The main reason for the increase was the decline of the coercive capacity of the state. This encouraged peasants, in times of hardship, to suppose that their best chance of survival was to become outlaws.[34] Rebellions broke out in 1628 in northern Shaanxi, an impoverished area which had shared none of the prosperity enjoyed by the Yangzi provinces and which may have been more severely affected by the deteriorating climate than the south of the country. The security of the area, which depended on military garrisons, had broken down, many official posts were vacant and the officials present failed to organize relief to combat a disastrous famine.

By then the dynasty was also facing an external threat from the Manchus, descendants of the Jurchen tribes who had founded the Jin dynasty in 1122. They had been reunified under Nurhaci (1559–1626), who, in 1616, established the Latter Jin dynasty in southern Manchuria. In 1629, his successor Hong Taiji launched the first major Manchu raid into China.

The Manchus withdrew, but Hong Taiji continued to adopt features of Chinese government and obtained the technology to cast cannon from Chinese military experts. In the late 1630s further Manchu raids diverted attention to the north and away from the internal rebellions. Li Zicheng, one of the rebel leaders, had attracted members of the gentry to his side. After he had captured Xiangyang in 1643 he established an administrative structure and announced tax reductions. The following year he declared the foundation of a new dynasty and marched on Beijing. Even at this point it should have been possible for the Ming to offer effective resistance, but it had lost control of large areas of the country, its military forces had collapsed, it was bankrupt, and the will to resist had almost disappeared. On 24 April 1644 Li Zicheng entered Beijing and that same night the emperor hanged himself.

Up to this point a Manchu invasion had seemed improbable. However, several leading Chinese generals, most notoriously Wu Sangui, the commander on the north east frontier, refused to join Li Zicheng and instead promised their support to the Manchus. They may have acted out of self interest, or they may have seen a better guarantee of maintenance of the status quo in the Manchus. In June 1644 the Manchus entered Beijing and assured the population that if they surrendered no harm would come to them. Li Zicheng's rebels were soon defeated. As the Manchus extended their rule to the Yangzi valley there were examples of heroic resistance, for example at Jiangyin, where the population was slaughtered after failing to comply with the order that men should wear the queue. It was not until 1662, when the last Ming emperor, who had fled to Burma (present-day Myanmar), was captured and executed, that the Ming dynasty was finally extinguished.

## CHAPTER THREE

# South-East Asia: The Khmer 802–1566

## HELEN IBBOTSON JESSUP

The phrase 'Khmer Empire' might not at first evoke a clear picture in the mind of the reader. It would not summon up an image of territory and conquest, as 'Roman Empire' would, nor of a set of laws, administrative infrastructure and language, as might 'British Empire'. Many Westerners may know little more of the Khmer than the name of their most famous capital city and religious centre, Angkor.[1] Yet Angkor was the nexus of a polity whose roots in southern Cambodia go back as far as the 6th century or earlier, and the centre of a canopy of civilization that by the 12th century had spread over a wide swathe of mainland South-East Asia.

Did the Khmer create an empire? Certainly their culture and language, which constitute a continuum of two millennia, prevailed for several centuries in a wider arena. This included modern north-eastern Thailand and most of the Mekong Delta area of Vietnam (regions where people still speak Khmer) and southern Laos. Art and architecture bear witness to Khmer hegemony in these regions, but Khmer control seems to have depended on vassals. It was often established through familial connections rather than military conquest. The relationship was different for the segment of central Vietnam that was called Champa, which became an important polity. The Khmer occasionally controlled it, but the balance of power fluctuated and there was intermittent warfare.

The greatest legacy of the Khmer may be the extraordinary art and architecture they created, which still has the power to astonish us today at sites such as Angkor Wat. Their monuments and sculpture gave physical expression to the Khmer concept of kingship, in which the king's right to rule depended upon his visible relationship with the gods. The reliefs and inscriptions preserved at these sites are also vitally important because they are one of our main sources of information about the Khmer. No other written records from the time survive, apart from the accounts of a few Chinese travellers to the region. Another remarkable achievement was Khmer mastery of water resources. From the earliest centuries they dug canals that linked many sites to major river arteries and lakes and provided transport networks as well as water for irrigation and ritual. They diverted streams (the Siem Reap River is almost entirely man-made) and dug enormous reservoirs, or barays; the Western Baray, more than 8 km (5 miles) long, still exists.

## Womb of Empire: The Early Centuries

The earliest written account of Cambodia comes from 3rd-century Chinese envoys,[2] who reported an agricultural society with walled palaces and villages, metalworking skills and writing that resembled Indian script. The Chinese called the country, which lay in southernmost present-day Vietnam and the lower Mekong Delta region, 'Funan', but we do not know what the Khmer then called it. Their rulers were given the title Fan, conceivably a transliteration of pon, a rank appearing in Khmer inscriptions in the 7th century. In 243 CE the ruler Fan Chan sent gifts of dancers and local goods to the Chinese court, indicating two-way communication.

Funan's capital was probably at Angkor Borei in Takeo province, near the sacred mountain of Phnom Da. Angkor Borei was a sizeable city linked by a network of canals and rivers to its port, Oc Eo, where archaeologists have excavated goods indicating connections with India, China and even the Roman Empire. Maritime commerce was the basis for Funan's prosperity, but by the mid-6th century entrepôt ports like Oc Eo were bypassed as improvements in shipbuilding enabled vessels to cross open seas instead of being forced to hug the coastlines. Funan's economy was, inevitably, affected.

## KEY DATES

| | |
|---|---|
| *c.*200–250 CE | First reference in Chinese records to Funan |
| 514–39 | Reign of Rudravarman, last king of Funan and first king of Zhenla |
| 802 | Jayavarman II consecrated as universal monarch (*chakravartin*) |
| 877–900 | Reigns of Indravarman I and Yashovarman I in Hariharalaya |
| *c.*900 | Yashovarman I moves the capital to the Angkor region |
| 921–42 | Reign of Jayavarman IV from Koh Ker |
| 1002–49 | Reign of Suryavarman I and extension of Khmer empire |
| 1050–66 | Reign of Udayadityavarman II; Baphuon temple and Western Baray reservoir constructed |
| 1113–45 | Reign of Suryavarman II and the building of Angkor Wat |
| 1177 | Champa invades Angkor and kills the king |
| 1181–1218 (?) | Reign of Jayavarman VII; he expels the Chams from Angkor and makes Mahayana Buddhism the state religion |
| 1296 | Visit of the Chinese envoy Zhou Daguan, who writes an account of life at Angkor |
| 1431 | Khmer capital moves from Angkor to the region of modern Phnom Penh |
| 1566 | End of reign of Ang Chan I, who returned the capital to Angkor for some decades |

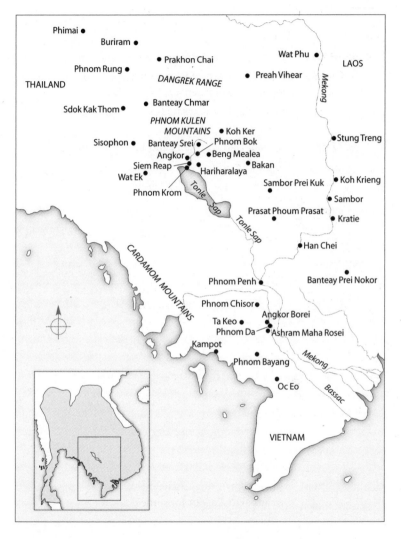

Map showing the extent of the Khmer Empire at its apogee under Jayavarman VII, r.1181–1218 CE.

The decline in Funan's fortunes at this time may be reflected in early 7th-century Chinese records, which state that Funan had been conquered by Chitrasena, a warrior from a polity the Chinese called Zhenla, described as a former vassal of Funan.[3] Local inscriptions in both Sanskrit and Khmer suggest that there were family connections among the rulers of Funan and Zhenla. According to the Chinese, Rudravarman – reported to be the son of a Jayavarman about whom nothing else is known – was the last king of Funan, yet in an inscription of 667 CE the same Rudravarman is mentioned as the predecessor of Bhavavarman I and other kings of Zhenla.[4] A likelier scenario is that Zhenla's emergence, rather than indicating hostile conquest, reflected a geographical shift of power to an inland centre where agricultural wealth countered the decline in maritime trade.

Written evidence of familial links between the Funan area and the more northerly Zhenla (centred in today's Sambor Prei Kuk) is reinforced by similar traits in the art of both regions, particularly in statuary. The spirituality and naturalism of an image from Phnom Da of Krishna (lifting Mount Govardhana to protect peasants from the destructive rainstorm created as punishment by the god Indra) relates strongly to the aesthetic of one of Cambodia's most remarkable treasures, an image of the goddess Durga from an early 7th-century sanctuary at Sambor Prei Kuk. The deity is portrayed slaying the buffalo demon Mahisha, and like the Phnom Da works she epitomizes the dynamic sculptural skills of the Khmer at this very early stage in their history.[5]

Architecture in both Funan and Zhenla shows remarkable sophistication. In Angkor Borei little remains beyond the ruins of many brick structures, but nearby, on Phnom Da, stands Ashram Maha Rosei. This small temple is made of basalt, which must have been brought a long distance, since the only Cambodian source is in Kratie province far to the north. The hauling of such massive quantities of stone to the steep site demonstrates a high level of social and technical organization. The meticulous planing and fitting of the stone blocks and the harmonious proportions of walls, pediments and roof are evidence of established architectural skills. These are not the experiments of beginners.

Extensive architecture demonstrating the achievements of early Khmer polities survives at Sambor Prei Kuk, where several dozen legible sanctuaries remain from a total of 257 identified structures. Three principal groups of monuments – designated North, Central and South – form the core of the capital of Mahendravarman I (r. c. 600–616) and his son Ishanavarman I (r. 616?–637/38), who called the city Ishanapura. Most of the temples are of fine brick. Some have door frames, false doors, lintels, colonettes and thresholds of sandstone, but in many these elements are carved into the brickwork. Many are square, some rectangular, including the two principal structures of the South and North groups; their inner sanctuaries rank among the largest in Cambodia. A particularly interesting group of temples is octagonal, a form unique to this region.[6]

A distinctive feature of the extant architecture at Sambor Prei Kuk is the depiction on the exterior walls of miniature monuments carved in intricate relief. Usually better preserved than the host building, they offer insight into how the architecture looked in its heyday. Peopled by kings, gods, guardians and attendants, often in lively poses, they let us glimpse the fabric of Khmer society. Fragments of the stucco that covered the entire structure remain in places.

Impressive though the art of Angkor Borei and Ishanapura may be, the polities had not extended far enough to be defined as empires. Nor had the realm of Ishanavarman's son, Bhavavarman II. Not until the reign of Jayavarman I (some time between 655 and 657) is there evidence of power extending to regions beyond the capital. The location of Jayavarman's capital is unknown, but it may have been called Purandarapura or Indrapura.[7] Inscriptions suggest that the establishment and merging of religious foundations (which owned land, and were therefore economically and territorially significant) now came under centralized rather than local control. For the first time inscriptions contain imprecations against defiance of royal edicts and mention functions within the royal retinue that hint at a growing complexity of administration. By the 8th century the title of pon had been replaced by *mratan*, a rank conferred, not inherited. The power of small chieftains was being subsumed by the strongest.

Jayavarman I probably died in 681 and was succeeded by his daughter Jayadevi. Her accession date is unknown but the first inscription naming her is from 713, by which time she would have reigned for thirty-two years. All the inscriptions from her reign were found in today's Angkor region and her capital was probably there. After 713, several centres can be inferred. Rulers included a succession of sovereigns in Sambhupura (in Kratie province on the Mekong), of whom three were queens.[8] This dynasty seems to have existed independently from at least the mid-8th century. The territory was well placed to take advantage of the trade associated with the fertile hinterland of the Mekong and its commercial traffic. Inscriptions prove that this dynasty dominated from the Stung Treng region in the north all the way to the delta area.

Another ruling group comprised kings whose names had the suffix -*ditya* ('sun') rather than -*varman* ('protected by'). They reigned in Bhavapura. Further kingdoms mentioned were Dhruvapura, Vyadhapura and Indrapura. There appear to have been a total of seventeen ruling houses in addition to the Bhavavarman to Jayadevi line. Most of these polities are recorded in a single inscription, but their multiplicity and distribution show that Cambodia was not yet centralized at an imperial level.

## Religion and Indian Cultural Influences

Khmer rulers mentioned in Chinese annals were entitled *Fan* and the earliest Khmer inscriptions use *pon*. These are Khmer words. By the 5th century kings' and chiefs' names include Indian vocabulary and use suffixes such as -*varman*.[9] It is not known when such Indian influences began in South-East Asia, but archaeological evidence suggests the first century CE or earlier. Probably the transmission was initially by traders, both Indians visiting the Khmer area and Khmer journeying to India. There is no evidence of permanent Indian settlements in the Khmer region.

Inscriptions show changes in succession and inheritance patterns, along with a vocabulary of governance, which may indicate that the Khmer were adopting an Indic social structure that better suited the ambitions of rulers with expanding territory.

The Khmer position of pon related more to moral than territorial authority, and inscriptions reveal that rank and land management passed not to the *pon*'s son but to his sister's son. Such matrilineal inheritance patterns are characteristic of many South-East Asian societies. Indeed, they probably account for the succession patterns among Funan kings. Even in Angkorian times (from the beginning of the 9th century until the mid-15th century) inheritance was seldom from father to eldest son, but sometimes to a younger son and often from uncle to nephew.[10] As has been argued (see note 4), when material prosperity expanded and small domains were consolidated into significant territory, it may have been expedient for chieftains to adopt Indic patrilineal descent patterns to guarantee the retention of power and wealth within the direct family line.

Besides the introduction of a male-dominated social hierarchy, Indian influences included the use of Sanskrit for many epigraphic records. Indic models also influenced sculpture. The form of Phnom Da and Sambor Prei Kuk statuary relates to the Gupta aesthetic, with its oval faces, refined features, and graceful hip-swayed posture (*tribangha*). In architecture, the Indian sanctuary tower, or *shikhara*, was adopted. Most important, Indian culture added Buddhism and Brahmanism to the religious beliefs of the Khmer, though they did not take over: inscriptions establish that local deities coexisted with Hindu ones. There is evidence of the importance of ancestor spirits (*neak ta*), which are still honoured today.

Associated with these spirits are origin myths revealing common elements in indigenous and Indian belief structures, in particular the *naga* (serpent) as ruler of the water and the underworld, and the mountain as home of the gods, which may explain the easy coexistence of two cultural strands. One legend relates the arrival of an Indian called Kaundinya, inspired by a dream to sail to the Khmer realm. He shoots an arrow into the vessel of its ruling queen, the daughter of the *naga* king. They marry; her father drinks up the waters of her territory and creates the land of the Kambus, a word for 'Cambodians' first cited in a Cham inscription of 817. Its earliest use in Khmer epigraphy occurs in the reign of Indravarman I (877–89); it is of course the basis for the modern 'Cambodia'. The extant Khmer version of the origin legend describes the umbilicus of the kingdom as the Kok Thlok tree.[11] The myth encapsulates the merging of Indic land-based culture with the water-based Khmer, whose myth of origin relates the emergence of the land from a lake.

However Indic culture was transmitted to Cambodia, it was thoroughly absorbed: Sanskrit inscriptions show high literary and epigraphic standards. Indeed, in the early 6th century, two monks from Funan were translating Sanskrit texts for China's Liang emperor.

### Chakravartin, the Universal Monarch: the Early 9th Century

There is little written information from the 8th century: only sixteen inscriptions survive. This has led historians to assume it was a period of decline, but the flowering of architecture and sculpture tells a different story. Temples such as Prasat Wat Kompong Preah and Prasat Phoum Prasat expand the scale and detailing of former monuments. Ak Yum, a now back-filled enormous mound at the south-west corner of the 11th-century reservoir of the Western Baray, provides the prototype for the apogee of Khmer architecture, the temple mountain. Statuary, particularly the lively images of female deities from the Kratie area,[12] also belies the idea of Cambodian stagnation. The paucity of information continued into the 9th century, and with one exception (see note 8) there were no inscriptions after 791 for more than eighty years, a period when enormous changes occurred. For information about this period we must look to retrospective inscriptions from the Angkorian period, of which the most informative is from Sdok Kak Thom, a temple now in Thailand near the Cambodian border at Poipet. The text was inscribed in 1052 by a family of priests who served the Khmer ruler for more than 250 years.[13] The family's founding ancestor, Shivakaivalya, came from Aninditapura and was given land by the king of Bhavapura. This area (all the sites mentioned were in the region near Banteay Prei Nokor in modern Kompong Cham province) was also the likely homeland of Jayavarman II, who came from Vyadhapura and founded a new line of kings. The Khmer text states that:

> His Majesty Parameshvara [the posthumous name of Jayavarman II] installed the kamraten jagat ta raja on Mahendraparvata and established [the family of Shivakaivalya] as permanent priests of the god.[14]

*Kamraten jagat ta raja* literally means 'Lord who is ruler of the world', a phrase translated into Sanskrit as *devaraja*. The term may refer to a linga, a statue or a sacred flame: its exact nature cannot be proved, and attempts to define it remain contentious.[15] The king swore that 'no-one outside the family should ever serve as priests of this god'. The commitment was maintained for 250 years, the succession as chief priest of the royal god passing from each priest to his sister's son. Next '…His Majesty came to reign at Mahendraparvata',[16] where a Brahman called Hiranyadama trained Shivakaivalya in magic rites. Reciting sacred Tantric texts, he established Jayavarman as *chakravartin*, or universal monarch. In addition, he installed the *kamraten jagat ta raja*, or *devaraja*.

The ceremony on Mahendraparvata (Phnom Kulen) signalled the peak of Jayavarman II's status, but it was not so much a sudden ascent to power as the culmination of a series of carefully planned movements that probably began around 770. The account of Shivakaivalya's movements as he followed the king in the relocations of his capital offers a framework to perceive Jayavarman's purposeful extension of territory. With every move, entire retinues of his officials and their dependants accompanied him in an almost transmigratory pattern. Areas where inscriptions name him as king include Purvadisha (probably in the north west) and Sambhupura, where he appears to have married either the last or the penultimate queen,[17] thus

extending his hegemony north from the Mekong basin. From there '…
His Majesty reigned in the city of Hariharalaya'. Now called Roluos, and
close to what became Angkor, Hariharalaya was strategically located near
the Tonle Sap Lake, the source to this day of extraordinary wealth in fish
and the nexus of rivers linked to the Mekong River. 'Then His Majesty
founded the city of Amarendrapura'. In the north west, beyond modern
Battambang, this was a fertile farming area near river connections to the
Gulf of Siam where Ishanavarman I and Jayavarman I had also established
a presence. Through these expansions and consolidations of his predecessors' forays, Jayavarman II gained control over an area bigger than modern
Cambodia.

Naming the site of Jayavarman II's consecration Mahendraparvata
('the mountain of Indra') invoked the power and sanctity of the peak that
was home to the king of the Brahmanistic pantheon. Mahendraparvata's
mountain symbolism was probably more significant than its territorial
importance: although Phnom Kulen gives rise to streams, maintaining a
water supply on its plateau must have been a major challenge, and later
the capital returned to Hariharalaya. Jayavarman died there, probably in
850, and was succeeded by his son, Jayavarman III.

## Hariharalaya: The Consolidation of Power in the 9th Century

Jayavarman II was extolled by subsequent kings as the paradigm of monarchy and the true founder of the empire. As an extender of the realm he
was undoubtedly among the most effective of rulers, but unlike most of
his predecessors and successors he left little material evidence of his presence. With one possible exception, there is no temple or statuary that can
confidently be attributed to his time.[18] Was this because he was too busy
with strategic expansion, staying in each capital too briefly to promulgate
monuments or inscriptions? Did his confident command require no
material props? Whatever the answer, none of the considerable body of
architecture and sculpture dating from the 9th century on Phnom Kulen
can be linked to him.

Little is recorded about Jayavarman III, who died in 877, but having the posthumous name of Vishnuloka he was one of the few kings in Khmer history to proclaim Vishnu as his patron god. This offers a clue to dating the 9th-century temple monuments on Mount Kulen/Mahendraparvata. Many of these monuments enshrined impressive statues of Vishnu, as distinct from the Shiva lingas (or later, anthropomorphic figures) that were usually the predominant images in Khmer temples.[19] The Vishnuite designation suggests that Jayavarman III was their instigator, while the impressive structures of the temples suggest a reign of consolidation and stability. We can speculate also that although the king resided in Hariharalaya, Mount Kulen/Mahendraparvata retained its symbolic status and was the chosen site for his sacred architecture.

Matrilineal descent was in play again with the ascension of Indravarman I (r.877–89), whose mother was related to Jayavarman II's wife. The Sdok Kak Thom inscription says:

> During the reign of His Majesty Ishvaraloka [posthumous
> name of Indravarman I] the …*kamraten jagat ta raja*… was in
> Hariharalaya…Vamashiva, grand-nephew of Shivakaivalya, was the
> teacher of the king.[20]

Vamashiva was not the chief priest of the *kamraten jagat ta raja*, but that priest's brother, indicating that the Shivakaivalya family not only provided in perpetuity the protector of the *devaraja*, but also the guru of the king's heir. The growing importance of this clan indicates the increasing complexity of the court and of the hierarchy of governance.

On his accession in 877 Indravarman vowed '…in five days from today I will begin to dig.'[21] This might refer to the construction of Indratataka, the first of the huge reservoirs created by Khmer monarchs, or to one of the two temples of his reign, Preah Ko and Bakong, or perhaps to all three. These three foundations established a precedent, namely, the improvement of public works such as ponds and canals and the building of an ancestor temple and a state temple (usually a temple mountain). The scope and complexity of Indravarman's constructions indicate the technical and organizational expertise that only a sophisticated state could command.

Preah Ko's foundation stele, after homage to Shiva, gives Indravarman's accession date and genealogy, and describes his royal possessions ('the venerable lion throne, the [palace]…and [pavilion]…made of gold to his own design'); praises his qualities ('…endowed with all virtue and irresistible heroism') and appearance ('…how then to distinguish between…his face and the moon?'); and compares him to several deities.[22] Stanza 28 provides the date (879/80) of the dedication of the divinity in each of Preah Ko's six towers, the three front (east) towers enshrining a god, the three rear towers a goddess. Inscriptions on some of the towers' lintels identify the deity within and associate it with one of Indravarman's ancestors, male in the east towers and female in the west.

The reverse face of the Preah Ko stele was inscribed in 893 by Indravarman's son, Yashovarman I, and describes donations to deities in two of the towers. The brick temple was supplemented in mid-construction by elements of sandstone.[23] The quality of building technique, the refinement of carving and the complexity of iconography establish a new level of ambition and scale for Cambodian temples and illustrate the growing power and confidence of the kingdom.

Bakong, Indravarman's state temple mountain, demonstrates this expansion. Its foundation stele is dated 881 CE. Given its immensity – the five-level pyramid, clad entirely in sandstone with a laterite core, rises almost 30 m (98 ft) above the ground with a footprint of 65 by 67 m (213 by 219 ft) – its construction must have been launched early in the reign. The pyramid is surrounded by smaller shrines, including eight brick towers described as:

> … housing the eight manifestations of Shiva … earth, wind, fire, moon, sun, water, ether and sacrifice.[24]

The imposing scale and the meticulous carving testify to the king's imperial ambitions, an expression of power echoed by the hieratic sculptures once enshrined in the towers. Their majesty and iconic detachment contrast markedly with the naturalistic images from Sambor Prei Kuk (see pages 76 and 78).

Evidence of monuments at Hariharalaya from the reigns of Jayavarman II or III is scant. This is also true for the likely site of the royal palace, an essential feature of the capital, but it has recently been suggested that the palace, built of perishable materials like all secular Khmer buildings, was situated in an elevated plain north of the temple of Prei Monti.[25] The discovery there of high-quality Tang Chinese and other ceramic sherds, indicating imported luxury items, lends weight to the case for a royal residence.

Inscriptions, both contemporary and later, praise Indravarman's prowess as a warrior, although no conquests are named. We know his power extended to near Ubon in the Mun valley in Thailand, because a text there dated 886 refers to him as freeing mankind from the burdens of birth and death.[26] Claims by his successor that Indravarman's kingdom extended from 'the sea to China' should be met with caution: the extravagance of royal eulogies was not always anchored to reality. However, Indravarman's Kambuja (a name for Cambodia first recorded in an 817 Cham inscription) can certainly be ranked as a considerable realm. Evidence of administrative control is lacking, so the farthest areas were possibly held in vassalage. Therefore, the kingdom could not yet properly be described as an empire.

Yashovarman I (r.889 – early 10th century) succeeded his father, and like him built a temple honouring his ancestors, the complex of Lolei erected in the middle of Indratataka on an artificial island, the first known example of a type called a Mebon.[27] Dedicated in 893, Lolei has four brick towers configured in two rows, and its remarkably fine lintels, colonettes and niches housing standing male (front) and female (rear) guardians are in the style of Preah Ko.

## The Roots of Angkor: The Beginning of the 10th Century

Around the turn of the 10th century Yashovarman I transferred his capital about 15 km (just over 9 miles) to the Angkor region, where he had already launched projects. The reason for the move is not certain. By 890 he had begun his own huge reservoir, known as Yashodharatataka (today's East Baray). It provides a staggering example of the hydraulic ambitions of the Khmer, since its construction entailed altering the course of the Siem Reap River. Twelve surviving inscriptions relate that the king created a hundred Yashodharashrama establishments, four of them on the baray's southern edge.[28] These hermitages were dedicated to many gods, including the Buddha, suggesting an ecumenical attitude characteristic of many Khmer monarchs.

At the heart of the new capital, Yashodharapura, the king established his state temple on the mountain he named Yashodharagiri (now Phnom Bakheng). Inscriptions indicate that it was intended as a microcosm of Mount Meru, home of the Brahmanistic deities. Hacked into the steep hillside and clad in sandstone, with its dominant location and rich iconography, this temple mountain embodies a new monumentality in Khmer architecture. Rising 65 m (213 ft) above the plain on five receding terraces on the levelled peak of the hill, it is crowned on its upper platform with five towers in quincunx formation. This arrangement comprises a central, slightly higher tower with four subsidiary towers around it and symbolizes Mount Meru, the sacred home of the Brahmanistic gods. The quincunx arrangement was to become a common form in Khmer architecture.[29]

The rare hills in the central Khmer plain make an impression disproportionate to their modest height and perhaps Yashovarman wished to expand his visibility by also crowning Phnom Bok, north east of his capital, and Phnom Krom, to its south near the Tonle Sap Lake, with temples. They comprise, among several structures, three towers dedicated to the trinity of Shiva, Vishnu and Brahma.

Like Indravarman, Yashovarman was extolled as a mighty warrior though no campaigns were specified. The epigraphic record is rich despite his relatively short reign, and its distribution gives evidence of a hegemony approaching imperial scale even though major architecture was still restricted to the capital region. By the time of his death (uncertain, but before 910) inscriptions indicate that that his kingdom stretched from near the present-day Shan states in Myanmar in the west to Champa in modern Central Vietnam in the east, and from Champassak in Laos as well as the Yunnan region in the north to the Gulf of Thailand in the south.

The next two kings were both Yashovarman's sons. Between 912 and 922 inscriptions cite Harshavarman I, and in 925 there is a reference to his brother, Ishanavarman II. They ruled in Yashodharapura but little is known about them and the period of their reigns produced few monuments. Khmer boundaries were unaltered during this period, perhaps because of the complications of the reign of Jayavarman IV (r. 921/28–942), who was the husband of the maternal aunt of Harshavarman and Ishanavarman.

## The Grandeur of Koh Ker

Between 921 and 928, while his nephews were ruling from Yashodharapura, the king who proclaimed himself Jayavarman IV reigned simultaneously as sovereign of the Cambodians from his estate at Chok Gargyar (Lingapura in some inscriptions, now called Koh Ker) about 80 km (50 miles) north east of Angkor. There is no evidence of conflict among the monarchs so it is conceivable that Jayavarman was a vassal king until the death of Ishanavarman II in 928, at which time he became *chakravartin*. This is described in the Sdok Kak Thom inscription:

> During the reign of His Majesty Paramashivapada [Jayavarman IV's posthumous name] the king left Yashodharapura to reign at Chok Gargyar and brought the *devaraja* with him.[30]

The high priest of the Shivakaivalya clan, Ishanamurti, established himself there. No date is given, but the supreme title was probably conferred in 928.

Koh Ker is in a dry region and the source of the prosperity enabling Jayavarman to execute his prodigious building programme is unknown. The remains of numerous ponds may indicate an extensive irrigation system, of which an early project was probably Jayavarman's baray, the Rahal. The Koh Ker complex comprises more than sixty structures. The grandiose proportions of the Koh Ker temples and their components are echoed by its statuary. Considering that the vast complex was built in just over twenty years, construction must have been continuous. It seems that architectural prowess sufficed for Jayavarman IV, as there is no evidence that he or his son and successor, Harshavarman II (who ruled from Koh Ker for just two years, 942–44) expanded the realm beyond its established borders.

## Return to the Heartland: Second Half of the 10th Century

Rajendravarman succeeded to the throne in 944. He returned to Yashodharapura, a name he retained, and by 947 had completed the temple of Baksei Chamkrong that had been begun earlier in the century. Its inscription says the king waged war against Champa and burned its capital. It also refers to the king's serious study of Buddhism. Rajendravarman seems to have had an ecumenical approach to religion, perhaps through the influence of Kavindrarimathana, a Buddhist who was the senior minister responsible for the magnificent architecture of his reign.[32]

Rajendravarman's first monument, the East Mebon temple mountain of 952 in the East Baray, was possibly his ancestor temple, though it is unusual in being a pyramid. In quincunx form (like Prasat Phnom Bakheng), it is distinguished by some of the most beautiful lintel and colonette carving in all Khmer architecture. Rajendravarman's state temple, Pre Rup (961), was dedicated just eight years later. Of red brick and laterite with sandstone door and stairway elements, it is also in quincunx form, with similarly high-quality carving and a spacious layout. The pyramid has three levels with a base of 50 m (164 ft) and a height of 12 m (40 ft) in harmonious proportions that make Pre Rup one of the most pleasing of Khmer monuments. Kavindrarimathana was also responsible for the three-towered Bat Chum (960), a rare Buddhist temple, and the beginning of a royal palace.

Temple construction was linked not only to the merit obtained from such acts of piety and the glory reflected on the donor, but also to the control of the land entailed for the support of the establishments and the retinues needed for their upkeep. A reign with prolific building projects in the heartland was almost certainly one of consolidation of power. Although trade with what is now north-east Thailand seems to have grown, the boundaries of the Khmer kingdom did not expand during Rajendravarman's reign, nor that of his son and successor, Jayavarman V. The period from Rajendravarman's accession in 944 until the death of Jayavarman V (r.968–1000 or 1001) was notable for the consolidation of social infrastructure that doubtless reflected a well-organized and peaceful state.

Jayavarman V was young at his accession. His guru, a Brahman called Yajñavaraha, came from one of the sacerdotal families whose influence had increased over the years. He founded the small temple of Banteay Srei, renowned for the perfection and intricacy of its relief carving, in 967, the year of Rajendravarman's death; it was dedicated in 968. Jayavarman V's long reign saw the construction of the temple mountain of Ta Keo, unfinished at his death and neglected in the turbulent decade that followed, and modifications to the Royal Palace and possibly its important small temple mountain, Phimeanakas. One foundation, Prasat Preah Einkosei of 968, bears two important inscriptions.[33] They provide detail about gifts, grants and concessions; varieties of livestock, crops and trade goods; and holdings of ritual vessels and statuary in precious metals. Thus they offer insight into the legal and financial complexities that Khmer society had achieved.

## Imperial Longings: The Ascent of Suryavarman

Why the reign of Udayadityavarman I, the nephew of Jayavarman V's queen, ended in 1002 after one year is unknown. He left no mark. The ancestry of his successor, Jayaviravarman I, is uncertain. His reign coincided with a claim to sovereignty by Suryavarman I, apparently of a princely family from the north east. Suryavarman made steady progress westward and finally achieved supremacy in 1010 by conquest:

> his sword broke the circle of his enemies…[and]…he won the
> kingdom in battle from a king surrounded by other kings.[34]

That his legitimacy needed affirmation can be deduced from the 1011 oath of allegiance carved on the gateway of the Royal Palace. Its 4,000 signatories swore eternal loyalty and dedication to the king. The oath was sealed by '…the cutting of hands' and defection entailed consignment to '…the thirty-second hell'.

Suryavarman's reign saw the breach of the unbroken line of inheritance of the chief priesthood of the *devaraja* by the Shivakaivalya family. The Sdok Kak Thom inscription states that that the king made Sadashiva, the current incumbent:

> relinquish the religious life in order to marry…the younger sister of
> his chief queen.[35]

Sadashiva was given the title '…*Kamsten Shri Jayadevi Pandita*, royal priest and chief of the workers of the first class'.[36] Although this was prestigious, it can be seen as an attempt by Suryavarman to establish his own claims to legitimacy by undermining the immutable authority of the clan.

Suryavarman was the first king to make sustained efforts to expand Khmer hegemony to the dimensions of an empire. He gained control of Louvo (Lopburi), the Mon-Dvaravati kingdom in the Menam valley of Thailand that extended to the Malay Peninsula. No wars against Champa were recorded in his reign. He proclaimed dominance over Khmer territory by establishing major temples at its peripheries. This involved the expansion of existing sacred places, as at Preah Vihear, the temple ascending the

I A Persian miniature of Chinggis Khan (on the green-armoured horse), fighting the Jin army. This may represent the Battle of Chabchiyal Pass (1211), which took place in a heavily defended mountain pass on the approaches to the Jin Empire.

**II** Illustration from Rashid al-Din's *Compendium of Chronicles* showing the sack of Baghdad by the Mongols in 1258. The besieging Mongols use a pontoon bridge and siege engine.

**III** A large medallion of silk and gold thread depicting an enthroned prince flanked by a Mongol general and an Arab or Persian vizier. The tapestry technique is Chinese, but the iconography suggests an origin further west. It was probably made or overseen by Chinese weavers in Il-Khanid Iran or Iraq around 1305.

**IV** Dong Qichang, *Wanluan Thatched Hall*, hanging scroll (Ming Dynasty,1597). Dong Qichang was the greatest Chinese painter and calligrapher of his age. He made a celebrated distinction between two schools of landscape painters. Artists of the 'Northern' School were professionals and court painters. Those of the 'Southern' School (including Dong) were amateurs and scholars.

**V** The Jin Shang Ling section of the Great Wall, 145 km (90 miles) north of Beijing. This section was reconstructed in 1567–72 by Qi Jiguang, who had become famous for his campaigns against Japanese pirates raiding the south coast. He also built sixty-seven watchtowers along this stretch.

**VI** Detail of a handscroll in ink and colour on silk by Qiu Ying (1494–1552) depicting candidates gathering around the wall where the results of the imperial examinations are about to be posted. This scene, dated 1540, illustrates the moment of the 'releasing of the roll'.

**VII** The central sanctuary tower of Angkor Wat, the world's largest religious monument, is 42 m (138 ft) high and the temple occupies 200 hectares. Its five lotus-bud towers represent Mount Meru, the home of the Brahmanistic gods, surrounded by four subsidiary peaks.

**VIII** A relief from the Baphuon temple mountain, Angkor Thom, Siem Reap, c. 1060. The steepness of this magnificent temple mountain caused many collapses through the centuries. A thorough reconstruction by a French-Cambodian team, completed in 2010, allows visitors to see its dynamic and naturalistic reliefs once more.

**IX** The monumental face towers of the Bayon temple at Angkor Thom, Cambodia.

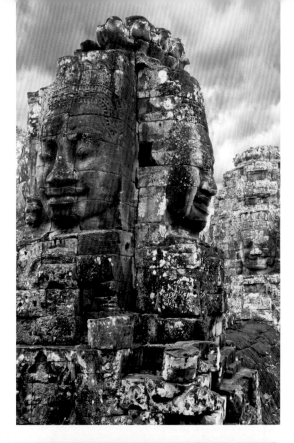

**X** A relief of *apsaras* from Angkor Wat. The 1,780 reliefs of *apsaras*, celestial dancers created during the Churning of the Ocean of Milk, are among Cambodia's most treasured carvings, The variety of stance, expression and costume offers a compelling insight into ideals of beauty in the court of Suryavarman II.

**XI** This famous 16th-century Turkish miniature shows the Ottoman navy at the French port of Toulon. As part of the Franco-Ottoman alliance against the Hapsburgs, the Ottoman navy under Hayreddin Barbarossa wintered in the port city in 1543.

**XII** The Battle of Childir (1578) near Kars, the first major Ottoman victory in the long Ottoman–Safavid war of 1578–90 over the Caucasus. The Ottoman army, commanded by Lala Mustafa Pasha, defeated the Safavids.

**XIII** The interior of the Süleimaniye Mosque, Istanbul, built by Mimar Sinan, Suleiman's chief architect, between 1550 and 1557. The mosque, considered the masterpiece of classical Ottoman architecture, was the centrepiece of a large complex that incorporated the tombs of Suleiman and his wife, schools, a hospital, a hostel, a public kitchen, a caravanserai, a Turkish bath and shops.

**XIV** Istanbul's Galata bridge over the Golden Horn, and the district of Galata with its famous tower, *c.* 1890. A Genoese trading colony under the Byzantines and the Ottomans, Galata remained a favourite place for the empire's European residents in the 19th century.

spectacular promontory on the Dangrek escarpment between Cambodia and Thailand.[37] Golden lingas called Suryameshvara were established in temples at the kingdom's furthest cardinal points, thereby making central authority visible in the outposts of the state for the first time.

Many of the temples Suryavarman erected were, like Preah Vihear, at the summit of hills, thus invoking the symbolic power of Mount Meru without constructing a pyramid temple. Among these are Phnom Chisor in the south and Wat Ek in the west. He expanded Wat Phu, on the sacred mountain of Lingaparvata, one of the earliest Khmer sacred sites (now in Laos). In addition he constructed shrines at Bakan, north east of Angkor, extended the temple mountain of Phimeanakas within the Royal Palace, and probably established part of Phimai in Thailand.[38] He erected no new temple mountain, puzzling for one of Cambodia's longest-reigning and most powerful monarchs. Perhaps the extensions of Phimeanakas satisfied his state temple needs. Perhaps the symbolism of the temple mountain as home of the *devaraja* and its Shivite linga, and the nexus of kingly power, meant less to him because he was possibly a Mahayana Buddhist, even though he maintained the Shiva cult and established linga throughout his realm.[39] His focus in the capital was conceivably on public works, including the creation of many ponds, suggesting that the city's population had grown. The enormous Western Baray, completed in the second half of the 11th century, was possibly begun in Suryavarman's reign. Such urban expansion with substantial infrastructure, along with the careful establishment of centres of authority at the farthest reaches of his realm, confirms the image of a sagacious ruler with a strong sense of imperial power.

Suryavarman I was succeeded by his son Udayadityavarman II (r.1050–66), described as well versed in sacred Hindu scriptures; he reaffirmed the importance of the *devaraja*, whose high priest was from the sacerdotal family of Saptadevakula, not the long-established Shivakaivalya's. Udayadityavarman's reign was plagued by a war with Champa in 1050, and soon after, a revolt in the south. That and a later uprising were put down by the renowned Khmer general, Sangrama. Inscriptions praise the king extravagantly but his outstanding contribution was building his temple mountain, the Baphuon, probably completed during his reign and lending its name to a style that characterized most 11th-century art. Inscriptions describe Baphuon as 'the mountain of gold', indicating that, like all Khmer monuments, its stone was stuccoed and probably also gilded. Baphuon is the most massive of the Khmer pyramid temples, with graceful narrative reliefs decorating its walls in profusion. The Western Baray, completed at this time, housed in the temple on its island, or Mebon, a remarkable bronze image of Vishnu Reclining in Cosmic Sleep. It would have measured about 6 m (20 ft) when intact.[40]

Harshavarman III succeeded his brother Udayadityavarman in 1066 and ruled until 1080 during a period of frequent warfare. He supported religious foundations but Khmer society did not change notably during his reign. He was succeeded by a king from another line, Jayavarman VI.

## Power in the North: The Late 11th Century

The first mention of Jayavarman VI (r.1080–1107) occurs in a Khmer inscription of 1082. The Mahidharapura rulers had probably long been vassals of the kings of Angkor, but what provoked Jayavarman's assumption of central authority is unknown. Although consecrated in Angkor, he possibly continued to live in Phimai, where the central sanctuary's distinctive cone-shaped tower foreshadows those of Angkor Wat. The region was prosperous and had been culturally distinguished.[41] The Buriram hoard of 8th-century Buddhas and bodhisattvas indicates the presence of Mahayana Buddhism in the area. Phimai was dedicated as a Buddhist temple, although it included Brahmanistic deities as well, perhaps a reflection of the syncretic tendencies of Tantric Buddhism. The slightly later Phnom Rung, another major temple, was Brahmanistic, so no conclusions can be drawn from architecture about Jayavarman VI's faith. His chief priest, Divakarapandita, who had been a high dignitary in the time of Udayadityavarman II, was also chief priest for

Harshavarman III and subsequently for Jayavarman's successor, his older brother Dharanindravarman I (r. 1107–13), indicating ritual continuity through four reigns.

Dharanindravarman reluctantly emerged from a meditative life to assume the throne on Jayavarman VI's death. Jayavarman's inscriptions were found in the northern regions, those of Harshavarman near Angkor, so there was probably continued resistance to the new dynasty. The rival factions were not brought under central command until the arrival of Suryavarman II, the young maternal great-nephew of the Mahidharapura kings. Inscriptions relate that after his education he 'was in the dependency of two masters' and '…bounding onto the head of the elephant of the enemy king, he killed him'.[42] This signified the defeat of Harshavarman's followers. Suryavarman then overcame his great-uncle, Dharanindravarman, in a combat lasting just one day. His assumption of power ended a period of turmoil in which, far from expanding, the Khmer kingdom was preoccupied with internal struggles.

## Suryavarman II and the Age of Angkor Wat

Suryavarman II (r.1113–45 or later) transformed the external relations of the Khmer empire as no previous monarch had done. Probably its most warlike king, he sent expeditions against the Dai Viet in the north of modern Vietnam in 1132 (in league with Champa), and against Champa in 1128, 1129 (a naval attack), 1147, 1148 and 1150.[43] Most of the campaigns were unsuccessful, including an attempt to install his wife's brother, Harideva, on the Vijaya throne, trying to exploit the rivalry between the northern Vijaya-based and the southern Panduranga factions of Champa. The 13th-century Chinese historian Ma Touan-lin records delegations to China from Kambuja; this was the first mention of Khmer embassies in Chinese annals since the 9th century. In 1116 two senior Khmer officials stayed in the Song court for a year.[44] Suryavarman's foreign outreach entailed further delegations in 1120 and 1128, at which time problems about trade were discussed and resolved. These references provide rare insight into economic matters: most Khmer inscriptions are concerned with religious foundations with little information about foreign commerce.

Khmer inscriptions from Suryavarman II's time were installed in the north, including at Wat Phu and Preah Vihear, so the king was presumably consolidating control of outer regions. Architectural activities continued in the Mahidharapura lands, and Khmer influence determined the style of monuments erected at this time in Lopburi. Relations with China presumably enhanced economic prosperity, and hegemony seems to have been maintained in the west (the Chinese mention that Khmer influence extended as far as Myanmar) and north. But abortive attacks on Champa and the Dai Viet make it clear that Suryavarman II's imperial ambitions did not enlarge his territory beyond the boundaries of his predecessors.

Regardless of his failed external ventures, Suryavarman's supreme achievement was as a builder. The small temples of Thommanon and Chau Say Tevoda in central Angkor, the meticulously constructed Banteay Samre at the eastern end of the East Baray, and the huge complex of Beng Mealea about 40 km (25 miles) north east of Angkor – to say nothing of the additions to Wat Phu – would alone guarantee his place among the great architect monarchs. Remarkable though these monuments are, they pale in comparison with Angkor Wat, one of the world's supreme architectural creations.

The statistics are impressive. The temple covers a rectangular area measuring 1,300 m on its north-south and 1,500 m on its east-west axis (4,265 by 4,922 ft). The perimeter moat is almost 200 m (656 ft) wide and more than 5 km (3 miles) in circumference, bordered on the inner side by a laterite wall 4.5 m (15 ft) high surrounding the outermost of four enclosures; the moat constitutes a fifth. Inside lies a broad open space, probably once the setting for hundreds of structures (in impermanent materials like all secular Khmer buildings) connected with the functioning of the temple. Successive enclosures lead, on rising levels, to the inner sanctuary terrace with its five towers in quincunx. The temple's mandala-like elements in plan and its five levels in elevation lend it double symbolism as a microcosm of Mount Meru, while in section its central tower, rising 42 m (138 ft) above the sanctuary, is matched by a well below the monument, constituting an *axis mundi* linking the underworld, the temporal world and the heavens.

Angkor Wat was dedicated to Vishnu and faces west, rare among the usually east-oriented Khmer temples; Suryavarman II was one of the few kings of Cambodia to worship Vishnu. It has been suggested that its orientation signified a funerary function, since west is the direction of death in Brahmanistic belief, but the west is also associated with Vishnu.

Massive though it is, Angkor Wat embodies an inspired mastery of proportion and detail, the richness of relief carving on pediments, lintels and panels – particularly the 1,780 *devatas*, the ravishing celestial dancers, or *apsaras*, in their myriad costumes and headdresses – always subsumed into the spatial whole of the majestic series of precincts. Among its wonders are the narrative reliefs lining the colonnaded galleries of the third enclosure in eight segments that extend about 800 m (2,625 ft). Some depict episodes from the Hindu epics, the *Ramayana* and *Mahabharata*. One famous panel depicts the myth of the Churning of the Ocean of Milk to create *amrita*, the elixir of immortality. The western face of the south gallery shows Suryavarman reviewing his army. Apart from its aesthetic achievement, the series offers invaluable information about armies, weapons, vehicles, dress, ceremonial materials, animals and vegetation.

The monument was invested with complex cosmological meaning, as a recent study has demonstrated.[45] Suryavarman II was probably Cambodia's most assiduous empire builder, but had he achieved nothing else, the construction of Angkor Wat would ensure his place in the pantheon of contributors to civilization.

### Buddhism as State Religion: The Reign of Jayavarman VII

Suryavarman II was succeeded by Yashovarman II (after 1150–65) about whom little is known. He was assassinated by a courtier who usurped the throne and ruled as Tribhuvanadityavarman until killed in battle during an invasion by Champa in 1177. Meanwhile Prince Jayavarman, son of a King Dharanindravarman of the Mahidharapura line, a Buddhist who may have ruled for a time at Angkor, had been in exile. Whether this was in Champa, as some suggest, or at Bakan in Kompong Svay is unknown, but he returned on hearing of Yashovarman's overthrow and prepared to regain the kingdom. After the 1177 Cham attack he led his forces to Angkor and in 1178 overthrew the invaders, killing the Cham king. In 1181 he ascended the throne. The land was in turmoil, and he had to quell a revolt in Malyang, in the west, just a year later, as well as restore the devastated capital.

In 1191 Jayavarman VII avenged the Cham defeat by overthrowing their king and seizing his lands. Control swung back and forth over the next few years but towards the end of the 12th century the Khmer were the masters of Champa. Chinese records describe the extensions of Jayavarman's realm to the Malay Peninsula, and by the end of the 12th century the Khmer empire had reached its apogee.

Although a few Khmer kings had been Buddhists, Jayavarman VII was the first to make Mahayana Buddhism the state religion. Supported by his Buddhist wife, Jayarajadevi, he promoted a doctrine of compassion and built public works. On Jayarajadevi's death he married her older sister, Indradevi, who was a renowned Buddhist scholar. Among Jayavarman's architectural projects were hospitals, chapels, fire shrines housing a sacred flame that had to be maintained at all times, and rest houses, as well as roads and bridges, all facilitating the pilgrimage route, the so-called Royal Road between Prasat Phimai and the Khmer capital. An inscription in the hospital chapel of Say Fong informs us:

> It is the suffering of the people that causes the suffering of kings, not their own.[46]

Statues of Jayavarman portray him in meditation, without crown or jewellery, in keeping with the humility of a practising Buddhist.

In addition to humanitarian projects and many monuments north of the Dangrek Range, the king embarked on a programme of temple construction that must have severely taxed the realm's resources. Among the largest were the complexes now known as Ta Prohm, in 1186, and Preah Khan, in 1191. The former was dedicated to Prajñaparamita, the bodhisattva embodying the Perfection of Wisdom, and honoured the king's mother and two gurus. The latter was consecrated to Lokeshvara, the bodhisattva of compassion, and honoured his father. They were vast establishments: Ta Prohm was inhabited by 12,640 people including 600 dancers, while almost 98,000 people served at Preah Khan. Both contained many subsidiary shrines as well as a huge central temple laid out on a linear plan. Although Buddhist in designation, both establishments had chapels dedicated to Brahmanistic deities, indicating that the usual Khmer ecumenical attitude to religion had been taken to a new level of inclusivity.

Jayavarman created a new city, Angkor Thom,[47] around the nucleus of his most important and mysterious construction, the state temple of the Bayon. Both temple and city were probably begun late in the 12th century. Unlike other temple mountains, Bayon lacks enclosure walls and a moat, but the entire city of Angkor Thom, which was protected by a moat surrounding a laterite wall 8 m (26 ft) high and 3 km (1.9 miles) per side, probably constituted the temple's precinct. A recent study explores the history of Bayon, but the identity of the dramatic faces on its multiple towers is still disputed.[48] Among the suggested entities are Lokeshvara, Brahma and Jayavarman himself.

The Bayon's narrative reliefs offer historical and mythological scenes, while depictions of daily life provide insight into Khmer society. The naturalistic and humane portrayal of deities and people in so-called Bayon style characterized free-standing sculpture as well, and the era is noted for its statuary in bronze and stone, particularly images of the king distributed throughout his realm.

Among the last of Jayavarman VII's enormous projects was the complex now known as Banteay Chmar in Banteay Meanchey province, a remote region near the western border. Dedicated to a deceased son of Jayavarman and generals who had defended him in battle, this heavily ruined and looted temple, the largest in Cambodia after Angkor Wat, houses more than 800 m (2,625 ft) of important historical reliefs in Bayon style.[49]

## The Waning Years?

Jayavarman VII probably died in 1218 (perhaps later) and was succeeded by his son Indravarman II (r.1219–42). Very little is known of the period but many of Jayavarman's architectural projects were possibly continued. Inscriptions dried up: the only record from Indravarman's reign is that of his death. His successor was Jayavarman VIII, who returned the state to Brahmanism and may have been responsible for the iconoclasm that destroyed many Buddha images. The growing power of the Sukhothai kingdom in Thailand eroded Khmer control and enabled Thai incursions into Khmer territory. Historians have postulated that the state was decaying, perhaps from the depletion of resources of water, agriculture, trade and manpower, but this is at odds with the account of Zhou Daguan, an envoy from the Yuan emperor in China who visited Angkor Thom in 1296–97, arriving in the year of the accession of Indravarman III (r.1296–1308). Indravarman was the first Cambodian king to adhere to the Theravadin sect of Buddhism, a belief system that has prevailed in Cambodia ever since. Zhou's rare first-hand report is the most informative of all outsiders' texts about Cambodia and has been the source of much of our knowledge about Khmer society.[50]

The Cambodia depicted in Zhou's account, which describes elaborate festivals and ceremonies and a court of pomp and prosperity, seems far from the declining society that has been postulated in most interpretations of the period. Until recently historians assumed the transfer of the Khmer capital from Angkor to the Phnom Penh region further south was the result of increasing harassment by Thai forces, who finally forced an abandonment of Angkor in a 1431 raid. It has been suggested recently that the move may have been made to take advantage of better connections for foreign trade offered by the new site, strategically located on the Tonle Sap and Mekong Rivers with both inland and overseas access.[51] Furthermore, not only were the Khmer victorious in some battles during these decades, but also the ruler Ang Chan I (1516–66) made Angkor the Khmer capital again, a move that would hardly have been possible had the Thai controlled the area. Even so, domination swung back and forth and the Thai retained control of much of the north-western areas of Cambodia from the 16th century until 1907 under the French Protectorate.

The 17th century saw the flowering of Khmer literary creativity including the creation of the Reamker, the Khmer version of the *Ramayana*. For much of the time between the 16th and 19th centuries, the kingdom was disturbed by ongoing confrontations with the Thai and later the Vietnamese as well as internal struggles for leadership. The beginning of French hegemony in 1863 saw confrontations that continued until the colonial period's end with Cambodian independence in 1953. Post-independence development, hearteningly prosperous during the 1950s, was undermined by the unrest provoked by the Vietnam War, the horrendous years of the Khmer Rouge (1975–79), and the decade of control by Vietnam until the United Nations-backed elections of 1993 established the present government.[52] This long and complex period is not relevant to any assessment of Cambodia as an empire: the days of glory waned after the 15th century and the imperial flame was extinguished.

## The Khmer Empire

How should the Khmer empire be judged? As an invasive controller of other polities it lacked the dominance of regimes such as Chinggis Khan's or the Romans'. Unlike the British Empire, it did not impose a new system of governance and law on its vassal territories. Unlike the maritime Indonesian kingdoms of Srivijaya, in Sumatra, or Majapahit, in East Java, its lands were contiguous with its heartland and the regime it promoted was based on a conception of kingship where the monarch's relationship with the gods provided the mandate for power. The visible expression of that relationship offered proof to the people of the monarch's right to his role. This underlying conception gave rise to what, in the end, constitutes the distinctive aspect of Khmer civilization: the continuous and prodigious creation of religious monuments, statuary and texts glorifying the gods and by association legitimizing the ruler. The ancient Khmer empire, as this chapter has suggested, should ultimately be defined by its incomparable legacy of art and architecture.

## CHAPTER FOUR

# Asia Minor and Beyond:
# The Ottomans 1281–1922

## GÁBOR ÁGOSTON

merging in western Asia Minor in the late 13th century, and finally
collapsing six centuries later during World War I, the Ottoman Empire
was among the militarily most formidable, bureaucratically best-ad-
ministered, and culturally most splendid empires in world history. Though
in principle an Islamic state, the Ottoman Empire was a multi-religious and
multi-ethnic polity that ruled for centuries with pragmatism and relative
tolerance over diverse peoples in the Balkans, Anatolia and the Middle East,
territories that have seen so much violence and unrest in subsequent times.
The Ottomans' longevity, cultural splendour and record of governance,
along with their significance in shaping the history of both modern Europe
and the Middle East, warrants a special place for them in world history.

## The Significance of the Ottomans in World History

The Ottoman emirate or principality, named after the founder of the
dynasty Osman I (d.1324), emerged in the late 13th century in north-western Anatolia (Asia Minor, roughly the territory of modern Turkey). The
Ottomans were one of many Turkic or Turkmen principalities that were
formed in Anatolia in the wake of the Mongol invasion of the 1240s,
which ended the rule of the Rum (Anatolian) Seljuq Turks and created
a power vacuum in the region. By the middle of the 15th century the
Ottomans had defeated and incorporated into their growing empire
most of the neighbouring Muslim Turkic emirates. They had also crossed

## KEY DATES

| | |
|---|---|
| **?–1324** | Reign of Osman I, founder of the Ottoman dynasty |
| **1453** | Sultan Mehmed II conquers Constantinople and ends Byzantine Empire |
| **1516–17** | Sultan Selim I conquers Mamluk Syria and Egypt |
| **1526** | Sultan Suleiman I defeats the Hungarians; Ottoman-Habsburg rivalry |
| **1555** | Ottoman-Safavid peace at Amasya stabilizes Ottoman-Safavid border |
| **1699** | Treaty of Karlowitz ends the Holy League's war against the Ottomans; Hungary ceded to Habsburgs; Morea ceded to Venice |
| **1768–74** | Russo-Ottoman War; Crimea becomes independent of Ottomans; Russia becomes protector of the Orthodox subjects of the Ottoman Empire |
| **1789–1807** | Reign of Selim III, attempt at modernization |
| **1839–76** | Tanzimat (Reform Era) |
| **1876–1909** | Abdülhamid II continues modernization |
| **1878** | Berlin Congress; Montenegro, Serbia and Romania gain independence from Ottomans |
| **1908** | Young Turk Revolution to save the empire through parliamentary democracy |
| **1914–18** | Ottomans defeated in World War I, Arab lands lost, Anatolia occupied by the Allied Powers |
| **1922** | Grand National Assembly abolishes Ottoman sultanate |
| **1923** | Treaty of Lausanne; Allies evacuate Istanbul; Republic of Turkey proclaimed |

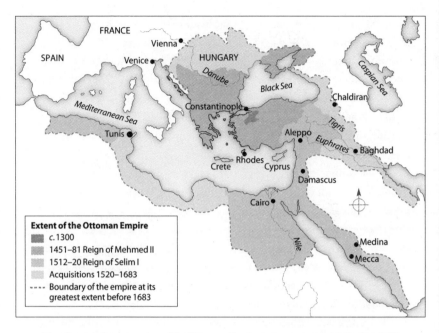

Map showing the expansion of the Ottoman Empire to its greatest extent before 1683.

the Hellespont and subdued the Orthodox Christian Slavic states of the Balkans, including medieval Bulgaria, Bosnia and Serbia. In 1453, Sultan Mehmed II (r.1444–46, 1451–81), one of the most talented Ottoman rulers, conquered Constantinople, modern Istanbul, the capital of the thousand-year-old Eastern Roman or Byzantine Empire. He made it the capital city of his own Ottoman Empire. The Ottomans called their new capital city Kostantiniyye (the Arabic/Ottoman Turkish form of Constantinople) on official documents and coins, while the name Istanbul (a corruption from a Greek phrase meaning 'to the city') was also used, especially by the common people. From the late 15th century to the late 17th century, Mehmed II's successors extended Ottoman rule to Hungary in the north and to Yemen in the south, to Algeria in the west and to Iraq in the east. In 1529 and 1683 the Ottoman armies marched on the gates of Vienna, the capital of the Austrian Habsburg Empire, but both times were defeated. Between the 1683 siege and 1699, an international coalition of the Habsburg Empire, Poland, Venice, the Papacy and Muscovy (as Russia was then known) managed to re-conquer most of Hungary. However, the Ottomans continued to rule over most of the Balkans until 1878 and in their Middle Eastern lands until World War I – a formidable accomplishment, even considering that Istanbul's control over provinces far from the capital was often nominal in the 18th and 19th centuries.

The Ottoman Empire was a crucial player in European power politics from the mid-15th century until its demise during World War I. Until the middle of the 18th century it was the only Islamic empire that challenged Christian Europe on its own territory. Ottoman-Habsburg rivalry in the 16th-century Mediterranean, or in Hungary in the 16th and 17th centuries, can only be compared to the 16th-century Valois-Habsburg struggle over Europe, or to the competition between the United States and the Soviet Union and their respective allies during the Cold War.

The Ottomans remained a major factor in international politics even after the heyday of their empire (15th–17th centuries) was behind them. In the 19th century, the Ottoman Empire's possible partition either by the European Great Powers (France, England, Germany, Austria, Russia) or by the emerging Balkan nationalist movements became a major concern in international relations, and was known as the 'Eastern Question'. For the Ottomans, it was a 'Western Question' and an era of reform and reordering, known in Turkish as Tanzimat ('Reordering', 1839–76). The main issues for the Ottoman government were: how to modernize and strengthen Ottoman military, fiscal, and bureaucratic capabilities in order to adapt to the new challenges of 19th-century modernization; how to counter the influence and meddling of the European Great Powers; and how to curtail the separatist movements of the Christian minorities of the empire.

The Ottomans built one of the longest-lived multi-ethnic and multi-religious dynastic empires in history. It bears comparison to the better-known Mediterranean empires of the Romans and Byzantines, or to the similarly multi-ethnic neighbouring dynastic empires of the Austrian Habsburgs and Russian Romanovs, or indeed to the other great Islamic empires of Asia: the Abbasid Caliphate (750–1258), Safavid Persia (1501–1722), and Mughal India (1526–1858). How did the Ottomans transform their small frontier principality in western Asia Minor into one of Islam's most splendid empires? How did they rule their multi-ethnic and multi-religious empire, and how did they survive the many challenges of the long 19th century?

## From Frontier Principality to Empire

The founders of the Ottoman dynasty masterfully exploited the power vacuum in Asia Minor caused by the Mongols' destruction of the Empire of the Rum Seljuqs in 1243 and by the Byzantine Empire's inattention to the region. Following their recapture of Constantinople from the Latin Crusaders in 1261, the Byzantines devoted most of their attention to re-establishing their rule in the Balkans, and neglected the defences of their Anatolian realms. The Ottomans were also lucky, in that the turbulent times of a Byzantine civil war offered opportunities for raids, often as allies of one of the warring Byzantine parties. Orhan I (r.1324–62), the son and successor of Osman I, became the supporter of one of the quarrelling emperors, John VI Kantakouzenos (r.1347–54), and in 1352 Ottoman troops arrived in Europe as his allies, establishing their first European bridgehead in Tzympe, on the European shore of the Dardanelles.

Through military conquest, diplomacy, dynastic marriages and the opportunistic exploitation of the Byzantine civil wars, the third Ottoman ruler Murad I (r.1362–89) more than tripled the territories under his direct rule. The empire now covered an area of 260,000 square km (100,400 square miles), evenly distributed in south-eastern Europe and Asia Minor. His son Bayezid I (r.1389–1402) extended Ottoman rule to the River Danube in Europe and the River Euphrates in Asia Minor, some 690,000 square km (266,400 square miles). Murad's and Bayezid's reigns were also important in the evolution of the Ottoman military, provincial and central administration. The famous Janissaries (from the Turkish *yeni çeri*, 'new soldiers') were established in the 1370s, originally as bodyguards of the sultan, in order to provide the ruler with a loyal military force that was independent of the Turkish warrior lords. By the time of the Battle of Kosovo against the Serbs in 1389, the Janissaries had become the sultan's elite infantry, numbering two thousand men. In the 1380s, the *devshirme*, or child levy system, was introduced to recruit soldiers for the Janissary corps. Under this system, Christian boys between eight and twenty years of age were periodically taken from Christian areas of the empire. After conversion to Islam and seven or eight years of service in Anatolian peasant farms, the boys joined the ranks of Janissary novices.

Murad also selected the first military judge (*kadıasker*), the head of the Ottoman religious hierarchy, and the first *sancakbeyi* or governor of a subprovince (*sancak*) was also appointed either towards the end of Orhan's reign or under Murad I. Later, under Bayezid, the subprovinces were organized into provinces, the first two being Rumelia (*Rumeli* means 'Greek Land', that is, the Balkans) and Anatolia (*Anadolu*) in Asia Minor.

Bayezid's spectacular conquests in the Balkans alarmed King Sigismund of Hungary (r.1387–1437), the strongest neighbour of the Ottomans in Europe. Sigismund organized a Crusade to halt the Ottoman advance, but the Crusaders were defeated in 1396 at Nikopol on the Danube. In the end it was not the European Crusaders but Timur (Tamerlane), a ruthless Central Asian military commander and a Muslim of Mongol descent, who temporarily stopped the Ottoman expansion by defeating Bayezid at the battle of Ankara on 28 July 1402. Bayezid was captured and died, and Timur reduced the extent of the Ottoman lands to what it had been at the beginning of Murad I's reign. The debacle at Ankara was followed by a decade-long civil war between Bayezid's sons (1402–13). Fortunately for the Ottomans, however, the basic institutions of the Ottoman state (the prebendal land-tenure system based on the so-called *timar* land grants or fiefs and the tax system, revenue and tax surveys, central and provincial bureaucracy and the military) had already taken root and large segments of Ottoman society had vested interests in restoring the power of the House of Osman.

Owing to these basic institutions and to the reunification and rebuilding efforts of Mehmed I (r.1413–21) and Murad II (r.1421–44, 1446–51), the Ottomans managed to re-establish control over much of their former territory. Through skilful diplomacy and military campaigns, Murad also saved the Ottoman state in the critical years of 1443–44, when it was attacked by the Karamanids, a Turkmen principality based in Konya in Asia Minor, and European crusaders led by Hungary, and threatened within by rebellions. The accession of Mehmed II to the Ottoman throne in 1451 began a new era in the history of the Ottomans and that of their neighbours.

## Empire and its Challenges

Mehmed II's conquest of Byzantine Constantinople on 29 May 1453 was of the utmost historical significance for the Ottomans and the peoples of the Balkans, Asia Minor and the Mediterranean. From an Ottoman perspective, the conquest eliminated a hostile wedge that had separated the sultans' European and Asian provinces. It also afforded the Ottomans a commanding position over the trade routes between Europe and Asia, the Mediterranean and the Black Sea, and a perfect logistical centre for mobilizing human and economic resources for campaigns to the east and the west. The conquest gave the young and ambitious sultan much-needed prestige in the Muslim and Christian worlds. He was now the 'Conqueror' (*Fatih*), the first Muslim ruler to accomplish the old dream of the Muslims who first besieged the city in 674 under the Umayyad Caliph Muawiya. Mehmed II also considered himself Caesar, the heir to the Byzantine emperors.

Mehmed II transformed Constantinople into the capital city of his empire. He repopulated the city through forced resettlements and built new commercial and residential quarters grouped around mosques or markets, of which the Conqueror's mosque complex and the Covered

Bazaar are the most famous. He abandoned the old capital city, Edirne, and moved into newly built royal palaces in Constantinople: first into the Old Palace and then into the New (Topkapı) Palace, whose location between the Golden Horn and the Sea of Marmara on the Seraglio Point offered an unmatched defensive position and spectacular views. Admired by foreign ambassadors and visitors, the Topkapı Palace housed the private quarters of the sultan and his family, including the imperial harem, where the women and children of the imperial household resided and were educated; the palace school that trained the chief bureaucrats of the empire; an administrative centre where the Imperial Council, the chief administrative body of the empire, held its meetings; and an outer section for servicemen and guards.

Mehmed II cemented Ottoman rule over Serbia in 1459 and Albania in the 1460s, eradicated the Genoese trading colonies in the Crimea, and made the Muslim Crimean Tatar Khanate his vassal in 1478, thus establishing Ottoman control over the Black Sea littoral. However, he met some failures too, such as his unsuccessful siege of Belgrade in 1456, and his expedition in 1480 against southern Italy and the Rhodes of the Knights of St John. More importantly, Ottoman rule in eastern Anatolia remained disputed. It was not until 1473 that Mehmed II managed to overcome his eastern Muslim rival, Uzun Hassan (r.1453–78) of the Aqqoyunlu ('White Sheep') Turkmen confederation, who ruled over eastern Anatolia, Azerbaijan, Iraq and western Iran. The Aqqoyunlus continued to resist the Ottomans until Mehmed II's grandson Selim I (r.1512–20) incorporated their lands into his empire. Mehmed II's wars, the expansion of the standing army, and his ambitious building projects strained the empire's resources. In order to meet these expenses he resorted to unpopular fiscal measures, such as repeated devaluation of the Ottoman silver coinage, extension of state tax-farming and confiscation of private lands. These measures all alienated large segments of society, including the old Turkish elite.

With the emergence of the rival Safavid dynasty in Persia, the threat to Ottoman sovereignty in eastern Anatolia became even greater. In 1501

Ismail, the head of the militant Shia Safaviyye religious order, defeated the Aqqoyunlus, declared himself Shah (ruler) of Persia, and made the Imami or 'Twelver' rite of Shia Islam the official religion of his new state. Shah Ismail I (r.1501–24) portrayed himself as Mahdi, the prophesied saviour of Islam. For the Turkmens and Kurds of eastern Anatolia the Safavid style of government, which resembled that of a nomadic tribal confederation, seemed a desirable alternative to the more centralized Ottoman rule, which jeopardized the nomads' way of life and social structure.

Since the ageing Bayezid II (r.1481–1512) seemed incapable of countering Safavid encroachments on Ottoman territories and Shah Ismail's proselytizing among the Turkmens, in 1512 his son Selim deposed him. Sultan Selim I defeated Shah Ismail at the Battle of Chaldiran on 23 August 1514 and extended Ottoman rule over eastern Anatolia. The battle is often cited as an example of the effectiveness of firearms in pitched battles. Selim's five hundred cannons and twelve thousand Janissary infantry musketeers slaughtered the Safavids, whose army, consisting mainly of light cavalry, lacked artillery and hand firearms. Selim's claim on the lands of the Turkmen Dulkadıroğlu emirate, situated in south-eastern Anatolia between the Ottoman, Mamluk and Safavid empires, strained Istanbul's relationship with the Mamluks, the Dulkadıroğlus' nominal sovereign.

To launch a campaign against the Sunni Mamluks of Egypt and Syria was problematic. The last Abbasid Caliph[1] resided in the Mamluk capital Cairo, and the Mamluk sultans were the protectors of Mecca and Medina and guarantors of the hajj. To justify his attack against the Mamluks, Selim secured a fatwa, or religious opinion. This accused the Mamluks of oppressing Muslims and justified the war against them by alleging a Mamluk-Safavid alliance, declaring that 'he who aids a heretic [that is, the Shia Safavids] is a heretic himself'.

Selim's forces met the Mamluk army north of Aleppo at Marj Dabik on 24 August 1516. Ottoman firearms, and desertions in the Mamluk camp, sealed the fate of the Mamluks. When Sultan Qansuh al-Ghawri (r.1500–16) died, apparently from a heart attack, his last remaining troops quickly fled. Aleppo and Damascus surrendered without a fight. The Ottomans followed the fleeing Mamluk army to Egypt and inflicted a second crushing defeat on 23 January 1517 at Raydaniyya, outside Cairo. Mamluk resistance collapsed when Sultan Tumanbay (r.1516–17) was captured and killed. With him died the Mamluk Sultanate that had ruled for more than two hundred and fifty years in Egypt and Syria. Its territories were incorporated into Selim's empire as the new Ottoman provinces of Aleppo, Damascus and Egypt, beginning the Ottoman era in the history of the Middle East.

Selim's conquests increased the area of the empire to 1.5 million square km (580,000 square miles), and revenues from Syria and Egypt accounted for approximately one-third of the total income of the Ottoman treasury. Selim's role as protector of Mecca and Medina and guarantor of the hajj afforded the House of Osman much-needed legitimacy in the Muslim world. On the other hand, Selim's wars against Muslims and the lack of any major campaign against the Christian 'infidels' lowered his standing in Muslim eyes. Thus his son and successor Suleiman I (r.1520–66) reversed his father's policy and embarked on an aggressive campaign against the empire's Christian rivals. Suleiman spent perhaps a quarter of his reign leading his armies on thirteen campaigns. These expeditions brought Iraq (1534–35) and Hungary (1541) under Ottoman rule, and threatened the Habsburg capital Vienna twice, in 1529 and 1532. Suleiman's victories at Rhodes in the eastern Aegean in 1522 and at Preveza in north-western Greece in 1538 made the Ottomans masters of the eastern Mediterranean. If Ottoman-Habsburg rivalry in Hungary and in the Mediterranean was one of the main confrontations that shaped the history of Europe, Suleiman's wars against Shah Tahmasb (r.1524–76) of Persia in 1534–35, 1548–49 and 1553 had decisive consequences for Iraq and the Safavid Empire. Ottoman conquests in Iraq (including that of Baghdad) were acknowledged in the 1555 Safavid-Ottoman Treaty of Amasya. The eastern border of the empire, established in 1555 and modified in 1639, was to remain essentially unchanged until World War I.

Under Suleiman I the area of the empire reached 2.3 million square km (888,000 square miles). A population of twelve or thirteen million at the beginning of the 16th century grew to some twenty to twenty-five million at the close of the century. Owing to its geopolitical situation, its control over vast human and economic resources in the Balkans, Asia Minor, Arabia and North Africa, and a central and provincial administration that was capable of mobilizing these resources to serve the state, the Ottoman Empire had become a superpower of its time. Europeans feared and respected the Ottomans, and called their ruler Suleiman I 'The Magnificent' for the grandeur of his court. To his subjects and to Muslims in general he was the 'Lawgiver' or 'Law abider' (*Kanuni*), for it was under his rule that sultanic or secular laws (*kanun*) were compiled, systematized and harmonized with the Islamic sharia law.

There is a view that the Ottomans declined after the reign of Suleiman, but in fact the empire continued to expand. In the latter part of the 16th century the Ottomans conquered Cyprus (1570–73)and some key Habsburg/Hungarian forts in Hungary. Although an international coalition of Habsburg Spain, Venice, Genoa and others – known as the Holy League – defeated the Ottomans and destroyed their navy at the Battle of Lepanto on 7 October 1571, the Ottoman recovery was quick. By the spring of 1572, they had built 150 vessels with all the artillery and equipment needed, a testament to the empire's tremendous human and economic resources and organizational efficiency. The Holy League collapsed when Venice concluded a treaty with the sultan in 1573 that left Cyprus in Ottoman hands.

The resurgence of Ottoman military might under the talented Köprülü grand viziers (1656–76) brought two key Habsburg forts in Hungary (Várad/Oradea in 1660 and Ersekújvár/Nové Zámky in 1663) under Ottoman rule, followed by the island of Crete in 1669 . In 1672, Sultan Mehmed IV (r.1648–87) personally led his armies to conquer the Polish fort of Kamieniec in Podolia, and made Cossack Ukraine an Ottoman vassal. At its largest the empire covered 3.8 million square km

(1,467,000 square miles), an area equivalent to 40 per cent of today's mainland United States. However, imperial overstretch and long, costly wars (against the Habsburgs in Hungary in 1593–1606, against the Safavids in 1570–92, 1603–11 and 1623–39, and the Cretan War of 1645–69 against Venice) put the empire's treasury in continuous deficit from 1592. Most of the conquered lands in Hungary and Iraq did not increase state revenue. On the contrary, their administration and defence required subsidies either from Istanbul or from the profitable inner provinces of the Balkan and Anatolian heartlands.

The military fortunes of the late 17th century also misled Ottoman politicians into thinking they could capture Vienna and defeat the Habsburgs. In 1683, grand vizier Kara Mustafa Pasha besieged Vienna, only to be defeated near Kahlenberg, at the edge of the Vienna Woods, on 12 September 1683 by the coalition forces of the Holy Roman Empire, Poland-Lithuania, Bavaria, Saxony, Franconia and Swabia. In the ensuing long war of 1684–99 against the anti-Ottoman Holy League of the Habsburgs, Venice, Poland-Lithuania, the Papacy and Russia, the Ottomans lost Hungary to Austria, the Morea and parts of Dalmatia to Venice, Podolia to Poland-Lithuania, and Azak (Azov) to Russia. Yet the Ottomans were far from defeated, as their victories against Peter the Great of Russia in 1711 and against the Venetians in the Ottoman-Venetian war of 1714–18 demonstrated. Although in the Austro-Ottoman war of 1716–18 Istanbul lost what remained of Hungary to Austria, it managed to recapture Belgrade and parts of Wallachia (modern Romania) in the Austro-Ottoman war of 1737–39. Still, the peace treaties of Karlowitz (1699), Passarowitz (1718) and Belgrade (1739) that concluded Istanbul's recent wars against the Habsburgs and their allies signalled the end of Ottoman military superiority. In 1699 at Karlowitz the Ottomans, for the first time in their history, acknowledged the territorial integrity of their opponents by accepting the creation of well-defined borders. The Karlowitz Treaty also marked the end of the European fear of the 'Turkish menace'.

## Military Might

From the 15th to the 17th centuries the Ottoman army was one of the best organized, paid, and supplied in the contemporary world. The bulk of the army consisted of the provincial cavalry forces, known as *timarlı sipahis* (timariot) after the military fiefs (*timar*) through which Istanbul compensated them for their service. In return for the right to collect revenues from his assigned fiefs, the Ottoman provincial cavalryman was required to provide his arms (short sword, bows), armour (helmet and chain mail) and horse, and to report for military service together with his armed retainers when called upon by the sultan. The *timar* system provided the Ottoman sultans in the 15th and 16th centuries with a provincial cavalry of some 50,000 to 80,000 men, while relieving the central Ottoman bureaucracy of the burden of revenue-raising and paying military salaries. The timariot provincial army also proved instrumental in maintaining law and order in the provinces. In addition, until the beginning of the 16th century another cavalry force known as the *akıncıs*, or raiders, remained militarily significant, and Suleiman I deployed 20,000 of them to support his Hungarian campaign in 1521.

The Ottoman sultans also established standing armies, beginning well before their European and Asian rivals. The Janissaries, established under Murad I, numbered 5,000 in the mid-15th century, and reached about 10,000 men by the end of Mehmed II's reign. They remained around 10,000 to 12,000 strong until the early 17th century, but their number rose rapidly to 37,600 in 1609, and to 54,000 by 1660. This sharp increase in the number of the armed Janissaries was one of the Ottomans' responses to the 'European Military Revolution', and more specifically to the military challenge of the Austrian Habsburgs, who considerably boosted the firepower of their infantry musketeers during the long war of 1593–1606 against the Ottomans. In addition to the Janissaries, the sultan's standing army also had six cavalry units whose number doubled between 1527 and 1567, from 5,088 men to 11,251. Out of all these forces, Mehmed II, Selim and Suleiman I could and did mobilize 70,000 to 80,000 men or more for major sultan-led campaigns, thus greatly outnumbering their opponents in the field.

The bulk of the Ottoman army (*azabs* or unmarried infantrymen, levied from and equipped by the peasants, cavalry timariots and akıncı raiders) used swords and bows. The Ottomans adopted firearms in the latter part of the 14th century, and established a separate artillery corps as part of the sultans' standing army in the early 15th century, well before their European opponents. In 1567, the corps (artillerists, gun carriage drivers, and armourers) had 2,671 men on its payroll. Initially the Janissaries were equipped with bows, crossbows and javelins. In the first half of the 15th century they began to use matchlock arquebuses, and Murad III (r.1574–95) equipped them with the more advanced matchlock musket. However, the Janissaries' traditional weapon, the recurved bow, remained a formidable weapon well into the 17th century. The Ottomans also established cannon foundries and saltpetre and gunpowder works throughout their empire and remained self-sufficient in the production of cannon, hand firearms, gunpowder and ammunition well into the 18th century.

Under Mehmed II and Bayezid II the Ottomans acquired the common naval technology of the Mediterranean, adopting the galley as their principal vessel. The size of the Ottoman navy was already impressive under Mehmed II, who employed 380 galleys in his naval expeditions against the Genoese-administered Crimean port town of Caffa in 1475. During the 1499–1503 Ottoman-Venetian war, Bayezid II considerably strengthened the navy, ordering the construction of no less than 250 galleys in late 1500 alone. The reorganization of the Ottoman navy under Bayezid II transformed the originally land-based empire into a formidable naval power. The navy was instrumental in halting Portuguese expansion in the Red Sea and the Persian Gulf, and in the Ottoman conquest of Mamluk Egypt in 1516–17 under Selim I.

After the conquest of Egypt in 1517, it became imperative for the Ottomans to control the maritime lines of communication between Cairo and Istanbul, and so they eliminated all hostile bases in the eastern

Mediterranean (Rhodes in 1522, Cyprus in 1570–73). Appointing Hayreddin Barbarossa governor of Algiers (in 1519) and grand admiral of the Ottoman navy (in 1533) and co-opting the corsairs of the Barbary states of Algiers and Tunis was a smart and economically efficient way to strengthen the Ottoman navy further, and extended Ottoman influence as far as Algiers and Tunis.

## Ruling the Empire

Although Europeans called the Ottomans 'Turks', they considered themselves *Osmanlı* (Ottomans), followers of Osman, the eponymous founder of the *Osmanlı* dynasty. In the early decades of the empire's history everyone who followed Osman and joined his band was considered *Osmanlı*, regardless of ethnicity or religion. Later the term referred to the Ottoman ruling elite, also known as *askeri* ('military') after their main occupation. The tax-paying subject population, Muslims and non-Muslims alike, was known as the *reaya*, the 'flock'. While the term 'Turk' is not entirely incorrect to denote the Ottomans – for the dynastic family and their followers were originally Turks – in actuality the descendants of Osman were ethnically mixed, through intermarriages with Byzantine, Serbian and Bulgarian royal houses and the dynasty's practice of reproducing through non-Muslim slave concubines. The population of the empire's Balkan provinces remained largely ethnically Slavic and Orthodox Christian in religion, despite voluntary migration and state-organized resettlements of Turks from Anatolia to the Balkans. Many Anatolian and Arab towns had a sizeable Christian and Jewish population, and few Turks lived in the Arab provinces. In short, it was a multi-ethnic and multi-religious empire ruled by the Ottoman dynasty.

The empire's elites considered themselves Ottoman – denoting their affiliation with the house of Osman rather than an ethnic or national identity – and used the word 'Turk' as a disparaging term for the uneducated Anatolian Muslim peasant population. These Ottomans spoke the Ottoman-Turkish language, which, with its Arabic and Persian vocabulary and inflections, was distinct from the Anatolian Turkish vernacular. They also produced, supported and consumed a courtly literature written in this language that would have been largely unintelligible to the masses.

The highest governmental organ of the empire was the Divan-i Humayun or Imperial Council, which evolved from the informal advisory body of lords and state officials of the early sultans. Originally a court of justice and appeals, the Divan also served as the supreme organ of government, and, in wartime, as a high command. Until Mehmed II, the sultans personally presided at the Divan's meetings, which usually took place near the gate (*kapı* or *dergah*) of the sultan's palace. Thus the term *dergah-i ali* or Sublime Porte first referred to the meeting place of the Divan and later came to denote the Ottoman government itself.

From the 1470s onward most sultans did not personally attend the meetings of the Council. However, the Council members were obliged to report to the sultan about their deliberations and ask for the sovereign's approval. 'Lying was mortal,' noted a 16th-century French diplomat, because the sultan was 'often listening at a window overlooking the said Chamber [of the Divan] without being seen or noticed.'[3]

In the absence of the sultan, the grand vizier, as the sultan's absolute deputy, presided over the Council. The grand vizier, other viziers, the governor-general of Rumelia, the grand admiral, and (from the latter half of the 16th century) the Agha, or commander of the Janissaries, represented the military. The *kadıaskers* or military judges spoke for the religious establishment (*ulema*) in the Council. Unlike the viziers, they were freeborn Muslims and graduates of the religious colleges (madrasas). Besides being the supreme judges of Rumelia and Anatolia, respectively, the two *kadıaskers* also supervised the judges (*kadı*) and the college professors (*müderris*) of the empire. The *sheyhulislam* ('Elder of Islam'), the chief jurisconsult (*mufti*) and head of the *ulema*, was not a member of the Council, but his written opinion was sought if the two supreme judges disagreed. These were his subordinates, for by the latter part of the 16th century the *sheyhulislam* had acquired the right to appoint and dismiss the *kadıaskers*, high-ranking judges, college professors, and heads of religious brotherhoods.

The bureaucracy was represented by the treasurers (*defterdar*) and the chancellor (*nishancı*) in the Divan. The *defterdars*, four of them by 1587, administered the royal revenues. The chancellor was responsible for authenticating all imperial documents by affixing the sultan's monogram (*tughra*), thus ensuring that all orders and letters issued from the Divan conformed to Ottoman laws and chancery practice. The chancellor also supervised the Divan's archives, which housed all the provincial revenue surveys and tax registers, classified in alphabetical order by province, as well as other official documents regarding fiefs and lands of religious endowments (*waqf*).

The clerks of the Divan (some 110 of them in the 1530s) worked under the supervision of the *reisülküttab* or 'chief of the clerks', who by the 17th century had become a quasi foreign minister. By this time, however, the Council had become less important than the office of the grand vizier, and the term the Sublime Porte or Ottoman government referred to his office.

Although the Ottoman Empire is often described as a meritocracy, it remained an essentially patrimonial system until the Tanzimat or Reform Era of 1839–76. Besides merit and career service, family ties, patronage and, above all, loyalty to the sultan were instrumental in attaining the highest offices of the state.

Starting with Suleiman I's wife Hurrem, a former concubine who married the sultan, women of the imperial harem also asserted exceptional influence on the sultans. Owing to her marriage to and influence over Suleiman, Hurrem had more than one son with the sultan and remained resident in the palace. This was a break with the former 'one concubine-one son' rule and with the practice whereby mothers of princes accompanied their sons to the provinces when they were appointed as prince-governors. The rivalry between Hurrem and Suleiman's first concubine Mahidevran marked the beginning of what is known in Ottoman history as the 'sultan-ate of women'. The emergence of 'favourites', both in the harem and among the *damads* (sons-in-law, men married to princesses), under Suleiman radically changed the way politics was played in Istanbul.

In theory, the sultans ruled with almost absolute power. In reality, however, the sultans' power varied greatly in different periods. From the late 16th to the mid-17th century the queen mothers and the wives of the sultans, backed and often manipulated by court factions and the military, wielded considerable influence through their protégés. In the 17th century, actual power passed to the grand viziers and the Köprülü family of grand viziers, in particular, attained unparalleled power between 1656 and 1691. From the mid-17th century until the late 18th century, most of the sultans reigned rather than ruled. In the 18th century the sultans' authority was further undermined as an emerging network of vizierial and pasha households (pasha was the highest title given to military and civil officials) and their protégés gained power in the sultan's court.

Until the 19th-century reforms, the Ottoman government, unlike the governments of modern nation states, was small, employing no more than fifteen hundred clerks. Its tasks were limited to a few key areas: the defence of the empire, maintenance of law and order, resource mobilization and management, and the supply of the capital and the army. Functions associated with government in the modern nation states, such as education, healthcare and welfare, were handled by professional organizations such as charitable trusts (*waqf*) and guilds, and by the empire's religious and ethnic communities (*millets*), who enjoyed considerable autonomy regarding education and religious and cultural life.

The Christian and Jewish clergy were exempted from taxes and their respective leaders (the Orthodox and Armenian Patriarchs, and the Jewish chief rabbi) were charged with the administration of their churches. They also liaised between the government and their communities: they collected taxes, dispensed justice, maintained law and order, executed Istanbul's orders and communicated their communities' grievances to the Ottoman authorities.

## Core Zones, Frontier Provinces and Vassals

With the expansion of the Ottoman realms it became necessary to create administrative subdivisions. Military commanders (*beys* or *emirs*) assigned to administer these territorial subdivisions received a standard (*sancak*) from the sultan as a symbol of power. Soon the word *sancak* was also used for the territory they controlled and it came to denote the basic military-administrative unit of the empire, translated as 'district' or 'subprovince'. It was headed by the *sancakbeyi*, that is, by the military commander of the subprovince. With further expansion of Ottoman lands there was a need to appoint a senior commander to supervise the *sancakbeyis*. The first such *beylerbeyi*, that is, *bey* (commander) of the (*sancak*)*beys*, was that of Rumelia. He was the commander-in-chief of the European provincial forces of the empire and the highest administrative official, governor-general, of the Ottoman province of Rumelia. In the 1520s there were 8 such provinces (*beylerbeyilik, vilayet*) consisting of some 90 subprovinces. By the 1570s, there were 24 provinces and 250 *sancaks*.

The government designated part of the sancak's agricultural revenues as fiefs (*timar, zeamet* and *has*) to be assigned to cavalrymen (*sipahi*) and to their military commanders, the *sancakbeyis*. The *sancakbeyi* was also responsible for maintaining law and order within his subprovince, with the help of his cavalrymen. He and the judge (*kadı*) of the *sancak* were responsible for collecting taxes, managing revenue, and assisting the officials appointed by Istanbul to carry out taxation surveys (*tahrir*). Surveys were done in a new *sancak*, and repeated every ten to thirty years to reflect changes in the size and composition of the population and the economic situation in the region. Taxes were then levied accordingly. One copy of the survey remained in the province, while the other was sent to the capital and was archived near the Imperial Council so that it could be consulted whenever needed. These surveys, along with the provincial law codes (*kanunname*) that summarized regulations on taxation and taxes and the registers that contained recordings of bestowals of military fiefs, testify to the Ottoman government's capabilities in data collection and processing. These documents, along with a host of financial records available in the Financial Department of Istanbul, as well as the copy-books of outgoing imperial orders, known as the *mühimme* defters (books of 'important affairs'), afforded the Istanbul government a long institutional memory. The scope of Ottoman administrative capabilities was impressive: in the main Ottoman archives in Istanbul today there are more than 370 *mühimme* defters that run to almost 110,000 pages, and cover the period from the mid-16th century to the mid-19th century. The number of revenue survey books in the archives is close to 2,000, the great majority of which concerns the 16th and 17th centuries. There are numerous extant surveys for strategically important *sancaks* such as Aleppo (24), Baghdad (9), Bosnia (36), Buda (12), Damascus (22), Diyarbekir (14), Erzurum (20), Karaman (20) and Silistre (19), most of them from the 16th – 17th centuries. In addition, the archives in Ankara house more than 2,300 survey books regarding fiefs and their beneficiaries, as well as the endowment deeds of charitable trusts.

The Ottomans showed great flexibility in administering their diverse empire. In the 15th-century Balkans, for example, Ottoman administrative units often followed the boundaries of the pre-conquest Serbian, Bosnian or Byzantine ones. Also, the Ottomans tried whenever possible to integrate cooperative groups from among the pre-Ottoman elites of conquered territories into the privileged Ottoman ruling class. For example, many Christian timariot *sipahis* were awarded Ottoman military fiefs after the conquest of their respective territories in the Balkans and in the former Byzantine Empire of Trebizond. In many places the old forms of property ownership were retained; the empire accommodated the previous systems of agriculture and mining, and sometimes adopted local practices regarding taxation and coinage. Similarly, the continuation of pre-Ottoman local communal organizations is well documented from Serbia, Bulgaria and Greece.

In eastern Anatolia and in Hungary the sultan accepted joint control, and shared taxation and jurisdiction with the local elite. When conducting daily business Istanbul often had to rely on village headmen, elders or notables of the province from Hungary to Greater Syria and Egypt.

Ottoman provincial administration can be visualized as a set of concentric circles: the closer the province was to Istanbul, the more control the government had over it. Thus one can talk about core zones, more remote frontier provinces, and loosely attached vassal or client states. In their core provinces in the Balkans and Anatolia the Ottomans distributed most of their revenues as military fiefs, and the beneficiaries served the state as soldiers and administrators. In the distant provinces such as Egypt, Yemen, Abyssinia, Basra, Baghdad or Tunis, the *timar* land-tenure system was not introduced, and tax revenues were collected with the help of tax farmers. The revenue had to cover the governors' salaries and other defence and administrative costs, and the surplus (if any) was sent to the Istanbul treasury.

The relative strength and limitations of the central government and the local elite showed great diversity in the core zones and the frontier provinces. In eastern Anatolia, where close to 20 per cent of the population were nomadic Turkmens and Kurds in the 1520s, Istanbul was forced to compromise and to rely on pre-Ottoman administrative practices. In these territories three different types of special administrative units were created: *ocaklık, yurtluk* and *hükümet sancaks.* In the *ocaklık* sancaks the tribal chieftain was appointed as district governor by Istanbul and had the right to pass his title to his son, but Istanbul surveyed his *sancak,* and distributed its revenue in the form of military fiefs to outsiders. During military campaigns, the *beys* (like other *sancakbeyis*) had to report to their respective governor-generals with their troops. The *yurtluks* were similar to the *ocaklık,* except the *bey* could not automatically pass his title to his son. The *hükümets,* again mainly territories of Turkmen and Kurdish tribes, were administered as hereditary lands by their tribal chieftains. In these areas Istanbul could not introduce the *timar* system and the *sancak* censuses, and there were no Ottoman officials or soldiers. The *beys,* however, were obliged to assist the Ottoman campaigns with their troops.

In the eastern provinces of Diyarbekir, Erzurum, Childir, Van, Baghdad and Shehrizor, between 25 per cent and 55 per cent of the *sancaks* were *ocaklıks* and *hükümets* as late as the 1670s.

Beyond the frontier provinces lay the vassal or tributary states of the empire, such as the two Romanian principalities (Wallachia and Moldavia), Transylvania (in historic Hungary), Ragusa (modern Dubrovnik), the Crimean Khanate, the Barbary corsair states in North Africa and the tributary states in the Caucasus.

However, the 17th and 18th centuries saw the devolution of Istanbul's power in the provinces to local communities and their leaders, known as *ayan* (notables). These *ayan* gradually replaced the central government's representatives in tax collection and jurisdiction. In the Russo-Ottoman war of 1768–74, the Ottomans also lost the Muslim Crimean Khanate, which was annexed by Russia in 1783. This was a major blow to Ottoman prestige, and triggered serious soul-searching and reforms.

### The Long 19th Century and the Ottomans' Staying Power

Ottoman military failures in the 18th century often led to unrest and rebellions, resulting in the dethronement of two Ottoman sultans (Mustafa II in 1703 and Ahmed III in 1730). The latter part of the century witnessed the emergence of the ayan: warlord-bandits, local notables, and governors. They strengthened their position during the Russo-Ottoman War of 1787–92, when they seized a host of vital administrative functions in the provinces, from troop recruitment to provisioning. The most powerful of the *ayan* carved out large autonomous polities, established their own armies, and waged wars against each other, bringing much suffering upon the subject population. Between 1792 and 1812, notables such as Osman Pazvanoglu in Bulgaria, Tepedenli Ali Pasha in southern Albania and Epirus, the Karaosmanoğlus in western Anatolia, the Tekelioğlus in Antalya, and the Kozanoğlus in Cilicia, in effect partitioned much of the Ottoman Balkans and Anatolia. Yet, threatened by Russia's ambitions in the Balkans, few of them sought independence. They realized that none of them was strong enough to withstand the Russians, and that they had access to the empire's resources only if they negotiated to legitimize their status with Istanbul.

Meanwhile, Ottoman power in Egypt was challenged by the Mamluk emirs and by Napoleon Bonaparte's invasion (1798–1802). Finally, in 1805, Mehmed Ali, an Albanian mercenary of the Porte, seized power in Egypt. Relying upon his European-style army, Mehmed Ali remained in power for forty years. In Serbia, the uprising of 1804 marked the beginning of a series of wars of national liberation. By the 1820s Serbia, Greece and Egypt had become, in effect, independent.

The Ottoman government responded to the many foreign and domestic challenges with vigorous reform. Just as in Europe, centralization and modernization of the military, bureaucracy, education and finances remained the major agenda of the Ottoman government during the long 19th century, a period that started with Selim III's reforms and ended with the demise of the empire in World War I. Selim III's reforms – labelled the *Nizam-i Cedid* ('new order') to differentiate it from the traditional Ottoman system or *Nizam-i Kadim* – were introduced in 1792 in the wake of yet another lost war against Russia. They focused on diplomacy and reform of the Ottoman military. The most visible result of the reforms was the creation in 1794 of the *Nizam-i Cedid* army, a modern provincial militia modelled on contemporary European armies and recruited from among the Turkish peasants and tribesmen of Anatolia. (The population of the Balkans was excluded because their ayan opposed it.) By 1807 this force numbered 23,000 troops. On the diplomatic front, Selim's reign saw the integration of the empire into the European diplomatic system through formal alliances with Sweden (1789) and Prussia (1790) against Austria and Russia; the declaration of neutrality in the First Coalition Wars against Napoleon (1793); participation in the anti-Napoleon coalition in the Second Coalition War (1799–1801) and, in response, Napoleon's invasion of Egypt; and the opening of Istanbul's first permanent embassies in London in 1793, and in Berlin, Vienna and Paris in 1795.

In 1807 Selim, whose legitimacy had been undermined by the Serbian and Wahhabi revolts, was dethroned and killed. A coup orchestrated by a rival faction of the court turned into an open revolt on the part of the Janissaries, the *ulema* and the Istanbul mobs. The position and status of these groups were threatened by Selim's reforms, and heavy taxation and debasement of the currency had jeopardized their living standards. However, Selim's reforms were to prove very important in the long run, for they initiated a genuine Islamic reform discourse that would offer an alternative path to modernity, in time giving legitimacy to many of the Western-inspired reforms. Thus the stage was eventually set for the more thorough reforms of the Tanzimat (Reform Era, 1839–76) and the Hamidian era (1876–1909), named after the ruling sultan, Abdülhamid II, which transformed the Ottoman Empire into a much stronger absolutist state.

Mahmud II (1808–39) continued Selim's reforms, and after meticulous preparation and propaganda – through which he won the support of the reform-minded *ulema* and military – in 1826 he destroyed and abolished the Janissaries, the main source of opposition to reforms. The Janissaries' execrable performance during the Russo-Ottoman wars of 1806–12 and the Greek War of Independence of 1821–31 (in contrast to that of Mehmed Ali's modernized Egyptian army) helped the sultan push through his military reforms. His new, European-style army, the Trained Victorious Troops of Muhammad (*Muallem Asakir-i Mansure-i Muhammadiye*), soon numbered 27,000 men, whereas his Victorious Reserve Soldiers (*Asakir-i Redife-i Mansure*), were 100,000 strong in 1836. The foundation of a modern bureaucratic state was laid by reinforcement of the permanent embassies; the opening of modern military, engineering and medical schools; the creation in 1834 of a modern postal service; the launching of the first official government newspaper in 1831; the abolition of state confiscation of the property of high dignitaries; and – most important – the creation of consultative councils to overhaul the judiciary and the government.

Modernization and rationalization of the Ottoman state proceeded at full speed during the Tanzimat (1839–76). Councils and ministries were created following European models and of these, the Ministry of Foreign Affairs (established in 1836) exercised great influence. Its rise was partly due to the growing significance of diplomacy in the face of diminishing Ottoman military capabilities, but also to the expertise of its ministers and staff. Their knowledge of European languages, societies, economies and government policies proved vital for modernizing the empire. In addition to this transition to ministerial governance, the other important development of the era was the creation of consultative councils and assemblies. Of these, the Supreme Council for Judicial Regulations (*Meclis-i Vala-yi Ahkam-i Adliye*) was the most significant. Although not an elected body, the council was vested with a semi-legislative authority, and thus played a crucial role in reforming the Ottoman legal system and central bureaucracy. By 1868, it had evolved into a Council of State (*Shura-yi Devlet*).

Another significant development was the opening of the first Ottoman Parliament in March 1877, under Sultan Abdülhamid II (r.1876–1909). While the parliament ultimately failed in its legislative functions, it proved a surprisingly effective forum for government criticism. It was suspended less than a year later, in February 1878, by Abdülhamid II, and reopened only after his deposition in 1909. However, it would be a mistake to portray Abdülhamid II as a bigoted reactionary, as earlier Ottoman historiography often did. On the contrary, he continued to modernize and centralize the Ottoman state, albeit in a characteristically autocratic fashion.

Abdülhamid II's government – greatly expanded and aided by modern technologies such as the electric telegraph and the railway – achieved a degree of centralization and efficacy never before seen in Ottoman history. By 1908, the number of government officials had risen to 35,000 as compared to the early 18th-century bureaucracy of 1,500. Most of these new government officials were professional bureaucrats, educated in specialized schools. The overland telegraph reached the port of Fao in the Persian Gulf by 1865, and under Abdülhamid II the system was expanded to link all the provincial centres with the central government via a telegraph station in the sultan's Yıldız Palace. The sultan's domestic surveillance system, feared by many, also relied heavily on the new technology. By comparison to European rail networks the Ottoman railroad system was modest: in 1911 its length was 6,448 km (4,030 miles) compared to Austria-Hungary's 22,748 km (14,218 miles) and Russia's 68,025 km (42,516 miles). Nevertheless, it enabled Istanbul to redeploy soldiers quickly to troubled or rebellious regions. Increasingly, however, lack of cash and growing Ottoman debt – which, from the establishment of the Public Debt Administration in 1881,[5] came under foreign control – hindered further modernization and undercut the authority of the Ottoman government.

The Ottoman army was based on conscription from 1848 onwards. However, owing to a lack of comprehensive censuses, and exemptions enjoyed not only by non-Muslims but also by Muslim town-dwellers and members of certain professions (such as civil servants and the religious establishment), its size was modest in comparison to its rivals. Its peace-time strength of 180,000 to 200,000 men on the eve of World War I was only half the size of the Austrian army, and perhaps one-fifth of the size of the Russian armed forces. Most of the soldiers were Muslim peasants from Anatolia. Non-Muslims were able to avoid military service by paying an exemption tax, despite the 1856 edict that gave equal rights to, and demanded equal service from, all the sultan's subjects regardless of religion. This system remained unchanged until the Young Turks introduced universal conscription irrespective of religion in 1909.

For the subjects of the empire the Tanzimat (Reform Era) brought equality before the law regardless of their religion and ethnicity. However, these reforms, by which Istanbul (like its many counterparts in Europe and Asia) tried to adapt the empire's inefficient economic and political systems to modernity, also meant tighter state control and oversight, and more efficient taxation and bureaucratic centralization, which many among the provincial elites and the subject population alike resented. Nor did the reforms serve the interests of the Great Powers. They favoured a weak empire that they could use to preserve the balance of power amongst themselves, and which offered cheap raw material and markets for their more advanced industries. Their criticism of the Ottoman government and urgings toward reform were often insincere, a mere pretext to interfere in Ottoman affairs. In 1878, for instance, the Great Powers expressed a preference for an appointed Christian governor to administer the empire's European provinces, rather than a constitution giving equal rights to all subjects.

The local power-holders threatened by Istanbul's centralization found a formidable ideology in the emerging idea of nationalism. The Ottoman elite tried unsuccessfully to counter this movement by putting forward alternative notions of citizenship, based on Ottomanism and Islamism. It was not nationalist ideology, however, or the supposed backwardness of the Ottoman state that led to the empire's demise. Rather, it was the combination of domestic and foreign opposition. The modern state apparatus lacked sufficient economic and social grounding. The economic reforms, often haphazard, remained insufficient in the face of constant wars and rebellions, the gradual contraction of the state's human and economic resources, and the economic and political pressure of the Great Powers. Inadequate economic development failed to create a modern society with higher literacy rates and a strong bourgeoisie and working class. Unlike the Russian Empire, which managed to survive in the form of the Soviet Union, the Ottoman Empire collapsed during World War I, just as Austria-Hungary did. The performance of the Ottoman army in the Great War surprised the Allies, costing them greatly in casualties, but the Ottoman Empire and its population also paid a staggering price: 15 per cent of the population was drafted, including almost half of all adult men outside the civil service. By the end of the war, 325,000 of these were dead and 400,000 wounded, and the empire was partitioned among the victors, leaving only a portion of central Anatolia in Ottoman hands. Although the Ottoman government acknowledged the status quo in the Mudros armistice of 1918, it was rejected by the Turkish national resistance. Led by the former

Ottoman general and Turkish national hero Mustafa Kemal Ataturk, the resistance managed to recapture Anatolia, upon which they abolished the sultanate and Caliphate (in 1922 and 1924), and proclaimed the Republic of Turkey in 1923.

## The Ottoman Achievement

The Ottomans ruled with flexibility, pragmatism and relative tolerance for centuries over peoples who followed multiple religions and spoke languages as diverse as Turkic, Greek, Kurdish, Slavic, Hungarian, Albanian and Arabic. At a time when most European monarchs sought to create religiously homogeneous empires by persecuting, expelling and killing all those who happened to follow other faiths, the Ottomans offered a new home to the Jews expelled from Europe and allowed the operation of Jewish and Christian churches, schools and printing presses. For centuries they maintained law and order in the Balkans and the Middle East. The atrocities perpetrated by the *ayan* against the local population in the late 18th century, or events such as the Armenian Massacre of 1915 (which took place amidst the horrors of World War I and Russian invasion, and in which hundreds of thousands of innocent Armenians lost their lives), should not negate the Ottomans' achievements in previous centuries. In the 15th and 16th centuries, the Ottomans brought economic stability, prosperity, and a great flowering of culture to many parts of their empire. The spread of local fairs, the establishment of new towns such as Sarajevo in Bosnia and the growth of population in the Balkans and Anatolia in the 16th century are all clear signs of economic prosperity.

Ottoman imperial architecture of the late 15th to 17th centuries rivalled that of Europe. The Topkapı Palace of the sultans, or the mosque complexes of Mehmed II the Conqueror (Fatih Külliyesi) and Suleiman I (Süleimaniye Külliyesi) in Istanbul were admired and envied by Europeans and proved that Ottoman architects were capable of producing buildings that were on a par with their contemporaries in Renaissance Europe in terms of both engineering and aesthetic genius.

The empire's location and its multi-ethnic and multi-religious character gave Ottoman sultans and subjects alike access to cultural traditions and scientific innovations from a vast area: from China to Persia, the Arab lands and Africa, and from Central Asia to Europe and the Mediterranean. For example, the Ottoman sultans imported vast quantities of Chinese porcelain for use in the Topkapı Palace, including the famous blue and white and celadon wares produced in China during the Yuan (1279–1368) and Ming (1368–1644) dynasties. The Ottomans' own tile industry, which reached an artistic zenith in the city of Iznik in the 16th century, produced an ingenious synthesis in which the influence of Chinese blue and white designs is evident, together with the heritage of Timurid Central Asia.

Another area of cultural productivity was the traditional Islamic arts of the book, including calligraphy, book-binding and miniature painting. Ottoman miniature painting emerged from the Persian tradition, but was also notably influenced by European portraiture and Mediterranean cartography, resulting in a distinct fusion of eastern and western styles. The subject matter of Ottoman painting was also distinctive, with its strong preference for documenting the history of the empire, including detailed representations of people, places, and events. This documentary quality makes Ottoman miniature painting a precious resource for the study of social life in the Ottoman court.[6]

The Ottomans placed great importance on the pursuit of scientific and religious knowledge in their realm, and invested heavily in these areas. In the highest-ranking Ottoman colleges (madrasas), which grew in number from 130 in the 15th century to 350 in the 16th, teachers from Damascus, Cairo and Samarqand taught Islamic subjects alongside the rational sciences (philosophy, logic, mathematics and astronomy). Civil and military medicine was a field of particular interest in an age of almost constant warfare. Classical Islamic medical texts such as the works of Ibn Sina (Avicenna), Ibn Baitar and al-Razi were studied and commented on throughout the empire from Sarajevo to Damascus and Cairo, just as they were at late medieval European universities from Vienna to Paris and Cambridge. In addition to some six hundred herbal drugs listed in Ottoman pharmacological treatises, the Ottomans also experimented with the use of music to treat the mentally ill, a practice they may have learned from their Seljuq and Ayyubid predecessors. The Ottomans had a rich tradition of bathing – a cultural legacy reaching back to the Roman Empire – and therapeutic baths were an integral part of Ottoman medical practice. Meanwhile, in the field of astronomy, the short-lived Istanbul Observatory (1579–80) headed by the Damascus-born chief astronomer Takiyeddin al-Rasid, was comparable to Tycho Brahe's in Uranienborg. Indeed, Takiyeddin's observations and calculations were often more precise than those of Copernicus or Tycho Brahe.

Of the traditional Ottoman crafts, textiles and tiles were the wonder of the time, especially in the 15th to 17th centuries. International commerce fostered a sharing of techniques and tastes to such a degree that Ottoman velvets, silks and brocades produced in Bursa are often indistinguishable from those produced in Venice or Florence. Ottoman carpets, robes (*kaftan*), fine leather goods, weapons and tiles became sought-after commodities in Europe and influenced the tastes of the elite. By the 18th century, the 'Turkish Menace' of the 15th to 17th centuries gave way to 'Turkish Fashion', and Ottoman rugs and tiles, as well as 'Turkish coffee', became popular commodities in Europe. Coffee had been consumed in the Yemen from the Middle Ages onward, and reached the Ottomans in the second part of the 16th century with pilgrims returning from Mecca. It became an instant success throughout the empire, despite periodic prohibitions on the part of the authorities, who found it difficult to control the sub-cultures that sprang from the coffee-houses (*kahvehane*) of Ottoman cities. Indeed, coffee-houses created a new space for discussing politics and criticizing the government, and the literature shared in them, as well as the folk shadow-puppet plays (*karagöz*), proved effective media for political satire.

Straddling the shores of the Bosphorus Straits and linking Europe with Asia, the Ottoman capital was the city that Napoleon Bonaparte called the capital of the world for its strategic location. In its heyday in the 16th century it was, like London in the 19th century or New York City in the 20th, the cosmopolitan hub of a world empire. In the age when European capital cities followed the religion of the ruling dynasty, Ottoman Constantinople was a multi-religious city with a population that in the late 15th and 16th centuries remained about 60 per cent Muslim and 40 per cent Christian and Jewish. The Ottoman capital was also a centre of international diplomacy, espionage and intrigues: the city of boundless opportunities for political, military, economic and cultural advancement.

## CHAPTER FIVE

# Persia: The Safavids 1501–1722

## SUSSAN BABAIE

T he Safavid Empire of 1501–1722 was the longest-lasting Persian polity in the history of Islamic Iran. Its alignment of ancient Persian ideas of kingship with Imami Shia doctrines of Islam created a distinctive culture whose powerful legacy can be traced in the later history of the region.[1]

The Safavid Empire grew out of a messianic venture in the north west of Persia, which became the anchor for the reemergence of a distinctly Persian empire not seen since the advent of Islam in the 7th century. Imami or Twelver Shiism (named for the twelve Shia imams) became the dominant religion, although Sunni Islam was prominent along with large communities, native or imported, of Zoroastrians, Jews and Christians. The territorial gains and losses of the Safavid period settled to an area more or less contiguous with the political boundaries of modern Iran. The Persian and Shia cultural identity of the Safavid Empire grew out of continual conflict or competition with neighbouring Sunni empires – the Ottomans, the Mughals and the Uzbeks – and political alliances and trade partnerships with Europe and Asia. A cultural synthesis, forged out of the ethnic, linguistic and religious groupings in Safavid society, revived the political concept of Iran, rooted in its long history, as a proto-nationalist phenomenon.[2]

### The Boy Becomes King

'The *padshah* [king] of the inhabited quarter of the globe'[3] was the four-teen-year-old Ismail (1487–1524), the charismatic young leader of the Safaviyye order. This was one of the numerous Sufi (mystical) orders that arose in western Asia in the wake of the Mongol invasions of the early 13th century. The order was founded by Sheikh Safi al-Din Eshaq (1252–1334) and centred on a shrine complex at Ardabil, near the south-western shore of the Caspian Sea. Leadership of the order was inherited; Ismail was a direct descendant of Sheikh Safi (a 'Safavid'). The order attracted numerous followers in the century and a half after its foundation, and became increasingly militant, wealthy and powerful. This led the Aqquyunlu Turkmens, the rulers of western Persia, to attempt to suppress the order. However, in the summer of 1501, the young Ismail and his followers defeated the Aqquyunlu, and captured their capital city Tabriz. Ismail was crowned Shah (King) of Iran, beginning the dynastic reign of the Safavids.

The author of a magisterial universal history, Mir Ghiyas al-Din Muhammad Hussayni (d.1525), known as Khwandamir, wrote of Ismail:

> The crown gained its renown from your head, O shah
> The throne gained its worth from your foot, O shah
> Your justice maintains the kingdom, O shah
> By your kingship the world became whole, O shah.[4]

Khwandamir underscores what became the characteristic features of the Safavid conception of kingship, that is, the divine right to rule based on religious authority and a claimed direct relationship to the ancient Persian kings. Thus the Islamic ideal of justice through caliphal rule was combined with a notion of powerful, all-conquering kingship harking back to the glories of the Achaemenid Empire. Khwandamir relates how the youthful warrior 'mounted the throne and placed the crown of the caliphate and world conquest on his head', legitimizing his authority by 'strengthening the Prophet's law' (that is, declaring Imami Shiism as the state religion) while reviving the ancient seat of Persian kingship.

To solidify the authority of Shah Ismail I, his family and followers constructed a network of symbolic narratives of legitimacy and practical instruments of rule that gave the Safavid ruler the absolute authority of

## KEY DATES

**1501–24**    Shah Ismail I founds the Safavid Empire, ruling from Tabriz

**1514**    Battle of Chaldiran: the Ottoman Sultan Selim I defeats Shah Ismail I

**1524–76**    Reign of Shah Tahmasb

**1520s–30s**    Creation of Shah Tahmasb's *Shahnama* (Book of Kings)

**1544–55**    Qazvin inaugurated as the new capital city

**1576–87**    Civil War and crisis of succession

**1587–1629**    Reign of Shah Abbas I 'The Great'

**1590/91**    Beginning of construction of Maydan-e Naqsh-e Jahan complex and the Chahar Bagh Promenade in Isfahan

**1598**    Isfahan becomes the new Safavid capital

**1604**    Forced relocation of the Armenian merchant families of Julfa on the Araxes and the founding of the New Julfa quarter in Isfahan

**1611–12**    Founding of Farahabad city (Caspian Sea) and urban development in the holy city of Mashhad, and the port of Bandar Abbas (Persian Gulf)

**1611–38**    Completion of the Masjed-e Jadid-e Abbasi (Royal Mosque) and Maydan-e Naqsh-e Jahan, Isfahan

**1642–66**    Reign of Shah Abbas II

**1647–50s**    Construction of the Chehel Sotun (Forty Pillar Palace)

**1722**    Afghan siege of Isfahan and capitulation of Shah Sultan Hussein

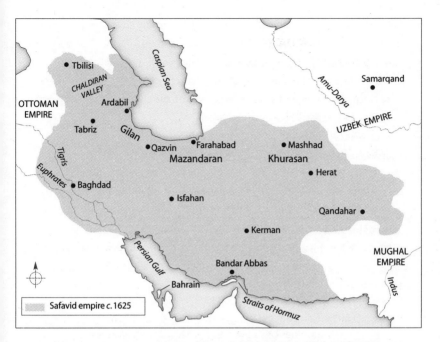

Map showing the Safavid Empire at its greatest geographical extent, during the reign of Shah Abbas I 'The Great' (1587–1629). Territorial rivalries with the Ottomans over the Mesopotamian provinces (Iraq) and Shia holy sites, and with the Mughals and the Uzbeks over the greater Khurasan region (including Afghanistan) raged throughout the Safavid period.

a god-king, albeit with mixed success. One narrative relied on a dubious genealogical tree that related the Safavids to the seventh Shia Imam Musa al-Kazim (d.799). This link was necessary in order for the Safavids to assume the authority embedded in the creed of Imami Shiism, which had distinguished itself from the Ismaili branch (the other major Shia group). Whereas the Ismailis considered the sixth Imam Jafar al-Sadiq to have been the last of the Prophet's family line, the Imami Shias upheld a genealogical continuity from the Prophet through to the Twelfth Imam. Having disappeared in 873, He is considered to be the Mahdi (Messiah), who will return as the redeemer of Islam. During His absence (the period of Occultation), authority to lead and rule remains contingent upon a number of prerequisites, one of which is the proof of blood lineage to the family of the Prophet. Thus the Safavid claim to blood relationship to the seventh Imam facilitated their assumption of the spiritual and temporal authority of Imami Shiism.

According to Shia tradition, the sole legitimate representative of the Mahdi, and the ultimate authority in His absence for the Imami Shia community, would be not a mere king, but the *mujtahid*, the scholar of Islamic law and source of juridical interpretations of the Quran and the traditions of the Prophet.[5] Ismail had taken power by force and could not claim to be the designated successor to the crown, so his bid for sovereign power rested on his claim to descent from the Imams. In this way, he could appropriate – and pass on to his successors – a divinely appointed status derived from the Shia doctrine of the infallibility of the Imams.

The other crucial component in the formation of the Safavid Empire was the role of Ismail as the *morshid-e kamel*, or grand master of the Sufi brotherhood of the Safaviyye. Their shrine at Ardabil had become the spiritual locus for the gathering, in the late 15th century, of the militant supporters of the family. As the *morshid*, Ismail wielded enormous spiritual and temporal influence over his fanatical followers, whom he was able to mobilize into a formidable military force.

The politicization of the Safaviyye had begun in earnest with Ismail's father Sheikh Haydar (master 1460–88). Haydar himself was closely associated with Sultan Uzun Hassan (r. 1453–78), the leader of the tribal confederacy of the Aqquyunlu Turkmens. A marriage of convenience between Haydar and a daughter of Uzun Hassan ensured that Ismail could claim royal blood, a significant link not only to the most powerful Turkmen dynasty of the 15th century but also to Calo Johannes, the Christian king of Trebizond, whose daughter was the wife of Uzun Hassan and hence Ismail's grandmother.[6] Haydar and his predecessors, though powerful leaders, had no claim to royal descent themselves.

It was Haydar who first organized his Sufi followers into an army, in order to pursue holy war against the majority Sunni ruling elites of the Aqquyunlu and other neighbouring Turkmen powers. The fighters were principally Turkmen tribesmen who had abandoned their Ottoman-controlled homelands in eastern Anatolia and joined the Safaviyye order. The army became known as the Qizilbash. The name, meaning 'red heads', was a pejorative designation bestowed by the Ottomans, but it was embraced by the Qizilbash as a badge of honour. *Qizilbash* derived from the red turban cap that was worn by the followers of Haydar and the Safavid shahs. Known as *taj-e Haydari*, it had twelve folds symbolizing allegiance to the twelve Shia Imams; it continued to be worn until the early decades of the 17th century, when Qizilbash influence diminished. Khwandamir credits the creation of the *taj-e Haydari* to a dream in which Haydar received instructions for its shape from Imam Ali. The Imam's intercession was interpreted as divine inspiration, lending further spiritual significance to the messianic mission of the Qizilbash and the Safaviyye.

Until the death of Uzun Hassan, Haydar's family ties kept his ambitions in check, but after that the Safaviyye became actively involved in the power struggle to dominate north-western Persia and eastern Anatolia. Although Haydar fell in battle in 1488, the Qizilbash continued to figure prominently in Aqquyunlu internal strife, using Haydar's three sons as pawns and fomenting blood enmity between the last of the Aqquyunlu rulers and the emergent Safavids. Ismail, only one year old at the time of his father's death, was sequestered in the Caspian seashore province of Gilan under the tutelage of a prominent Shia theologian. It was not until 1499 that Ismail, then twelve years old, emerged from hiding and went to Ardabil to assume leadership of the order. This move was interpreted by Safavid historians as a symbolic parallel to the emergence of the Mahdi at the End of Time and the fulfilment of the dictum 'God sends at the beginning of every century someone to renew the faith'.[8]

With such messianic zeal and the extensive support that rallied around the young master, the Qizilbash Sufi fighters enabled Shah Ismail I to launch successful campaigns in the vacuum left by the internal struggles of the Aqquyunlu in the north west, and the weakened Timurids (1370–1506) in the north east. The Timurids (descended from the Mongol leader Timur) had already been dislodged from their last capital, Herat, by the Uzbek Shaybanids (1500–98). The Safaviyye family's supporters helped unseat nearly all the kings of the western regions. In the east, Ismail wrested some of the former Timurid domain out of Uzbek hands, adding the Khurasan and Herat provinces to his empire by 1510. In short, within only nine years, Shah Ismail's messianic leadership had (temporarily at least) reunited under a single banner a vast region stretching from Transoxiana and Afghanistan to the southern Caucasus, eastern Anatolia and Iraq and encompassing today's Iran.

The administration of the new empire was dominated by the chiefs of the Turkmen Qizilbash, who formed the military aristocracy and held the posts of governors of the provinces. As governors, they oversaw the education of the Safavid princes. This system ensured confederate rule while keeping in check royal prerogatives. However, the Qizilbash tutors of the Safavid princes would prove in time to be formidable threats to the royal household.

Owing to their zealous loyalty to the Safaviyye and their invaluable military role in bringing Shah Ismail I to power, the Qizilbash tended to hold all the superior positions in the empire as generals and governors. The Persians, or Tajik, mostly occupied lower ranks of the bureaucracy as viziers and in various positions in the royal secretariat and financial administration. This early division of official posts along ethnic lines flexed and transformed, however, during the 16th century. The structure of the state administration was divided into two broad categories: state (*mamalek*) and crown (*khasse*). The state lands or provinces were administered by the emirs or tribal chiefs of the Qizilbash, who wielded considerable influence in imperial affairs through control of the economic and military resources of their provinces. At first the ratio between state and royal lands was decidedly in favour of the Qizilbash-controlled domains, so that the Safavid royal household and the shahs remained dependent upon the loyalty of the Qizilbash governors and generals. The master-disciple relationship set up by Ismail unravelled almost as quickly as it had been forged. The esoteric and militant practices of the Safaviyye order would prove to be incompatible with the Safavid Empire as it became centralized.

The success of the Safavid dynasty depended on the political theory of kingship that linked the family blood of Ismail and his successors to Ali and the family of the Prophet, to the venerable Sheikh Safi and his Sufi devotees and to the lineage of kingship that he could claim through the Aqquyunlu household. Shah Ismail I certainly saw himself as both the rightful bearer of the heritage of ancient Persian kingship and 'the heir to the Imamate',[9] making him the natural leader of the Muslim community. This bold claim is nowhere more in evidence than in his ecstatic religious poetry. There, under the nom de plume Khatai ('the Sinner'), he declares with an audacity unheard of before or since:

> I am God's mystery. I am the leader of all these *ghazi* warriors.
> My mother is Fatima, my father is Ali; and I am the *pir* [leader] of the Twelve Imams.[10]

Ismail's personal charisma intermixed with popular narratives that compared him to Abu Muslim, a warrior who had led Arab-Muslim armies in north-western Persia against the Umayyads (661–750), the first Muslim ruling dynasty. Abu Muslim defeated the Umayyads, bringing the pro-Shia Abbasid dynasty (750–1258) to power. This narrative of a Persian warrior helping to establish a Shia state had compelling echoes of Ismail's own deeds. Also, like the Twelfth Imam, Abu Muslim was expected to return.[11] Thus, Ismail's complex and multi-faceted formulation of a divinely inspired mission fitted perfectly into the messianic fervour of the time. The zeal of his followers allowed Ismail to rally effective armies able to capture territories and take over the cultural resources concentrated in the principal cities of the Aqquyunlu and the Timurids. Unconventionally, Ismail kept Tabriz, the capital city of the Aqquyunlu (and their predecessors the Qaraquyunlu) as his own capital. This surprising choice – to keep the capital of a defeated foe – asserted Ismail's ties with the Aqquyunlu aristocracy and represented Tabriz as the geographical and psychological seat of an unbroken chain of authority and legitimacy. This must have seemed a necessity to the new ruler, with his enormously ambitious designs to invent and install his own Persian and Shia model of kingship.

## Architecture and Art under Shah Ismail I

Not much remains of Safavid Tabriz and, in fact, little monumental architecture was sponsored by Ismail. The warfare during his reign and the constant movement of resources to expand and consolidate the new frontiers seem to have left little time or funds for large architectural projects or urban development. The most important building works were additions to the shrine of Sheikh Safi in Ardabil. The small medieval convent and burial site of the Safavid ancestors was being turned into their dynastic icon of spiritual legitimacy. Most of the constructions in Ardabil were funded and supervised by members of the family and their Qizilbash devotees, as were the few other projects elsewhere in Safavid Persia during this period. Curiously, no major mosque of the congregational variety was constructed under Shah Ismail I. Such mosques were usually commissioned on the ascent of a new dynasty or the accession of a new king in an established dynasty. Before the accession of Shah Abbas I in 1587, Safavid shahs did not follow suit, for reasons discussed below.

Architectural projects require enormous funds and may have been sacrificed for the sake of the war chest. Nevertheless, the making of other arts – manuscripts, textiles and luxury objects – continued to flourish, if not peak, under Safavid patronage. Conquest encompassed the intellectual and artistic riches of the conquered. The royal ateliers of Tabriz, famed since the early 14th-century Il-Khanid times for their assembly of international talent from China to Europe, were reinvigorated by artists from the Timurid workshops of Herat. The astoundingly inventive and fresh style of painting that emerged from the Safavid atelier in Tabriz, especially under the patronage of Shah Tahmasb (r.1524–76), Ismail's son and successor, represented just such a synergy. Among the masters was Sultan Muhammad, who had been in the Aqquyunlu atelier in Tabriz and became director of the royal *ketabkhane* (scriptorium) under the Safavids, and Behzad, the ageing master from the late Timurid atelier in Herat.

This fresh synthesis was not limited to painting and book-making skills; it extended into all the artistic productions under the Safavids in the first half of the 16th century. Carpets and textiles, exquisitely detailed and decorated metalwork (cups, jugs, pen-boxes), engraved, inlaid and bejewelled jade and metal wine cups, leather and lacquer book-binding, illuminated manuscripts graced with calligraphy from the greatest scribes – the range of materials, and the technical skill and creative subtlety of the Safavid visual arts at that time, is astounding. Less appreciated in later centuries was a parallel new synthesis in Persian poetry.[12] Complex interweaving of mental images, metaphoric and verbal acrobatics, and endlessly interlaced word plays on the language of master poets; these, although growing out of 15th-century Timurid developments, became quintessentially associated with Safavid taste.

Persian cultural effervescence in the early Safavid period had been fuelled by two important factors traditionally upheld by all Turco-Mongol overlords in greater Persia since the 11th century: to educate the new princely clan in the classical repertoire of Persian arts and letters, and to deploy the human resources from all the conquered terrain. Ismail's greatest contribution was to revive the Tabriz scriptorium and commission a copy of the *Shahnama* (Book of Kings) for his son Shah Tahmasb. This was the most spectacular project to come from the assembly of great masters in Tabriz.[13]

The masterpiece of the poet Firdausi (d.1010), the *Shahnama* recounts the conflict between pre-Islamic Iranian warriors and kings and their Turanian (Turkic) enemies, usurpers of the Persian crown. Part imagined, part historical, it grew out of the encounter of Islam with the ancient past of Persia. It proved so versatile that every Muslim who aspired to high culture in the Persian-speaking world adapted to its ideals by assuming the guise of its heroes and kings, and it became a potent instrument of princely education. By commissioning a copy for his son, Shah Ismail I was connecting the Safavid claim to power to the ancient idea of the Persian throne. The *Shahnama* of Shah Tahmasb was thus a representation of the most Persianate ethos of Muslim kingship. The 70,000 couplets of the *Shahnama* provided cultural ammunition appropriated by nearly every Muslim king – but most efficiently by the Safavids – to legitimize their sovereignty over the cultural world of Iran.

Imami Shiism was not an invention of the Safavids, but under their patronage it was infused with a cultural identity deeply rooted in the pre-Islamic past of Iran, and cognizant of the many ethnic and lingual groupings under its banner. Ismail, his ancestors and heirs were not ethnic Persian-Tajik. They spoke a Turkic language and even wrote in it. The propagation of the Imami creed depended on imported Arab-speaking theologians, while the empire's administration benefited from the inclusion of converted Christians from the Caucusus. Therefore the Safavid appropriation of the Persian language and Persian stories and symbols was politically, not ethnically, motivated. The Safavids succeeded in formulating, for the first time in Islamic Iran, a cultural identity that fused their Imami Shia faith with a uniquely Persian sensibility. Their leadership renewed a sense of ownership of Islam that was distinctly Persian, even though the rulers and many of their subjects were not. The Safavids propelled Imami Shiism to imperial prominence and their legacy has had a lasting impact as a marker of a political theory, and later a national identity, for Iran.

The Safavid copy of the *Shahnama* was begun on the orders of Shah Ismail I after 1514 and completed mostly under the discerning patronage of Shah Tahmasb in the 1520s and 1530s. With 258 unusually large-scale and imaginatively represented paintings of the escapades, loves and battles of kings and heroes, ravishingly rich illuminations, and a binding of superb workmanship, this *Shahnama* is the grandest copy ever produced.

## The Fall of Ismail and Reign of Shah Tahmasb

In August 1514, Shah Ismail I and his armies met a horrible defeat at the hands of the Ottoman armies of Sultan Selim I (r.1512–20) at the battle of Chaldiran. The debacle is blamed on Ismail's arrogant assumption of infallibility, on the logistical miscalculations of his ineffectual generals, and on in-fighting among the Qizilbash. Safavid territorial losses in eastern Anatolia were almost permanently fixed, while battles over regions in north-western Persia and the southern Caucusus were to continue for another century. The Safavid capital of Tabriz, located near the disputed north-western frontiers, proved all too vulnerable. The city was occupied by Sultan Selim for only a week, but this proved symbolically devastating.

The defeat was crushing enough, but Ismail's fall was all the deeper, given his previous status.[14] His invincibility was shattered. His inability to protect his Qizilbash men-at-arms from the slaughter undermined his authority and spun him into deep depression and a retreat from affairs of state.

Ironically, his retreat may have been the impetus for a different kind of political strategizing. His energies were diverted toward reorganizing the administration, moving the imperial sponsorship of Imami Shia doctrine away from its more mystical and esoteric practices, and attending to the education of future shahs, principally his son Tahmasb. After Chaldiran, Ismail wished to create a more equal balance of power between the Qizilbash emirs and the Persian-Tajik land-owning nobility. His reforms were limited in scope, if indeed implemented at all, but this desire to reduce the exclusive rights and privileges of the Qizilbash heralded a significant political realignment. Tahmasb, his eldest son, was under the tutelage of Qizilbash emir Div Sultan in Herat, the cultural capital of the deposed Timurids and an important centre of artistic production. Herat and, by extension, the province of Khurasan – important for its resources and especially as a buffer against Uzbek territorial ambitions – was controlled by Div Sultan, but his authority hinged on the presence of his ward, prince Tahmasb. When Ismail died in 1524, the emir-tutor brought the ten-year-old Tahmasb Mirza (his princely title) to the capital, assuming for him a *de facto* rule over Safavid realms. This bold move unleashed the fury of rival Qizilbash tribes. A period of intense intra-tribal rivalry for control of the Safavid throne followed, with Safavid princes used as pawns. Civil war raged until 1533, when Tahmasb finally quelled the unrest.

Although it began in chaos and with threats from the Ottoman and Uzbek frontiers, Shah Tahmasb's fifty-two year reign (1524–76) was largely prosperous and culturally brilliant. He normalized the shattered Safavid polity, established a religious hierarchy loyal to the crown and capable of implementing the sharia laws, and transformed Qazvin into the new capital city. Well aware of the danger of unchecked Qizilbash rivalries and power, he entrusted the highest military and administrative positions to the Persian-Tajik nobility and learned class as well as to his own family.

Tahmasb centralized authority in the Safavid king to a far greater degree than before. This was achieved by introducing a third element into the administrative structure, namely the *ghulam* (slave) category of service.[15] During three campaigns against the Ottomans in the Georgian and Circassian territories between 1540 and 1554, Shah Tahmasb stabilized his control by installing a loyal Georgian governor in Tbilisi in 1554. Tens of thousands of captives were converted to Islam and routinely recruited into the Safavid armies as royal bodyguards and special forces. Leadership of some of the corps was almost exclusively given to a Georgian, Circassian or Armenian *ghulam* commander, and so the inner circle of power was populated by people whose loyalty to the shah transcended tribal and family relationships. In time, this strategy curtailed the influence of the Qizilbash by making personal politics paramount over tribal ones, though it was never entirely successful. By the 17th century, the *ghulams* had acquired enormous wealth and influence, and began to play a major role not only in the maintenance of the empire but also in its cultural output.

During the reign of Tahmasb, the Safavid realms were continually under attack from the Ottomans on the west and north west, and the Uzbeks from the north east. The Qizilbash civil war of the first decade of Tahmasb's reign and the chaotic internal situation at the Safavid court coincided with five Uzbek invasions into Herat and Khurasan. Intermittently, Tahmasb was preoccupied with the more dangerous Ottoman encroachments on the western front. The Ottoman Sultan Suleiman I (r.1520–66) initiated fresh attacks on Persia after negotiating a cease-fire with his Austrian enemies in January 1533. Less than a year later, his grand vizier, Ibrahim Pasha, occupied Tabriz. Suleiman himself arrived in the city in September 1534 on his way to capture Baghdad, which then remained in Ottoman hands (except for a brief period in the 17th century). Tahmasb recovered and then relinquished Azerbaijan twice more (1535 and 1548) and Tabriz was again occupied for several days in 1549.

The trauma of these repeated captures and recaptures left Tabriz in ruins. The city's position, near the contested Safavid-Ottoman frontier, rendered it ineffectual as the principal seat of empire, and this must have been the reason for Tahmasb's decision to relocate the capital. In 1555 the Shah officially left Tabriz for the city of Qazvin, to the south east.[16]

## Architecture and Art under Shah Tahmasb

Qazvin was an old city that functioned as the urban centre of a significant military and agricultural region. Tabriz had been inherited as Ismail's capital with few architectural changes, but Qazvin was extensively refashioned to serve as the imperial seat. Planning was begun a decade prior to the transfer of the capital. A vast tract of land north of the city walls was purchased, and a protected royal precinct (*daulatkhane*, literally 'the abode of rule') was built there, alongside an existing public square. Qazvin had good access to water, a scarce commodity, through an extensive system of subterranean canals (*qanat*) that flowed from the mountains to the north.

On its south side, the walled palace complex opened onto a long and narrow public square (a *maydan*); on its north side were the new garden-mansions of Safavid high society. This planned urban development underscores the political significance of the relocation. In order to be a true capital, even one grafted onto an older city, it had to be conceived afresh.

The Safavid historian Qomi wrote that the rectangular space of the royal precinct was built by:

> skilled engineers and artful builders ... [who] designed a square
> garden named Bagh-e Saadat (garden of felicity) and in the midst
> of that garden, [they] designed excellent buildings and lofty pillared
> kiosks and vaulted porches and pools.[17]

The commencement of building in 1544–45 coincided with Tahmasb's official statement of renunciation (*taube*) of worldly pleasures. A second 'Edict of Sincere Repentance' in 1556 included dancing, music, wine, sodomy and the magical pleasures of painting in its list of 'pleasures'. The 'Sincere Repentance', recounted in Tahmasb's memoir (*Tazkere*), represented a self-portrait of disciplined religiosity and an advocacy of the accepted dogma of Imami Shia theology. His patronage of the established laws and of the clerics who would interpret and implement those laws was in sharp contrast to the unorthodox religious practices and beliefs that were prevalent among the earlier followers of Ismail, the Safaviyye order and their Qizilbash cohorts. These developments during the reign of Tahmasb further aligned the leadership position of the Safavid shah with the Imami Shia adaptations of religious laws (sharia).

Tahmasb's renunciation of the pleasures of painting diverted some resources away from the royal atelier in Tabriz, but was not as detrimental to the creation of manuscripts as some have assumed. The exodus of artists from Tabriz may have given impetus to other centres of manuscript production. One of the greatest examples of this realignment was the commissioning of a luxury manuscript, *Haft Awrang* ('Seven Thrones'), by Prince Ibrahim Mirza (1540–77), a grandson of Shah Ismail I and a nephew of Shah Tahmasb.[18] Ibrahim Mirza astutely recruited dispersed master artists and craftsmen and supported an important scriptorium in Mashhad. His commission of the first Safavid copy of the *Haft Awrang* was at once homage to the dynastic tradition of patronage of cultural monuments and a statement of aesthetic taste. It reflected the same mastery of the arts as were generated from the royal atelier for the great *Shahnama* of Shah Tahmasb or for the famed pair of Ardabil carpets (1539–40), masterpieces of Persian carpet design and weaving.[19]

Other artists of Tahmasb's court found lucrative opportunities at royal ateliers in Mughal India and Ottoman Turkey. This migration of talent contributed to new styles of painting in those courts in the second half of the 16th century. Meanwhile, mural painting came into vogue at the Safavid court, and was used to decorate the new pavilions in the palace precinct in Qazvin.

The shah's court was not the only patron of the arts. Competition for the ownership of de luxe copies of manuscripts generated satellite centres of production such as Shiraz, where speculative luxury copies were made for the Ottoman elite. Ottoman high culture, like that of the Mughal Empire, was permeated in this period with Persian literary and artistic ideals and courtly practices. While Safavid-Ottoman territorial conflicts raged and the ritual cursing of the Sunni sultans of Turkey took place on the streets of Tabriz and Qazvin, Ottoman collectors vied for cultural sophistication by seeking to possess greater, more expensive and glamorous Persian works of art.[20]

The craze for deluxe Persian manuscripts may have been refuelled by the sumptuous diplomatic gift despatched in 1567 by Shah Tahmasb on the accession of the Ottoman Sultan Selim II (r.1566–74). Wishing to maintain the truce he had negotiated with Selim's father Suleiman I, he spared no effort in impressing his good intentions on the new sultan. An exceedingly elaborate congratulatory letter was composed under Tahmasb's direct supervision and sent with some thirty camel-loads of gifts and treasures from the royal library, notably the *Shahnama* of Shah Tahmasb.[21]

## Civil War and the Accession of Shah Abbas I

Cultural production of the end of the 16th century was overshadowed by the political upheavals that followed the death of Shah Tahmasb in 1576 and nearly unravelled the empire. The Second Civil War in 1576 pitched Qizilbash emirs, Persian and Georgian dignitaries and members of Tahmasb's family, especially his daughter, Pari Khan Khanum (d.1578), against one another.[22]

Women of the royal house, taking advantage of their blood heritage and never as sequestered and ineffectual as might be assumed, became prominent. Their monumental patronage is exemplified by Pari Khan Khanum. She was Safavid through her father but was born to a Circassian mother, evidence of the gradual but decisive emplacement of the new elite from the Caucasus within the royal household. She was highly sophisticated, a poet of note and a generous patron of the principal Shia shrines in Safavid Persia. Also, she was instrumental in the power politics that brought her brother, Prince Ismail, to the throne as Ismail II (r.1576–77).

The new shah tried to restore order by eliminating all brothers and cousins who could threaten his rule, but then his sudden and mysterious death unleashed renewed political manoeuvering. Palace intrigue replaced Princess Pari Khan Khanum, the *de facto* ruler during the reign of her brother, with Khayr al-Nesa, the spouse of Ismail's half-blind brother Muhammad Khodabande (r.1578–87). Khayr al-Nesa, not of Turkmen origin, was supported by an alliance between her kin from the Mazandaran region of the Caspian Sea shore and the Persian-Tajik elements within the Safavid administration. Before she too was purged (strangled in the harem in 1579 on the pretext of an unlawful love affair), the queen-consort had nearly monopolized the most important functions of the empire, outraging the Qizilbash emirs. Her death unleashed new unrest and an especially virulent retaliation against the Persian, and especially the Mazandaran, aristocracy.

The situation exposed the empire to attacks from its neighbours. The Ottoman-Safavid wars were renewed and Tabriz was lost again in 1585 along with territories in Transcaucasia and Kurdistan. On the eastern front, while Uzbek attacks on Khurasan were resumed in 1578, the more significant threat came from the temporary secession of Khurasan from the central government in 1581. The secession was short-lived, but it had the far-reaching effect of propelling the Safavid prince Abbas Mirza onto the political stage. As was the custom, Abbas Mirza's education had been entrusted to the Qizilbash governor of Herat, Morshed Qoli Khan of the Ostajlu tribe. He was ostensibly educating the potential heir in the art of statesmanship, but actually playing him off against competing forces while Muhammad Khodabande was distracted by threats from the frontiers. Following the successful plotting of his tutor and governor-protector, Abbas Mirza ascended the throne in Qazvin in 1587 in the absence of Sultan Muhammad Khodabande. Khodabande evidently returned to his capital subsequently, but did not challenge the usurper.

The sixteen-year-old Shah Abbas I (r.1587–1629) began his reign in the midst of dauntingly chaotic circumstances but accomplished such an extraordinary realignment of the Safavid Empire that he earned the title of 'The Great'. Threats of further hostilities with the Ottomans in the west and the Uzbeks in the east compounded the effects of the protracted period of internal and external strife, which had left the Safavid domain in a state of severe economic decline. Shah Abbas I implemented shrewd measures that restored the empire and concentrated power into an absolutist centre of authority, the shah himself.

### Isfahan, the Safavid Capital 1598–1722

This second century of the Safavid Empire was dominated by the city of Isfahan and by a decidedly different flavour of imperial and social life.[23] Beginning with the official transfer of the capital to Isfahan in 1598, this period is striking in its relative political and social stability, its economic vitality and the associated expenditure on monumental architecture, urban development and the arts, as well as its confident advocacy of a fully developed Persian-Shia political culture.

The 'reforms' implemented by Shah Abbas I entailed a relative curtailment of the power of the Qizilbash emirs. One such policy involved the modernization of the armies through the introduction of new formations of musketeers and the artillery corps. The English brothers Robert and Anthony Sherley, along with other Europeans, advised the shah on such matters when they arrived at the court in 1598. That early venture ended in disaster for the envoys, but the English played an important role later in the reign of Shah Abbas when they helped drive the Portuguese out of Hormuz and in effect opened the Persian Gulf maritime routes to expanded European trade.

Leadership in the new military formations went mostly to people of non-Turkmen origin, especially those from the *ghulam* slave elite from the Caucasus. Their loyalty was further secured because they were paid directly out of the royal treasury and not through the old revenue assignments controlled by the tribal chiefs and the Turkmen military aristocracy. This meant an eclipse of the feudal system of the earlier Safavid structure, in which the state revenues were controlled by the Qizilbash governors for the maintenance of their troops and their province. To raise royal income, Shah Abbas I systematically converted more provinces into lands of the royal domain, thus diminishing the exclusive control held by the Qizilbash governors over those resources. Alongside his restructuring of the military, he promoted members of the *ghulam* elite to high ranks in the administration. A concomitant feature was Shah Abbas I's elimination of all his male blood relatives and the emphasis on new marriage alliances outside the traditional Safavid and Qizilbash nexus of power.

The Georgian, Circassian and Armenian royal women, or their converted compatriots who had been incorporated into the Safavid royal household, became key players in the harem and the court by virtue of bearing a potential male heir. Alongside this shift was a change in the practice of sending princes to Qizilbash tutor-governors. Instead, they remained in the harem in Isfahan, concentrating the shah's control over the competition from within and rival plots from without, an effective strategy that curtailed the power of the Qizilbash but opened the door to greater harem intrigues.

The centrepiece of Isfahan was the Maydan-e Naqsh-e Jahan (the Image of the World Square). There, the shah built a theological college (madrasa) for his father-in-law adjacent to the royal chapel-mosque in Isfahan, also known as the Sheikh Lotf-Allah Mosque (1602–19). Its significance lay in the enormous investment devoted to creating such an architectural gem, and its location in the heart of the new capital city. The building is extraordinary, for it departs from the usual formula of devising a protected space of royal seclusion within a city's main congregational mosque. Here, the royal chapel was turned into a discreet mosque. The interior was reserved for the royal retinue, but the public could see the tiled entrance-way and the elegantly decorated golden dome from the outside.

The Maydan measures 83,000 square metres (893,405 square feet) in area, second only in size to Tiananmen Square in Beijing. Exceptionally, it was designed as a rectangle with two-storey peripheral façades opening onto rows of shops. The four sides of the Maydan were strategically articulated by the placement of monumental structures: the royal bazaar (Qaysariyye, begun in 1590/91) on the north side linking the new urban centre to the old through its vaulted markets; the Ali Qapu Palace (1590/91–1615) on the west, serving also as the ceremonial entrance into the palace precinct; the Sheikh Lotf-Allah Chapel-Mosque on the east; and the spectacular new congregational mosque (the Royal Mosque, 1611–38) on the south.

Indeed, the Maydan, with its bazaars, mosques and palace, and its daily markets, spectacles, martial performances and polo, was the quintessence of an extraordinary venture in architecture and urbanism that made Isfahan one of the most famous cities of the 17th century.

When Shah Abbas I ordered this vast project in 1590/91, he was anticipating the official move from Qazvin to Isfahan in 1598. The timing was not coincidental because 1590/91 CE corresponded to the year 1000 AH in the Islamic calendar, [25] making it a millennial threshold. In the same year, Shah

Abbas had suppressed the resurgence of a millenarian movement challenging the legitimacy of the shah and associated with Nuqtavi Dervish Khosrau, a popular preacher.[26] The enterprise of building a new capital city, and the particular design of the Maydan, was intended to maximize the message of renewal and the fulfilment of a new Safavid patrimony.

During the 16th century, no Safavid shah had dared sponsor the construction of a main congregational mosque because of the debate among Imami Shia scholars over the permissibility of performing congregational Friday prayer during the absence of the Mahdi (the Twelfth Imam). This particular religious impasse had preoccupied Safavid society and had prevented the shahs from exercising what was traditionally both a prerogative and a duty of Muslim royal patronage, the founding of a congregational mosque. Their Sunni rivals, the Ottoman sultans and the Mughal emperors had done so; and even mocked them for being unable to lead congregational prayer.

By the end of the 16th century, and with the help of imported scholars from Jabal Amil in southern Lebanon, the impasse was removed. Shah Abbas I's patronage of the two great Amili religious scholars of the age, Sheikh Lotf-Allah and Sheikh Baha'i, contributed to a new formulation of Shiism through teaching and the writing of treatises aimed at propagating normative doctrinal practices and aligning them with imperial agendas.[27] The institutional adoption of Friday prayer at the end of the 16th century lifted the burden and allowed for the imperial patronage of congregational mosques. This was a political victory of enormous magnitude – nothing less than a fresh conceptualization of the empire, its new capital city and its urban centre. The first and only congregational mosque ever built in the capital cities of the Safavid Empire was the gigantic Masjed-e Jadid-e Abbasi or Royal Mosque (popularly known, after the 1979 formation of the Islamic Republic of Iran, as the 'Imam Mosque') on the south side of the Maydan-e Naqsh-e Jahan in Isfahan.

Isfahan and the Maydan represented a political impulse to establish an imperial capital that would rival contemporary Constantinople or Agra.

They also expressed the concept of an imperial seat at once sacred and secular. Safavid Isfahan contained ritualized spaces for social encounter, where the king observed his subjects in the public square and where he was observed in the aura of kingship. Such strategies appealed to expectations rooted in ancient Persian notions of kingship as well as in Shia Islamic practice. The Imami Shia model of kingship required the shah to make himself accessible to a degree quite unlike anything practised in the Sunni world. Thus the entire Maydan design may be read as the imprint of a spiritual mapping of Safavid kingship.

Other motivations for choosing Isfahan as the capital may have been economic. The Safavid-Ottoman conflicts of the 16th century had imposed trade limitations on the land routes from Iran to Europe, making it necessary to expand maritime trade via the Persian Gulf. Moreover, in the middle of the 16th century the English had opened a link with Persia via Norway and the White Sea and through the Volga and the Caspian Sea. This bypassed two hostile barriers, the Ottomans in the west and the Portuguese (until 1622) in the Persian Gulf. The resulting political stability and the ending of major wars, especially the lasting peace with the Ottomans on the north-western borders, paved the way for a boom in the economy. Monumental projects were undertaken throughout Persia with major bridges and caravanserais dotting the trade routes. Trade, particularly with Europe and India, expanded to unprecedented levels, maximizing exports of Persian products, especially raw silk, textiles, and carpets.[28]

## Cosmopolitanism and Kingship

As elsewhere in the 17th century, trade and the lure of greater riches – including gold and silver from the Americas and exotic commodities from the east – determined the political and military networks of cooperation and competition. The Portuguese held tightly onto their interests in the Persian Gulf, posing a serious threat not only to Safavid economic ambitions but also to those of their European rivals. The Safavid annexation of the Island of Bahrain in 1607–08 was one of the steps towards the recovery of Safavid control; and with English help the Portuguese were forced out of Hormuz after more than one hundred years of occupation.[29]

Isfahan in the 17th century exuded a cosmopolitanism that could be called proto-modern. Its denizens were well aware of their place in the wider world. Merchants, be they Armenian, Persian, Indian or a combination of those, conducted commerce on the international networks out of their mansions in Isfahan. In turn, European and Asian merchants, envoys and adventurers sought favourable concessions and lucrative employment at the Safavid court or the city's marketplaces. The encounters are represented in the commercial deals, political negotiations and cultural exchanges that permeated the daily life of the city. Such cultural encounters are represented in the mural paintings decorating the houses of the elite.[30]

Members of the *ghulam* and other elite members of the Safavid household in the 17th century routinely undertook monumental patronage both for themselves and on behalf of the shahs. Ganj Ali Khan, the Kurdish boyhood friend and close companion-in-arms of Shah Abbas I 'The Great', oversaw the building of a new urban ensemble in the city of Kerman in south-eastern Iran in the first decade of the 17th century.[31] His square, inspired by the Maydan in Isfahan, was on a smaller scale and had a strong commercial motivation. Kerman became a centre for the production of raw wool, carpets and ceramics.[32] By the latter part of the century, these commodities featured prominently in trade across Eurasia, reaching as far as Dejima (Nagasaki), as well as Amsterdam and other European centres.

Other cities were redeveloped for a combination of political, commercial and religious reasons: Mashhad as a pilgrimage centre with huge revenues; Farahabad in Mazandaran as a political and commercial centre for the production of silk; and Bandar Abbas on the Persian Gulf as a port city, the Safavid link to maritime routes. The Safavid players in the great game of international trade and the dissemination of new commodities and styles were diverse in their social origins and had far-reaching influence on shaping the cosmopolitan flavour of Isfahan.[33]

**XV** Shah Ismail (1487–1524), the charismatic founder of the Safavid dynasty of Persia, victorious in battle against the Uzbeks in Transoxiana. This is a folio with paintings in ink and pigments from a 17th-century copy of the *Tarikh-e alam-ara-ye Shah Ismail* (The World-Adorning History of Shah Ismail).

**XVI** Soaring minarets flank the monumental entrance-way to the Royal Mosque on the south side of the Maydan in Isfahan. This was the first and only congregational mosque to be built in any of the Safavid capital cities and thus marked a significant development in the institutional establishment of Shiism as the dominant religion of Safavid Persia.

**XVII** In its earthenware material, blue and white glazes and dragon motif, this plate exemplifies the popularity, since the Mongol period, of Chinese porcelain among Persian ceramicists and their Dutch patrons. Dutch merchants presented some of these Chinese-inspired Safavid wares in European markets by mixing them with Chinese true porcelain.

**XVIII** (Opposite) 'The Court of Gayumars', from the famous *Shahnama* for Shah Tahmasb, depicts the legendary first king of Persia on a mountaintop holding court over his kingdom. Trees are in perpetual bloom, rocks burst in fiery colour, their edges hiding animal and human faces, humans are introduced to civilizing arts, and wild animals are tamed. Its richness of minute detail, intensity of colours and dynamic composition led this painting and its artist Sultan Muhammad to be singled out in a contemporary art-historical text as the most wondrous of the age.

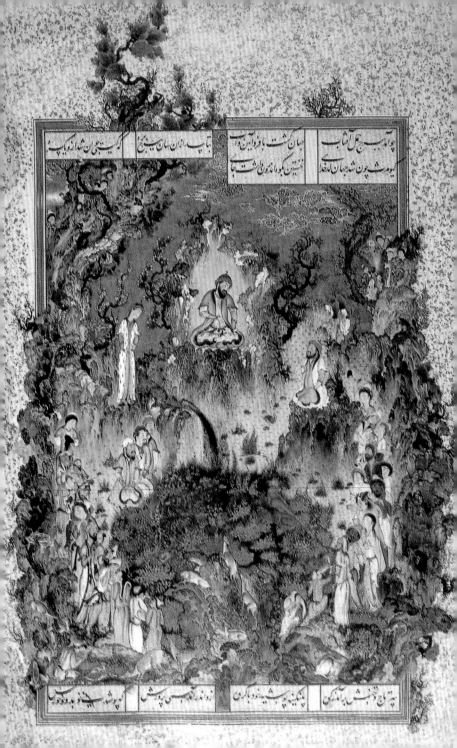

**IXX** The tomb of Akbar's father, Humayun, in Delhi is set in a garden modelled on those introduced by Babur. The tomb was probably intended as a dynastic mausoleum, although it was never used as such.

**XX** This illustration from a *Baburnama* (History of Babur) shows the first Mughal emperor directing the construction of a walled terraced garden, through which intersecting channels of water flow. Babur believed that creating regular symmetrical gardens brought order to India, which he considered unruly and chaotic.

**XXI** Elite females were responsible for embellishing Mughal cities with mosques, serais, wells, gardens and more. Nur Jahan, an active patron of architecture, built this exquisite marble tomb, set in an ordered, regular garden, for her parents. Today it is named after her father, Itimad al-Daula, the Mughal finance minister.

**XXII** This may be a portrait of the formidable queen, Nur Jahan, entertaining her husband Jahangir and prince Khurram, the future Shah Jahan. This queen was a powerful figure and European traders in particular feared her influence, for she had control over major trade routes and taxes on traders.

**XXIII** Aurangzeb spearing an enraged elephant while his father, Shah Jahan, and his brothers watch. The sixth Mughal emperor, known for his military skills and bravery, won many battles but left the empire weakened by continuous warfare and uprisings.

**XXIV** This dynastic portrait depicts Timur (centre) flanked by his descendants down to Aurangzeb; it reminds us that the Mughals are an extension of the Central Asian Timurid dynasty. Mughal rule lasted until 1858, but even after their demise the memory of their extraordinary wealth and cultural contributions stayed alive in the subcontinent.

**XXV** A print representing Japanese curiosity about the 'Black Ships': American warships so named for the billowing black smoke from their steam engines.

**XXVI** Samurai from the Satsuma domain, one of the domains that led the Meiji Restoration overthrow of the Tokugawa Shogunate. The mixture of Western and Japanese military uniforms and weapons can be clearly seen.

**XXVII** Female students bid farewell to *kamikaze* pilots with flags and cherry blossoms. The blossoms, symbols of the ephemeral nature of life, were associated with the sacrifice of the young pilots on suicide missions.

Indians must be singled out as one of the most important cultural partners in this cosmopolitan venture.[34] The 17th century witnessed a renewed flowering of Indo- Persian relationships, despite territorial competition over such strategically and commercially important cross-roads as Qandahar, in present-day Afghanistan. There were deep cultural ties through the migration of artists, poets, physicians and other skilled and creative people who sought patronage at the substantially richer Mughal court, and through trade, which was Asia-wide in scope but had India as a major anchor and attraction for Persian interests. The shift eastward came after the permanent resolution of the Safavid-Ottoman conflicts. The Ottomans retook the Mesopotamian territories, especially Baghdad and the holy cities, in 1638. However, the Safavids did not relinquish those cities without leaving their brand of Imami Shiism in place for centuries to come.

The Sunni Mughal Empire represented the arch-enemy (aside from the Uzbeks in Central Asia, another source of constant conflict) but it was also the source of lucrative trade and of new fashions and styles of painting and textile designs. Until well into the 19th century, Mughal India and Safavid and post-Safavid Iran remained intertwined in inspiring and informing the production of high culture as well as in the exchange of knowledge in all kinds of technological and military ventures. Europeans – envoys, merchants, missionaries, travellers, artists and artisans – were another important group in Isfahan's social composition.

In such charged cosmopolitanism, Safavid rituals of kingship took on a particularly convivial form. Feasting in the company of the shahs became a hallmark of the royal ceremonies in Isfahan. Palaces, most famously the Chehel Sotun (Forty Pillar Palace, c. 1647–50s), were constructed to accommodate such rituals.[36] With a vast and high-ceilinged pillared porch (*talar*) on the main façade, these palaces were unique to Safavid Isfahan, where they served as the principal sites for ceremonial feasts and other royal rituals of conviviality. The choreography of the feast and the personal involvement of the shah declared the legitimacy of Safavid rule. The feasts called upon the memory, preserved in the *Shahnama*, of ancient Persian kingship, when feasting had been a celebration after victory. The Safavid rulers saw themselves placed in a continuum of history that reached back to the Achaemenids and their royal processionals and feasting events at the ancient capital Persepolis. It was a measure of the strength of this belief that the Safavids provided the lavish architectural and garden spaces and urban sites for such performances.

These rituals of conviviality, with their studied manipulation of distance and proximity, served as a political instrument for the shah's role as the deputy on earth of the Awaited Messiah. This was a distinctly Imami Shia and Persian ceremonial and so a uniquely Safavid posture of kingship. Mughal emperors and Ottoman sultans remained almost completely aloof from such large-scale displays of royal hospitality. Music, conversation, food and drinks animated the Safavid royal rituals; in no other early modern example of absolutist empire do we find rulers hosting such events in person. The French king ate while courtiers watched; the Habsburgs and Ottomans (like their Byzantine predecessors) assumed a posture of transcendence that could not allow for the display of such lowly human acts as eating. In sharp contrast, the *talar* palaces of Isfahan were designed specifically for the exact hierarchies and etiquette of such gatherings, for which there were no contemporary equivalents.

## The Later Safavids

The implementation of a centralized and absolutist structure of power, initiated largely by Shah Abbas I 'The Great', was carried out mostly by his successors. Shah Safi I (r.1629–42), Shah Abbas II (r.1642–66), Shah Sulayman (r.1666–94) and Shah Sultan Hussein (r.1694–1722) ruled as absolute monarchs but without the personal control that Shah Abbas I had wielded. All were born and educated in the inner sanctum of the harem in Isfahan, tutored by the *ghulams* and the eunuchs, and prohibited while growing up from entering into direct contact with statesmen of the realm. Shah Safi I and Shah Sultan Hussein displayed great cruelty or total apathy in office. Shah Abbas II and Shah Sulayman were more personally engaged in affairs of state and were important patrons of art and architecture. The shah's role was never insignificant, but in this latter part of the Safavid age new networks of relationships became increasingly important: women of the harem; eunuch *ghulam* allies; other members of the slave elite who filled some of the ranks of the military, administration and governorships; the Persian-Tajik elements within the supreme secretariat; the remaining Turkmen governors and generals; and especially high-ranking *ulema* (religious scholars).[37]

The last phases of the Safavids have been viewed as steady decline, attributed by modern scholars to weaknesses in the imperial structure and the ineffectual role of the kings.[38] A more nuanced picture would delineate an imperial polity experiencing the pressures of emergent 'globalization' and European ascendancy as much as any in Asia. Even in such conditions, Safavid Persia was not in the least restricted in its display of cultural competitiveness. Shah Abbas II, like Shah Tahmasb, trained in the art of painting, reputedly with a couple of European artists employed at court; he was a vigorous patron of manuscripts and paintings and a discerning patron of architecture, and was involved in an area of development in Isfahan that centred on the beautifully designed and engineered Khwaju Bridge.[39] His successor, Shah Sulayman, oversaw the construction of the exquisite Hasht Behesht Palace and sponsored artists with styles ranging from a super-realist hybrid of European and Persian modes to revivals of earlier styles.[40] Even the much-maligned reign of Shah Sultan Hussein offers more than the doomsday scenario portrayed in contemporary and later accounts.

Transformations through the 17th century led to the unprecedented rise of the office of the *mujtahid*, the influential theologians who emerged late in the century as a unified front within the court. Gradually gaining socio-economic and political power, they posed a challenge to the position of the monarch towards the end of the reign of Shah Abbas II and during those of his successors. By the second half of the 17th century, the expanded powers of the harem and the court officials had created an atmosphere of factional rivalries that undermined the coherence of budgetary policies. The situation was aggravated by the insatiable demands of the harem and the court, which devoured much of a state budget already stretched by high military expenditure, inflation, declining trade balances, excessive taxation and corruption among officials. In these conditions the enhanced position of the theologians paved the way for an outright seizure of power during the rule of Shah Sulayman and Shah Sultan Hussein.

Shah Sultan Hussein promoted a pietistic version of Imami Shiism that produced masterpieces like the Madrasa of Chahar Bagh, a monumental example of Safavid architecture in its final years.[41] On the other hand, it exposed him to the influence of his tutor Muhammad Baqer Majlesi, a learned and powerful theologian whose impact on the political restructuring of the *ulema* was far-reaching. This was when the policy of 'religious cleansing' took a harsh turn: Sufis were expelled from Isfahan, while pressure was put on Zoroastrians, Jews and Christians to convert. The immediate impact undermined the economic role of non-Muslims, particularly Armenians.

The policy created discontent among the persecuted, especially the Sunnis. Those on the eastern frontiers, in present-day Afghanistan, began to consider secession.[42] The movement gained momentum when the rebellious Ghazali tribe was brutally suppressed by the Georgian armies of the Safavids in 1704. The leader of the tribe, Mir Vais, was dispatched to Isfahan as a prisoner but stayed there as a guest of the shah. In 1709, after his return to Qandahar, he staged a revolt and took the city from the Safavid governor. A succession of misfortunes, made worse by the military weaknesses of the Safavid armies, rendered ineffectual efforts against Mir Vais. In the face of grave revolts in the north east, aggravated by Russian attacks on the south-west coast of the Caspian Sea, Kurdish skirmishes in the west, and problems with the ruler of Oman in the Persian Gulf, Shah Sultan Hussein moved his court to Qazvin in 1717–18 in the hope of raising a more effective army.

The Safavid court returned to Isfahan in 1721, having been humiliated in its attempts to quell unrest and recover its lost cities. With the central government and the military force in disarray, Shah Sultan Hussein retreated to the royal pleasance at Farahabad and embarked on building a new suburb south east of Isfahan and beautifying it with pleasure pavilions. On 8 March 1722, the Afghan forces, steadily marching from Qandahar through Kerman, finally arrived at the outskirts of Isfahan, where, despite numerical superiority, the Safavid troops suffered a crushing defeat. Three days later Mahmud, the Afghan leader, captured Farahabad and made it his headquarters while his troops plundered the helplessly abandoned Armenian quarter of New Julfa.

Isfahan was under siege for nearly seven months, during which the trapped citizens faced severe famine and shortages of fuel and other necessities. Finally, on 21 October 1722, the Safavid shah capitulated to Mahmud. He and his family were imprisoned, and four years later were massacred. Isfahan was plundered and many citizens slaughtered. The collapse of the central government did not, however, end the Safavid dynasty. In the ensuing anarchy five Safavid princes became nominal rulers in different parts of Persia. None managed to regain overall control. Instead, the old tribal system again rose to the occasion. Nader Quli Beg, a talented and ambitious general from the Afshar tribe who had supported the last Safavid puppet king, dethroned him and declared himself Nader Shah (r.1736–47).[43] He founded the short-lived Afsharid dynasty, abandoned Isfahan for his new capital of Mashhad, and attempted to conquer India.

The 18th century witnessed a revival of tribalism, internecine feuds and the fragmentation of Persia. The establishment of the Qajar dynasty (1779–1924) by Agha Muhammad Khan, the leader of one of the Qizilbash Turkmen tribes who had originally helped the Safavids to power, reconstituted a centralized monarchy, consolidated most of the territorial gains of the Safavids, and marshalled Iran's strategically important position in the modern era.

**The Significance of the Safavids**

Unlike all other dynasties that ruled Islamic Persia, the Safavids emerged from within a reigning royal lineage and embodied a regal status already infused with spiritual authority. Shah Ismail I's descent from both the Aqquyunlu dynasty and the Safaviyye order engendered unprecedented loyalties and imperial ambitions. To maintain its politico-religious authority and the territorial integrity of the empire, the Safavids, especially during the reigns of Shah Tahmasb and Shah Abbas I 'The Great', introduced new formations in military, administrative and court hierarchies. Their success depended, in large part, on how they strategized political action in response to the strengths and weaknesses of their allies and rivals: the Qizilbash tribal forces and European trade partners, and the Ottomans, Uzbeks and Mughals. Under Safavid rule, Persia underwent a profound transformation from a feudal to an early modern world economy. It was stimulated by new commodities of exchange and social elites, like the Armenian community and the *ghulams* in Isfahan, who became influential in international trade and in the patronage of art and architecture from within an expansionist, centralized and absolutist imperial framework. The cosmopolitanism of Isfahan, the Safavid capital from 1598 until 1722, attracted multitudes. Its fame and efficiency as a mega-city was anchored on the conceptual and functional grandeur of its urban design, on the concentration of political, economic and cultural resources found there, and on its accommodation of myriad interest groups including ethnic and religious communities, as well as transient foreigners, and European diplomatic, missionary and commercial agents. The potent realignment of Persian ideologies and icons of kingship with Imami Shia doctrines and practices of Islam revived the ancient idea of Iran and recast it in a distinctive cultural image. The Safavid Empire is pivotal in the history of Islamic Persia, its legacy contributing to the formation of the modern nation-state of Iran and to the politics of the region today.

## CHAPTER SIX

# India: The Mughals 1526–1858

## CATHERINE ASHER

The Mughals were a Sunni Muslim dynasty who ruled over a predominantly Hindu South Asia from the 16th to the mid-19th century. The first Mughal, Babur, was descended from the mighty Central Asian warlord Timur, who by his death in 1405 had conquered a large band of territory extending from Central Asia to the Persian Gulf. Babur and his descendants thought of themselves as Timurids, but they were known as Mughals (a corruption of the dynastic name Mongol) since they were also related to the great Mongol conqueror Chinggis Khan. By the late 15th century, Timur's successors ruled a much-reduced empire from their capitals at Samarqand and Herat, but their courtly culture, with its splendid architecture, calligraphy and illustrated manuscripts, was considered the most magnificent in the entire Islamic world. The Mughals wished their own achievements to equal those of the Timurids. After a slow start, by the late 16th century the Mughals had built an empire of extraordinary wealth and power. Their achievements equalled, or perhaps even surpassed, those of their Muslim contemporaries in Safavid Persia and Ottoman Turkey, transforming culture in the modern states of India, Pakistan and Bangladesh even to this day.

## The Beginning of Mughal Rule

Babur (d.1530) was a Central Asian prince who spent much of his life in search of a principality that he could claim as his own. After a series of false starts, Babur successfully invaded northern India and defeated the last independent Sultan of Delhi in 1526. Babur was extremely proud of this victory, noting that the Delhi Sultan had a much larger army than his; however, Babur had the benefit of superior horses and artillery.

Babur lived for only four years after his conquest of north India. During this time he introduced to India the Timurid tradition of building walled gardens with running water courses, for Babur believed that his ability to shape India's unruly terrain was a symbol of his ability to govern. In his own personal memoir, known as the *Baburnama*, he mentions gardens often, which indicates their importance to him. Illustrations created in the late 16th century and intended for inclusion in editions of Babur's memoirs often show the new emperor directing the construction and planting of his gardens, a demonstration of the significance that

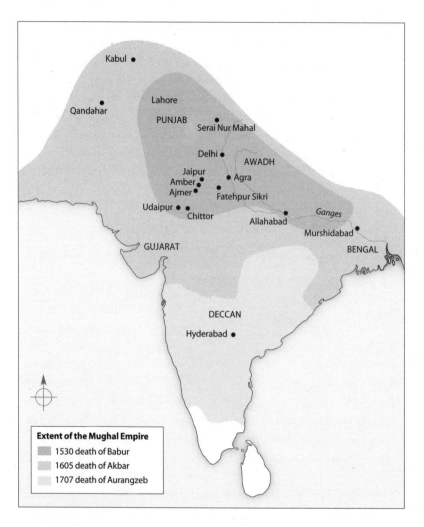

Map showing the extent of the Mughal Empire from its inception in 1526 until the beginning of the 18th century. After this time Mughal authority began to diminish and its territory shrank. Just prior to the end of the empire in 1858, its authority was confined to the Delhi region.

gardens retained for his successors. Once Babur had introduced this particular type of garden to India, it became an essential ingredient of Mughal architecture. Perhaps the most famous example is the mid-17th century Taj Mahal, the tomb of Shah Jahan's favourite wife, which is set in not one but two gardens with running water and pools.

Babur died in 1530 and was succeeded by his son, Humayun, who lacked Babur's charisma and military skill. He ruled for ten years, then was forced out of India by a low-born but brilliant warrior and administrator, Sher Shah Sur. Two significant developments occurred during the fifteen-year Sur interregnum. The first was that Sher Shah introduced a number of economic and administrative innovations, which the next Mughal ruler, Akbar, would refine and perfect. These included standardized coinage and systematic methods of measuring land for taxation purposes.

The second development took place in Safavid Persia, where Humayun was sheltered by Shah Tahmasb, the Safavid ruler. Tahmasb had been a keen patron of painting, especially illustrated manuscripts, but as he aged and became increasingly orthodox in religious matters he began to dismiss his court artists. Humayun took advantage of this by inviting some of the most outstanding artists to work for him. So, when the way was clear for Humayun to return to India and reinstate Mughal authority in 1555, he brought with him painters who had reinterpreted Timurid painting in Shah Tahmasb's Safavid court. The presence of these artists would help transform artistic production in the Mughal court.

### Akbar (r.1556–1605): Conquest and Consolidation

Humayun's return to India was short-lived. Just one year later, in 1556, he tumbled down a steep flight of stairs in his library in Delhi and died. Akbar, his twelve-year-old son, succeeded him on the throne. Akbar inherited a highly unstable state, and owing to his youth a high-ranking Central Asian noble in Humayun's court acted as regent. By 1560, however, Akbar had sent his unpopular regent on pilgrimage to Mecca and begun to assume the reins of power himself. The tasks before him were formidable, but thanks to Akbar's remarkable abilities as a statesman and military strategist, during his almost fifty-year reign he was able to consolidate Mughal authority over the whole of northern India and develop a highly sophisticated concept of state.

One of Akbar's first tasks was to expand and consolidate his territorial holdings. He was able to take control of major fortified cities to the east, west and south of Delhi, thereby gaining domination over the north Indian heartland. Next, he systematically extended his territories in all directions. Thus Mughal rule stretched from Gujarat on the west coast to Bengal on the east, although Bengal remained troublesome into the reign of Akbar's son and successor, Jahangir (r. 1605–27). By his death in 1605, Akbar's empire extended from Kabul in Afghanistan to the Deccan in south India.

It was Akbar's policy not to suppress or punish former independent princes but rather to incorporate them into the Mughal administrative system, while at the same time allowing them to remain as active heads of their own ancestral lands. An excellent example is the case of the Rajput Hindu Kachhwahas, whose ancestral landholding was Amber, close to Jaipur in modern Rajasthan. The Kachhwahas were a minor Rajput house, but were the first of all the numerous princely states in western India to acknowledge Mughal authority. The tie was further cemented when Akbar married a Kachhwaha princess. The marriage gave this Rajput house an enhanced status in Mughal eyes, although some of their Rajput counterparts, especially the Sisodiyas of Chittor (later Udaipur) frowned upon the union. Because of the Kachhwaha's new status Raja Man Singh, who was head of the Kachhwaha Rajput house, was Akbar's highest-ranking noble. He served as a military commander and governor of several provinces. Kachhwaha princes went on to serve the Mughals in exalted positions into the 18th century.

Akbar built an elite body of nobles who were prepared to serve him faithfully, but his method differed considerably from that of the contemporary Ottoman and Safavid empires. They relied heavily on non-Muslims who had been captured on military campaigns, or else acquired through a levy system, and then converted to Islam. These converts, trained in the customs of the Ottoman or Safavid court, owed their allegiance solely to the ruler. Mughal India had a dominant non-Muslim population so such a tactic would have backfired, especially since conversion to Islam was not on the Mughal agenda. All the same, Akbar's initial concern was to diminish the influence of the Central Asian nobility who had dominated under Babur and Humayun. He wished to have a multi-ethnic nobility and thus he incorporated Persians and Indians (both Muslims and Hindus) into his administration, among others. Nobles were assigned a numerical rank and their pay was based on this rank. In addition, the highest-ranking military commanders were assigned a number of troops to serve under them. These troops and their commanders made up the Mughal military. Men with the closest relationship with the emperor reported to him directly. Those who served in the provinces were required to attend the court once a year; for those serving in the capital, it was once a day. Those of lower rank reported directly to the noble under whom they served, thus creating a system in which the king stood at the apex of a pyramid and authority filtered down from him.

One of the reasons that Akbar's army was such a highly successful military machine was that the troops were always paid, for the Mughal state was extraordinarily wealthy. India was rich in resources such as land and gold. The highest-ranking nobles were not paid directly in cash, however, but were assigned land-holdings from which they received an income. The revenue from the most fertile lands, which were divided between the Mughal treasury and the highest-ranking nobles, was usually predictable, owing to carefully calculated land measurements and the averaging-out of crop yields over a decade (a system first introduced by Sher Shah). The lands assigned to each noble were generally changed on a regular basis, so that the nobility could not build up a power base away from the capital and thus threaten the emperor.

## Akbar's Concept of State

Islam had been a political power in north central India from the late 12th century. In many areas Islam became politically dominant and conversion was widespread, but this did not occur in the Indian subcontinent. Akbar realized that to maintain the support of his multi-ethnic nobility, and particularly his multi-cultural population, he needed to recognize and acknowledge religious and ethnic diversity. Thus he developed a policy known as *suhl-i kul*, which means literally 'peace to all'. It was, in essence, a statement of what in the 21st century we might call universal toleration. This policy meant that subjects were free to practise their own religion. Further, they were taxed according to the land they held or farmed, and not according to their faith (according to Islamic belief, non-Muslims were ordinarily required to pay an additional tax).

To help promote his policy of *sulh-i kul* Akbar ordered the translation into Persian of Hindu epics that were originally written in Sanskrit, the language of Hindu religious texts. Persian was increasingly becoming the lingua franca of the Mughal court. This translation project had two motives. The first of these was Akbar's genuine belief that translating these texts would encourage harmony among India's populations. The irony is that he appointed an orthodox Muslim, by the name of al-Badauni, to translate the two most famous Hindu epics, the *Mahabharata* and the *Ramayana*. Al-Badauni was not best pleased with the honour: he wrote a secret history of Akbar's reign in which he expressed his discomfort and distaste at having to work on texts that dealt with polytheism and with deities who assumed human and animal forms – concepts antithetical to Islam.[2] Akbar also had these manuscripts illustrated, which he believed increased their educational value. His personal copy of the *Ramayana*, which bears a completion date of 1588, included 176 superb illustrations. Illustrated pages from other texts are housed in various museums around the world today. Akbar's mother and at least one Muslim noble also commissioned illustrated *Ramayanas*, suggesting that the court took an active role in promoting Akbar's official policies.

The second reason for Akbar's promotion of the Persian language was his wish to have a single court language that transcended ethnic and religious divisions. His grandfather, Babur, had spoken and written in a form of Turkish, but his own father Humayun preferred Persian. A range of Indic vernaculars were emerging, but they lacked the status of Persian, whose grammar and vocabulary were well established. In addition, Persian was not primarily a language of religious texts, and so was preferable both to Arabic, the language of the Quran, and to Sanskrit. With Persian as the court language, many non-Muslim students were inclined to enter the schools that Akbar was in the process of secularizing, and learn Persian. Thus non-Muslims could enter the service of the Mughal court as scribes, or in any number of low- to middle-level roles.[3]

Akbar's desire for a multi-religious, multi-cultural, tolerant state probably derived in part from his own genuine interest in religion. About 1562 Akbar became devoted to a Sufi (mystic) Muslim saint, Sheikh Muin al-Din, of the Chishti order. For seventeen years Akbar visited the saint's tomb in Ajmer annually. He was also attracted to a living Sufi, Sheikh Salim Chishti, who correctly predicted the birth and survival of sons and heirs, at a time when the king was worried that no child of his would survive infancy. In honour of Sheikh Salim Chishti, Akbar built a palace known as Fatehpur Sikri around the saint's simple abode. There he invited men from a number of religious persuasions, including Muslims, Hindus, Jains, Parsis (Zoroastrians) and Portuguese priests residing in western India (Goa), to engage in religious discussions. These discussions often turned into heated debates, but they ultimately encouraged Akbar to introduce the veneration of light and fire, borrowed from these various religious traditions, into his court ceremonial. Akbar never renounced Islam, as is often thought, but he was certainly the least orthodox of all the Mughal rulers. Many people believe that Akbar created a new religion, known as the Din-i Ilahi, but it was nothing of the sort. It was an attempt to ensure the absolute loyalty of Akbar's closest nobles by casting himself as a living saint.

In 1575 Abu al-Fazl, a son of a liberal-thinking Muslim intellectual family, joined the court circle and transformed the perception of Akbar from an excellent emperor to a semi-divine ruler who was endowed with god's light. This young man was a theologian trained in the illumination philosophy of a 12th-century Sufi, which professed that a state benevolently ruled over by a king possessing god's light would be an enlightened one. Abu al-Fazl wrote Akbar's official history, the *Akbarnama*, in which he interwove the factual events of history with a depiction of Akbar as a semi-divine being. In the opening text Akbar's lineage is traced back to a princess who was miraculously impregnated by a ray of divine light. For centuries this light had been hidden in his predecessors, but it became manifest in Akbar. Abu al-Fazl presents Akbar as above ordinary mortals. His illuminated status gives him access to divine revelation, allows him to have close personal relationships with his subjects as if he were their father (an ancient Indian concept of kingship) and encourages harmony among various social, ethnic and religious groups. In essence, Akbar's policy of *sulh-i kul* was evidence that he was fully enlightened and semi-divine.

## Akbar's Patronage of the Arts

Akbar maintained the Timurid interest in the arts. Babur had been obsessed with the construction of gardens and his son, Humayun, had built some architectural follies, although only a mosque he constructed in Agra survives. Akbar, in part owing to the length of his reign and the empire's stability at the time, gave full attention to artistic production. His interests included the creation of carpets, shawls, numerous textile types, manuscripts, architecture and more. Much scholarly study has focused on the illustrated manuscripts and architecture of Akbar's time.

Akbar inherited the Persian artists that Humayun had brought with him from India and added a number of Indian artists to the Mughal atelier. Akbar's artists were kept active throughout his lengthy rule and the range of works they produced was prodigious. Two particularly notable manuscripts were executed early in his reign, each very different in style and subject matter. One was an illustrated *Tutinama*, Book of the Parrot, which, rather like the famous *1001 Nights*, is a series of stories inside stories. Its illustrations suggest that the artists who worked on them trained in the bright, bold colours and angular lines of Indic painting. They are small in scale with illustrations averaging about 12 cm (4¾ in) in height. The text of this small-format book concerns a wise parrot telling a series of tales to a young wife whose husband is away on a sea journey. The purpose is to prevent her from going out at night to meet a potential lover, whom she has seen from her window. The book's overall theme concerns the control of women, and it was probably intended as a warning to the women of Akbar's harem. It was begun in the 1560s, a period in which Akbar's former wet nurses, mature women who meddled in court affairs, were creating havoc for the young king. This was also a period when Akbar was marrying young women from important Hindu and Muslim families as a way of achieving favourable political alliances and ensuring the longevity of the Mughal house.

A much larger manuscript project, the *Dastan-i Amir Hamza* (The Adventures of Amir Hamza), was undertaken over a fifteen-year period during the 1560s and 70s. The project was led by two painters who had originally come from Persia with Humayun, and the text is said to have had 1,400 large-scale illustrations, some of which are 93 cm (about 36 in) in height. This multi-volume manuscript was looted in 1739 when the Persian ruler Nader Shah sacked Delhi, and the majority of the illustrations were lost. Painted not on the usual handmade paper but on cloth, the illustrations were held up for the young Akbar to see as the text was read to him from the back, for although Akbar was highly intelligent he was unable to read. (He probably suffered from what today we would diagnose as dyslexia.) Full of action and adventure, the *Dastan-i Amir Hamza* concerns the fictitious encounters of Hamza, an uncle of the prophet Muhammad, with villains, giants, demons, dragons and sorcerers. These stories must have appealed to the young king, who was engaged in his own military campaigns to consolidate the nascent empire.

In addition to the illustrated translations of classical Hindu epics discussed earlier, Akbar commissioned a wide range of other illustrated manuscripts, ranging from classical Persian literature to histories that focused on the Mughals' history and historical lineage. The illustrations in these manuscripts developed a mature, naturalistic Mughal style of painting that combined Indic, Persian and European elements. European art was first introduced by Jesuits visiting the Mughal court. They brought illustrations of Christian subject matter, which fascinated the Mughals. The priests were hoping to convert Akbar and his court, but the Mughals were particularly interested in depictions of Mary, who, like the princess progenitor of the Mughal house, was miraculously impregnated. Elements derived from European art were used in both painting and architecture during the reigns of the next two Mughal emperors to highlight their semi-divine status.

Of all the manuscripts focusing on Mughal history the most significant is Abu al-Fazl's history of Akbar, the *Akbarnama*. Most scholars believe that the 116 illustrations from this text that are now held in the Victoria & Albert Museum in London, and which were executed between 1586 and 1590, belong to the copy that the author presented to Akbar. Roughly half of the illustrations feature Akbar, who is always depicted as calm, cool and collected even in the face of calamity. One good example of this is a double-page composition that depicts Akbar at a battle to win the Rajput stronghold of Chittor. Gunpowder had accidentally been ignited, causing much pandemonium and even death. Akbar is easily recognizable. He wears a simple white robe associated more with saints and holy men than kings and he is proportionally larger than those around him. While everyone else panics, the great king is decisively taking control of the situation.

Relatively few of his subjects would ever have been able to see propagandistic paintings such as those in the *Akbarnama*, but architecture provided a considerably more accessible way to assert Akbar's Timurid origins and his extraordinary status. The tomb he completed in 1571 for his father, Humayun, in Delhi was designed by architects from Central Asia and adheres to the plans and elevations of Timurid tombs. However, the materials used (red sandstone and white marble trim) belong to the Indian tradition and would become the hallmark of Mughal imperial architecture.

In 1571 Akbar began construction of his palace of Fatehpur Sikri. It remained his official residence until 1585, when pressing political issues north of Lahore forced the court to shift. The monumental entrance to the palace at Fatehpur Sikri was built as a celebration of his conquest of Gujarat, but it also publicly proclaimed his profound devotion to Sheikh Salim Chishti. The saint's exquisite white marble tomb is just inside the entrance. This part of the Fatehpur Sikri complex, accessible to anyone, served to popularize Akbar with ordinary people. Not only Muslims but also Hindus visited the tombs of mystic saints. The irony is that the Sheikh's tomb was completed about the time that Akbar began to lose interest in saint veneration and instead started to cast himself as a living saint.

Other sections of the palace were intended for administration and public access was limited. One of the entrance gates, the royal entrance, is marked by two carved elephants. In India elephants had long been considered the imperial mount. Akbar attributed special importance to elephants, for he believed that they could only be controlled by wise and intelligent men. When he was eighteen, as illustrated in a double-page composition from the Victoria & Albert Museum's *Akbarnama*, he mounted a crazed elephant that, in Abu al-Fazl's words, 'turned the gall-bladder of the lion-hearted to water',[5] and survived unscathed. The elephant tore across an unstable pontoon bridge, causing pandemonium. As the painting indicated, the emperor's ability to ride such a beast and survive unharmed was a sign of God's contentment with him.

The Fatehpur Sikri palace also featured Akbar's public viewing window, known as a *jharoka-i darshan*. It specifically proclaims the emperor's illumined status, but equally highlights one of the institutions of

Mughal governance. Akbar presented himself each morning at this public window, located in an exterior wall, so any subject might see him. In this practice, the Islamic notion that kings must be accessible to their subjects is combined with the Hindu practice of *darshan*, that is, beholding in the sense of auspicious sight. Akbar's appearance in the window parallels the manner in which Hindu deities are revealed to devotees. In a Hindu temple devotees assemble to await the revelation of gods. With great anticipation they stand before the closed curtain. Once it is opened, the devotees have *darshan*, that is, they behold images of the deities. Akbar, positioned in his window, enacted the role of an enlightened father to his children and a spiritual master to his followers. Emperor, deity and saint were conflated into a single vision, thus visually blurring the role between the ruler and the divine.

## Jahangir (r.1605–27) and Shah Jahan (r.1628–58)

In 1600 Akbar's son, Prince Salim, the future Jahangir, rebelled and established a counter court in Allahabad, a city about 500 km (310 miles) from Agra, then Akbar's capital. This move did little to shake the stability of Mughal authority. Just before Akbar's death in 1605 emperor and son were reconciled and Salim succeeded to the throne. He took on the titles Nur al-Din Muhammad Jahangir Badshah Ghazi, which translates as 'Emperor Warrior Muhammad World-Seizer [who is] the Light of the Religion'. Not a particularly distinguished military general, Jahangir entrusted campaigns to his sons, in particular to Khurram, the future Shah Jahan. Khurram led the most important military exploits of Jahangir's reign. He forced the most recalcitrant of all the Rajput houses, the Sisodiyas of Chittor/Udaipur, to accept Mughal authority and he was able to extend Mughal authority south into the Deccan, although maintaining sustained authority over territories in the Deccan remained a challenge.

Two incidents under Jahangir would see serious repercussions in the reigns of subsequent rulers. One was Jahangir's execution of Arjun, the fifth guru of the Sikh religion. Sikhism had been established in the 15th century as a conflation of Islam and Hinduism and was generally centred on an area north of Delhi known as the Punjab. The execution of Arjun was not religiously motivated, for Jahangir largely followed Akbar's tolerant religious policies. Arjun had openly given his support to Salim's son in the matter of the succession and Jahangir perceived that as a threat to his authority. However, Arjun's death sparked off a situation in which the Mughals and Sikhs became increasingly hostile to one another, eventually leading to increased militarism on the part of the Sikhs.

The second incident was the emperor's imprisonment of a leading Muslim theologian, Sheikh Ahmad Sirhindi (1564–1624). He was an outspoken critic of the Mughal religious policy that ignored the sharia, the Islamic religious law that governs how Muslims should live every aspect of their life. Sirhindi's views were well known, for he wrote numerous letters that were distributed across the subcontinent. His influence continued after his death, ultimately causing the Mughals to adopt a much more conservative attitude towards Islam.

In 1611 Jahangir, who already had a number of wives, married a Persian widow in her thirties. She was extremely intelligent and reputed to be very beautiful, although normally in 17th-century India a woman of thirty would have been considered beyond marriageable age. Women in Mughal India held considerable importance, notwithstanding Akbar's difficulties with manipulative court women early in his reign. Akbar had consulted his own mother often about affairs of state and treated her with the greatest respect. Women of the court lived in a large guarded harem. There, they had access to the same activities and entertainments that men had in their own quarters, but the artists, storytellers, masseuses, educators and so on were all women. Contrary to common belief, women did not simply remain immured in the harem. They moved with the court when it travelled, including going on hunting expeditions.

Jahangir's Persian wife quickly became his favourite, and he bestowed on her the title Nur Jahan, 'Light of the World'. She was the daughter of the Mughal finance minister and her brother also held a position of great authority in the court. Jahangir mentions her several times in his memoirs, the *Jahangirnama*, indicating her intelligence, her care for the emperor, and her great skill in shooting. Jahangir wrote:

> …the scouts had cornered four lions. I set out with the ladies of the harem to hunt them. When the lions came into view, Nurjahan Begum said, 'If so commanded, I will shoot the lions.' I said, 'Let it be so.' She hit two of them with one shot each, and the other two with two shots, and in a twinkling of an eye the four lions were deprived of life with six shots. Until now such marksmanship had not been seen. … As a reward for such marksmanship I scattered a thousand ashrafis over her head and gave her a pair of pearls and a diamond worth a lac of rupees.[6]

The emperor consulted Nur Jahan over affairs of state and she held considerable power of her own, especially when Jahangir's health began to decline due to his excessive alcohol consumption. Coins were minted in her name, which was extraordinary, and drums were sounded to announce her presence in court. Khurram, Jahangir's militarily gifted son, was the emperor's favoured heir apparent, but by 1619 Nur Jahan realized that he would be no pawn in her hand and she began to press the claim of another son. She arranged for this son to be married to her daughter from her first marriage. As a result Khurram rebelled, but after several years he acknowledged his father's authority once more. After Jahangir died in 1627 a prolonged war of succession broke out among the princes. Khurram, supported by powerful factions at court, emerged victorious. He acceded to the throne in 1628, adopting the title his father had given him after a successful military campaign: Shah Jahan, 'King of the World'.

Shah Jahan was extremely proud of his Timurid roots and also adopted the title that had been used by Timur, 'Meteor of the Faith'. He seems to have taken this latter role seriously, as he provided more mosques than any of his predecessors, fasted during the month of Ramadan even when on the battlefield, and visited the shrine of Sheikh Muin al-Din Chishti in Ajmer on a regular basis. Shah Jahan also forbade the construction of some new Hindu temples and pulled down some older ones. However, his support of his son, Dara Shukoh, a mystic who wrote treatises claiming Islam and Hinduism had a good deal in common, suggests that Shah Jahan may have been less orthodox in reality than the public image he wished to present. The individual personalities of the previous Mughal rulers show through clearly in their public personas, but the same is not true of Shah Jahan. We have only the official image of an aloof, formal emperor.

Shah Jahan's thirty-year rule was marked by a sense of prosperity and wealth unequalled even during Akbar's reign. Military campaigns included further efforts to stabilize and increase Mughal authority in the Deccan, although the Deccan issue would remain a problem until the early 18th century. Shah Jahan was eager to expand Mughal territory into the Timurid homelands of western Afghanistan and Central Asia, but his efforts to do so were fruitless. There was some internal disruption, particularly from vassal chiefs who wished to assert their independence from the Mughals, but these problems were resolved with relative ease. Fewer high-ranking Hindu officers were included in the Mughal administrative system than had served under Akbar and Jahangir, while Persians leaving Safavid Persia found new favour. Alongside these developments, Shah Jahan made changes to Akbar's organization of the nobility. Owing to the increasing numbers of men serving in the system, the pay scale was adjusted to cover the inflationary new numerical ranks now issued and the nobility were required to support fewer troops.

In 1657 Shah Jahan became ill. Many believed that the emperor would die, and a war of succession began among his sons. In fact Shah Jahan recovered, but by then the emperor's third son, Aurangzeb, had claimed the Mughal throne. He imprisoned his father in his fort in Agra from 1658 until his death in 1666.

## The Arts under Jahangir and Shah Jahan

Patronage of the arts assumed an increasing importance under these two Mughal rulers, as they showcased the continually refined imperial image. Buildings became more sumptuous, while painting often focused on an imperial image that was iconographically charged with symbolic meaning.

Jahangir made considerable reference to architecture in his own memoirs, suggesting the particular significance it held for him. However, most of the buildings he had erected were later torn down by his successor, Shah Jahan, who replaced them with his own structures. Today, Jahangir is best remembered for his patronage of painting, which he also mentions in his memoirs. He gave his favourite artists titles such as 'Rarity of the Time' and 'Wonder of the Age', but he also prized himself as a connoisseur of art:

> I derive such enjoyment from painting and I have expertise in judging it that, even without the artist's name being mentioned, no work of the past or present masters can be shown to me that I do not instantly recognize who did it. Even if it is a scene of several figures and each face is by a different master, I can tell who did which face. If in a single painting different persons have done the eyes and eyebrows, I can determine who drew the face and who made the eyes and eyebrows.[7]

Under Akbar many illustrated manuscripts were produced, but Jahangir favoured albums composed of single-page illustrations alternating with splendid examples of calligraphy. Many illustrations for the *Akbarnama* focused on military victories or extraordinary feats accomplished by Akbar, but those for the *Jahangirnama* are quite different. Some depict Jahangir enthroned, or celebrating a Hindu festival with his ladies of the harem. Others are portraits of rare animals that had been presented to him, for example, a turkey and a zebra. Jahangir describes the animals depicted in the *Jahangirnama* in great detail, particularly the turkey, noting that he had its likeness drawn so that the 'astonishment one has at hearing of them would increase by seeing them'.[8]

In addition to portraits of humans, animals and birds, Jahangir's artists also produced a series of allegorical illustrations. Among these paintings is a double-page composition in which Sheikh Muin al-Din Chishti of Ajmer hands Jahangir, who holds a globe, the Timurid crown. By the 17th century, support for Muin al-Din and the Chishti line of Sufi saints, who were venerated by large sections of the Indian population, validated the Mughal dynasty. Shah Jahan and his daughter invested in this concept even more fully with their construction of elegant white marble buildings at India's most important Sufi shrine, in Ajmer.

Other illustrations done by Jahangir's master artists display Jahangir's ongoing rivalry with the Safavid ruler Shah Abbas I, whom he called 'my renowned brother'.[9] The two rulers corresponded by letter and sent each other considerable gifts, each attempting to outdo the other. Jahangir's position was an awkward one, for the Safavids had given the Mughals protection in one of their darkest hours when Humayun had been forced out of India. Both rulers claimed Qandahar, but the Mughals often lost the city to the Safavids. The desire on Jahangir's part to be seen as equal to, or perhaps more important than, his Safavid brother probably inspired two illustrations which are both now in the Freer Gallery of Art in Washington, DC. In one the two rulers, who never met in person, are seated together on a throne with Persian verses above and below suggesting they are both kings who dispense justice and peace in their realms.[10] The second picture, which according to an inscription was executed in response to one of Jahangir's dreams, depicts the two rulers as less than equal.[11] The two kings stand on a globe and embrace one another, but Jahangir, on a powerful lion, towers over Shah Abbas, who stands on a meek lamb. The lion covers India and Persia on the map, while Shah Abbas's sheep is being edged into the Mediterranean. Behind the heads of both rulers is an enormous halo supported by two European-style cherubs.

Under Akbar the royal personage had been rendered as disproportionally larger than other figures. First under Jahangir, and then under Shah Jahan, the imperial image often has a halo and is usually shown in profile (since that view is less prone to distortion). Small cherubs often crown the king or support his halo.[12] Paintings of Shah Jahan often include holy men beneath the ruler's throne, indicating his concern with religious matters, or a lion and lamb in peaceful coexistence, indicating his execution of justice. The common device by which the kings are shown standing on a globe of the world is a visual play on their two names (Jahangir means 'World-Seizer', and Shah Jahan 'King of the World').

Shah Jahan was an active patron of painting; his commissions included a sumptuous illustrated chronicle of his years as prince and the first ten years of his reign. However, he is best known for his prolific patronage of architecture. His varied constructions ranged from a tomb for his father to hunting lodges, palaces, gardens and mosques. Today his most famous work is the Taj Mahal,[13] which he built as a mausoleum for his favourite wife Mumtaz Mahal, niece of Nur Jahan, who died in 1631 giving birth to her fourteenth child. It was probably intended to be Shah Jahan's own tomb as well. The Taj Mahal's official name, the Illumined Tomb, is the same as that of the tomb of the prophet Muhammad in Medina. Shah Jahan thus cast himself as a Perfect Man, an Islamic theological concept, likening him to the prophet Muhammad, who, in Muslim eyes, is the model human.

Today this enormous tomb, set in two gardens with water courses and a reflecting pool, is on the itinerary of virtually every tourist who visits India, yet at the time of its construction (1632–48) it was a private monument which would have made little impact on wider Indian society. Ordinary Muslim people in India would probably have had a much greater appreciation of Shah Jahan's white marble mosque and the towering gateways he added to the important shrine of Muin al-Din Chishti at Ajmer, and of the enormous congregational mosque he provided in Delhi in the 1650s.

However, while these mosques are, of course, religious structures, it would be incorrect to view them as having no political or dynastic implications. The mosque at Ajmer was built to celebrate Shah Jahan's victory, before his accession to the throne, over the Sisodiya Rajputs of Chittor/ Udaipur. His great congregational mosque in Delhi was surely intended as a visual response to the splendid mosques that his Safavid 'brother' Shah Abbas I had built in Isfahan, and also to the imperial Ottoman mosques that graced Istanbul and Edirne. The fact that Shah Jahan's mosque was intended to glorify his own name and the Mughal line is clearly indicated by the inscriptional panels that run across its façade. The letters of those epigraphs are written in such a manner that they appear to be verses from the Quran in Arabic; however, they are actually encomiums praising Shah Jahan, written in Persian.

The Delhi mosque, built on the city's highest hill, was a focal point of Shah Jahan's new city, Shahjahanabad, meaning 'the Abode of Shah Jahan', which he built between 1639 and 1648. The walled city consisted of broad avenues with canals, numerous gardens, an enormous serai for travellers and a palace fit for the King of the World. The palace stood beside a large river and its white marble chambers were intended for the sole use of Shah Jahan and his immediate family. The nobility would gather in the Public Audience Hall to attend the king. Those of the highest rank would stand closest to Shah Jahan's elevated throne, which was known as a *jharoka*. This throne was replete with symbolic imagery which must have been understood by those in attendance. Its bulbous baluster columns, supporting a curved roof, derive from European illustrations of holy people and royalty and symbolically show the enthroned Shah Jahan as a semi-divine world ruler.

Shah Jahan provided the palace and main mosque, but many of the women of his court were responsible for embellishing the city with gardens, inns and smaller mosques. This was not a new tradition. Previous Mughal queens and princesses had taken responsibility for the development of other Mughal cities, for example, Lahore, Agra and Delhi under

Humayun and Akbar. During the reign of Jahangir, Nur Jahan had embellished Agra with gardens and built serais along major highways where merchants could retire and taxes be collected. Her serai in Agra no longer survives, but another magnificent one, known as Serai Nur Mahal, on the Delhi-Lahore road remains intact. Contemporary European travellers claimed she commissioned this in order to be remembered by posterity.

Nur Jahan's most important project, however, was the tomb she completed in Agra for her parents, which is known as the tomb of Itimad al-Daula. The tomb is constructed from white marble and is heavily inlaid with semi-precious stones. The exquisite inlaid designs, depicting cypress trees, fruit, wine vessels and abstracted flowers, were intended as visual metaphors for paradise, and the tomb building is set in a fine garden.

## Aurangzeb (r.1658–1707) and the Later Mughals (1707–1858)

History has tended to treat the lengthy rule of the sixth Mughal, Aurangzeb, with hostility. He is often deemed to be a religious orthodox fanatic responsible for the downward spiral of the formerly liberal and powerful Mughal Empire. It is true that Aurangzeb was personally much more traditionally devout than any of his predecessors and his personal desire to follow the sharia was clear. For example, he banned the wearing of gold cloth at court, but he realized that unless he presented himself as a supreme leader with a rich and powerful court he would lose face and perhaps even followers. Nevertheless, he ceased presenting himself at the public viewing window since he considered the practice to derive from non-Islamic traditions. He also dropped the previous Mughal practice of employing court artists and court musicians. It is possible, however, that Aurangzeb's public demonstrations of commitment to the sharia were intended to compensate for an act that was not at all compliant with sharia, his imprisonment of his father. He reinstated the tax on non-Muslims that had been abolished by Akbar, making him unpopular with those who now bore an increased economic burden – that is, the greater proportion of his subjects.

However, Aurangzeb's religious policies were less strident than are generally imagined. He did engage in some destruction of Hindu temples, but this was for reasons of political retaliation against disloyal nobles. During the first decades of his reign, Aurangzeb's main cultural commitment was the construction of mosques. He built one in Lahore that far surpassed Shah Jahan's Delhi mosque in size.

The Mughals had been attempting to subdue the Deccan in the south of India since the time of Akbar. Success was usually fleeting, but for Aurangzeb containing the south became an obsession. Throughout his reign problems in the Deccan plagued the Mughal army. His initial problems were with the rebel Maratha, who excelled in guerrilla war tactics that gave them tactical mobility against the ponderous and slow-moving Mughal forces. This ended in victory for the western-Indian based Shivaji. Shivaji died in 1680, but his son Shambuji and his successors continued to cause havoc for the Mughal army. In 1681 Aurangzeb shifted his residence to the Deccan, thus leaving north India without much imperial attention, though the move did give him apparent control over the south.

At the time of Aurangzeb's death in 1707, the Mughal Empire covered nearly the entire subcontinent. The extent of the empire was, therefore, apparently much the same as it had been at the end of Akbar's reign. In fact, the underlying situation was quite different. Akbar bequeathed to his successors the foundations of a strong, stable empire, but by the time Aurangzeb died, the empire's fabric was weakened by continuous warfare in the Deccan as well as uprisings in north and western India. As a result, the empire was in dire financial straits. The system created by Akbar was plunged into crisis by the pressure of warfare, the inflated ranks of the nobility and the fact that there was no longer enough productive land to go around. As a result, factionalism among the nobility grew and the concept that a noble was a loyal member of the large imperial family disappeared. Now it was every nobleman for himself.

After Aurangzeb's death in 1707, the Mughal Empire endured, at least officially, for another 150 years. The British imprisoned and exiled the last

Mughal ruler in 1858 after the emperor had become the unwilling leader of an uprising by Indian soldiers, known variously as the Indian Mutiny or the First War of Independence.

Shah Alam Bahadur Shah succeeded Aurangzeb in 1707. However, constant political turmoil prevented him from entering the long-standing Mughal capital, Delhi, after his coronation. That city again became the imperial residence in 1712, but the empire continued to suffer seriously from financial problems, political intrigue, inadequately prepared rulers, and invasions. Delhi itself was sacked by the Persian ruler Nader Shah in 1739 and again in the 1750s by the Afghan Abd al-Durrani, who entered India four times. In fact, as Delhi became increasingly vulnerable, it also became virtually all that was left of the Mughal Empire. The Shia nawabs of Murshidabad, Awadh and Hyderabad established their own successor states, while Jat, Maratha, Sikh and Hindu rulers asserted their independence, carving out numerous kingdoms from what had been a single empire. During the 18th century, the British East India Company, which had come to South Asia for trading rights, successively extended its sway as a territorial ruler over much of the subcontinent.

Although the Mughal Empire was in financial straits in the 18th century, this does not mean that all individuals were similarly affected. Rather, we find a situation in which the nobility might be more impoverished than the emerging merchant class. Trade and manufacture continued to expand. Raw goods moved across not only the Mughal Empire but also across its former territories to make the products desired in India and abroad. Cotton grown in the Deccan was shipped to the Coromandal coast in the south east, or Gujarat in the west, to be woven, dyed and/or printed. Raw silk from Bengal was transported to western India, where workers produced highly sought-after woven textiles. Some of these products were consumed internally while others were exported to South-East Asia and Europe. Trading companies from various European countries were trying to get a foot in the door, and Indian merchants were at times cut out of lucrative business situations.

The changing distribution of wealth meant a change in patronage systems for the arts. In Mughal India many artists, artisans and literary figures left Delhi for more lucrative employment in successor states such as Awadh to the east or the Rajput states to the west, which were beginning to expand and flourish. However, this does not mean artistic production in Delhi ceased. Many mosques, tomb complexes, mansions and gardens continued to be constructed, but there was a change both in scale and in materials. Architectural projects were now considerably smaller and expensive stones such as marble and even red sandstone were largely replaced by stucco and brick. The identity of patrons also changed. Royalty did not abandon building altogether, but their patronage was often directed at the tombs of Chishti saints in Delhi itself (since Ajmer was now outside Mughal territory). Even imperial tombs, now almost always situated at a saint's tomb and not in an independent garden, usually comprised a simple marble tombstone enclosed by a marble lattice left open to the air. This is a reflection of the increased orthodoxy of the time as well as the changed economic status of the state. During the 18th century a number of nobles and their wives continued to provide small mosques, but by the 19th century merchants, and in one case even a milkmaid, were sufficiently wealthy to provide and inscribe their own religious buildings.

The Mughal successor states experienced a variety of conditions. Many of these states looked back to the Mughals as a model of the sophisticated use of symbols of power and culture. This was true even of Shia Muslim rulers, though the Mughals were Sunni. Even the British, after they had deposed the Mughal dynasty in 1858, adopted much Mughal ceremonial in their own courtly practice both in India and in England. Long after the Mughals had ceased to exist, a sense of their formidable power, their wealth and their ability to display their achievements through artistic, architectural and courtly performance remained vitally alive in the memories of their successors.

At the height of their power in the 17th century, the mighty Mughals ruled over most of the Indian subcontinent. They were an extraordinarily wealthy house, well able to compete in military might as well as in cultural achievement with their international neighbours and rivals, the Safavids of Persia and the Ottomans of Turkey. It is impossible to know the exact population of Mughal India, but it was probably about 100 million, making it many, many times larger than that of the Safavid or Ottoman Empires. Mughal India was rich in land, natural resources and sheer human power to manipulate its remarkable resources. Is it any wonder that the name Mughal, often written as 'mogul', is still used in this century to designate one who has extraordinary power to direct and control?

## CHAPTER SEVEN

# Japan: The Meiji Restoration 1868–1945
## ELISE KURASHIGE TIPTON

T he Japanese empire was short-lived, in comparison with the other Asian empires in this book. It lasted only fifty years, from its first territorial acquisitions in 1895 to its unconditional surrender in 1945. Nevertheless, at its height during the Second World War the empire spread across most of North-East and South-East Asia – occupying Korea, Taiwan, Micronesia, and the former British and Dutch colonies in South-East Asia and wielding de facto control over Manchuria, central and eastern China, and French Indochina. Most tellingly, the Japanese empire was the only non-Western empire of modern times. This significance was not lost on contemporaries in the West or in other parts of Asia, and memories of the more brutal aspects of Japanese imperialism linger even into the 21st century.

Before 1895, Westerners had seen Japan simply as the producer of beautiful, but strange and exotic, arts and crafts, which were displayed at world's fairs and expositions such as the 1876 Philadelphia Centennial Exposition. However, Japan's military defeat of China in 1895, and the consequent expansion of its influence over Korea, focused Western attention. The victory over China demonstrated that Japan had come a long way since the early 1860s. Now Western governments and commentators praised Japan's military accomplishments, representing Japan as civilized and progressive. American foreign service official Harold Martin's assessment of the war between China and Japan was typical:

> …the success of Japan in Korea means reform and progress –
> government, social and commercial – in that unhappy country.…

The success of the Chinese means the forcing back of the Koreans to Oriental sluggishness, superstition, ignorance, and anti-foreign sentiment. It is a conflict between modern civilization, as represented by Japan, and barbarism, or a hopelessly antiquated civilization, by China.[1]

This highlights the fact that Japanese imperialism was born in an age of European colonialism and empire, when territorial acquisitions were a symbol of national status and prestige.

However, ten years later when Japan defeated a white nation, Russia, forebodings of threat and the Yellow Peril would be mixed with further praise. During the next few decades of the 20th century, differences in the perceived national interests of Japan and the major Western powers would be exacerbated, and the growing forces of nationalism on the Asian continent would conflict with Japan's expanding imperial ambitions. The resulting war extended Japan's empire briefly, but ended with the atomic bombings of Hiroshima and Nagasaki. Defeat led not only to the loss of the empire, but also to occupation by foreign powers for the first time in Japanese history. Both the Japanese people and their Asian neighbours suffered as victims of Japan's aggressive expansionism.

Understanding the origins and development of Japan's empire requires an examination of Japan's nationalist goals in the context of international politics and diplomacy during the second half of the 19th century. Understanding Japanese leaders' broad goals makes their colonial ambitions comprehensible and even unsurprising, though they should not necessarily be seen as part of a planned conspiracy. At the same time, empires are not static. Changes within the regional and international environment after World War I as well as domestic social, economic and political circumstances help to explain how and why Japanese leaders became estranged from the Western powers and decided to pursue aggressive expansionary policies in the 1930s.

## KEY DATES

| | |
|---|---|
| **1868** | Meiji Restoration, overthrow of the Tokugawa Shogunate |
| **1876** | 'Opening' of Korea |
| **1894–95** | The Sino-Japanese War and acquisition of Taiwan |
| **1902** | Anglo-Japanese Alliance |
| **1904–5** | The Russo-Japanese War |
| **1910** | The annexation of Korea |
| **1 March 1919** | First of March Movement for independence in Korea |
| **1931** | The Manchurian Incident |
| **1932** | The establishment of Manchukuo |
| **1937** | Beginning of war with China and the 'Rape of Nanjing' |
| **1940** | Tripartite Pact with Italy and Germany |
| **December 1941** | Attack on Pearl Harbor |
| **1942** | Occupation of South-East Asia |
| **August 1945** | Atomic bombings of Hiroshima and Nagasaki; Japan surrenders |

## 'A Rich Country, Strong Army'

In January 1868 Meiji Restoration leaders carried out a coup that overthrew the Tokugawa Shoguns, who had ruled for more than two and a half centuries (1603–1868). The coup came after fifteen years of tumultuous politics, civil war and a transformation of the world view of the Meiji leaders. The Meiji leaders rode the wave of the anti-Western Restoration movement, but they rejected radical terrorism against Westerners in order to try to save Japan from becoming a semi-colony like China. This involved creating a highly centralized political system, under the theoretically restored rule of the divinely descended emperor, in addition to organizing modern

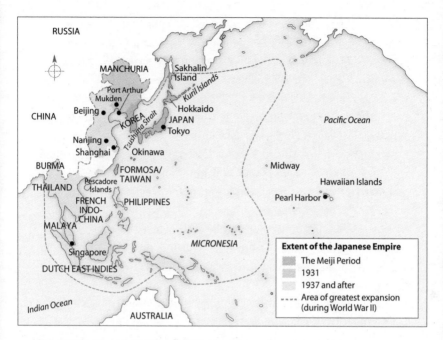

Map showing the growth of the Japanese Empire.

Western-style military forces. The Meiji leaders encapsulated their nation-alist goals and approach to reform in two slogans: 'a rich country, strong army' and 'Japanese spirit, Western techniques'. In their new world view, international politics consisted of a struggle among nations to achieve power and status. Enriching the country and strengthening the military would be the means to Japan gaining a place at the top of the hierarchy of nations equivalent to that of the major Western powers. Their broad modernization programme, based on Western models, aimed to abolish the unequal treaties imposed by the Western powers during the late 1850s using gunboat diplomacy. As in China, the unequal treaties forced Japan to open 'treaty ports' to trade and privileged foreigner settlements and deprived Japan of the ability to regulate import duties or to prosecute foreigners under Japanese law (extraterritoriality).

There were reforms not only in strategic manufacturing and military industries, but also in society and culture. Western powers would treat Japan as an equal only if they viewed Japan as 'civilized': that is, like Western societies. For example, the Japanese government hired many Westerners to advise and teach the Japanese how to construct Western-style buildings and to paint in the style of Western art academies, as well as to establish Western-style laws and administrative systems. Being 'civilized' also meant that Japanese elites adopted Western styles of dress and social behaviour, including Western ballroom dancing and beef-eating. Moreover, the desire to gain Western approval was evident in attempts to proscribe behaviour considered indecent by Westerners. Consequently, when the government ordered public bath owners to create separate areas for men and women and to erect screens at the door, a newspaper article explained that this was to prevent foreigners from laughing at the Japanese.

Westernization and industrialization were not undertaken entirely for the purpose of achieving treaty revision, however; they were seen as useful in their own right. A mission led by court noble Iwakura Tomomi set out in 1871 to study Western societies and to try to revise the unequal treaties. Impressed by Western economic strength, the leading oligarch Okubo Toshimichi became convinced that industrialization should be pursued for its own sake, not only as the basis for a modern military. Consequently, he cut short his stay abroad to stop a planned expedition to Korea by the caretaker government, led by former Restoration army leader Saigo Takamori. This did not mean that Okubo ruled out foreign expansion entirely; however, he believed that further domestic reforms and industrialization took priority. Nevertheless, his opposition provoked Saigo's angry withdrawal from the government, and Saigo subsequently became the rallying point for disgruntled samurai whose privileged ruling class status was abolished. Saigo eventually led the Satsuma Rebellion in 1877, during which the traditional samurai forces were defeated by the new army of largely peasant conscripts.

In the meantime, Japan was extending its territorial borders to what we now think of as Japan, while carefully taking opportunities to increase its presence in Korea. Hokkaido and the Kuril Islands in the north became an internal colony in 1869, and the indigenous Ainu people were relocated to make way for Japanese settlers. In the south the incorporation of Okinawa as a prefecture in 1879 destroyed the Ryukyu Kingdom and began a programme of assimilation to eliminate the Okinawan dialect and other distinctive cultural practices. Japan also made an aggressive move against Korea in 1876, though this was not intended to prompt an invasion as in Saigo's plan. Under advice from an American hired by the foreign ministry, Japan 'opened' the 'Hermit Kingdom' Korea, using gunboat diplomacy similar to that which the American Commodore Matthew Perry had employed to open Japan in 1853.

The opening of Korea indicates the strategic importance that the peninsula increasingly played in this era of international rivalries. It was concern about the fate of Korea that underlay the beginnings of Japan's empire-building. For a thousand years Korea had acted as a bridge for transmission of the cultural achievements of China. In the late 19th century, however, Japanese military and political leaders came to see Korea as a 'dagger' pointing at the heart of Japan. Moreover, seeing the rush of European powers to add colonies to their empires in Asia and Africa, by the end of the 1880s a number of Meiji leaders came to think that colonial conquest constituted an essential part of Japanese nationhood and independence. Foreign Minister Inoue Kaoru concluded that 'we have to establish a new, European-style empire on the edge of Asia'.[2]

During the late 1870s and 1880s Japan sought to keep Korea from falling under the control of China or of the major Western powers, notably Russia. Rivalry with China for influence on the Korean monarchy grew, as represented by the emergence of pro-Chinese and pro-Japanese factions in the court. The latter favoured Meiji-style reforms. In 1894 a rebellion by the anti-Western Tonghak religious movement in Korea provided the incident that sparked Japanese intervention. When China responded to the Korean government's request to help suppress the rebellion, Japan sent troops too and so began the Sino-Japanese War.

## Building the Nation through War

The Sino-Japanese War stimulated widespread support and a wave of nationalism among the Japanese people as well as accolades in the Western press for the apparent Japanese underdog's victory over the Chinese behemoth. At the start of the war China was expected to win because its navy was much larger than Japan's – 'virtually invincible'.[3] However, the Meiji government had invested in small, fast modern warships, modelled its navy on Britain's, and started its own ship-building industry. Its army and navy were well organized, trained and equipped, in contrast with the Chinese military forces, which were riddled by regional rivalries and whose discipline and morale were low because of corruption and poor leadership as well as inadequate munitions. The Japanese military forces won battles on land and sea, occupying not only Korea, but also the Pescadore Islands and Formosa/Taiwan, and invading Manchuria.

The foreign press, such as the *Illustrated London News*, enthused about the Japanese victories as the accomplishments of the West's able pupil:

> The enthusiasm in Japan continues, and the spectacle of this Eastern nation fighting and manoeuvering and organizing with a verve and intelligence worthy of a first-class European war has sent a thrill of admiring wonder through the military world.[4]

Japanese people living in the United States at the time became popular dinner party guests, and American hostesses took to wearing Japanese kimonos. Americans praised the Japanese victories as if they were boasting about their own country.

The Treaty of Shimonoseki in April 1895 ended the war after less than nine months. It gave Japan huge reparations to pay for the war, its first territorial acquisitions of Taiwan, the Pescadores and the Liaodong

Peninsula in southern Manchuria, and economic concessions in China that began Japan's participation in the treaty port system. Taiwan was mainly a prestige symbol; more significant was Chinese recognition of Korea's independence, ensuring no further intervention on the peninsula. However, Japanese elation over the victory was cut short when Russia, France and Germany forced Japan to give up the Liaodong Peninsula. This 'Triple Intervention' indicates growing concern among Western powers about Japan's emergence as a regional power.

Both at home and at the front there was widespread support for the war among ordinary Japanese. Youth magazines and other popular sources, such as songs and children's games and toys, as well as major newspapers, reveal that despite hardships, the war stimulated the spread of military values in Japanese society and heightened popular nationalism. Education authorities used the war to emphasize loyalty to the state and the importance of the emperor. Stories of war heroes past and present filled textbooks, while physical education programmes adopted more military-style exercises. Mock battles involved boys as soldiers and girls as nurses to strengthen the idea of all Japanese people's involvement in the war, serving the nation. The media and war artists focused attention on individual soldiers, who were welcomed back to their villages as local heroes. The state exploited soldiers' funerals to promote the value of national self-sacrifice and designated 'special' Shinto shrines to commemorate war dead. At this time the Yasukuni Shrine in Tokyo acquired its position of exceptional respect, because the emperor himself paid tribute to the souls of the war dead enshrined there.

These developments occurred in the context of various efforts since the late 1880s to forge national unity and a distinctive Japanese identity. Reforms in education explicitly aimed to make primary schools a vehicle for nation-building and create loyal imperial subjects willing to sacrifice themselves for the nation. National unity was also the objective for introducing a constitution in 1889. The new emperor-centred political system used Bismarck's Germany as the model and successfully brought in leaders of the opposition movement. Intellectuals and other non-governmental leaders also contributed to this creation of a Japanese identity when they criticized what they saw as indiscriminate borrowing from the West during the previous two decades. The backlash against Western borrowing did not mean that Westernization ended, however. Nor did it mean that the goal of achieving equality with the West was abandoned at either state or popular level.

In fact, the war contributed to the desire of ordinary as well as elite Japanese to distance Japan from the 'backward' peoples of Asia. Here we see the beginnings of Japanese imperialism being built on concepts of a racialized hierarchy of Asian peoples, which is evidence of an acceptance of Social Darwinian racial theories prevalent in the West during the late 19th century. Woodblock prints, which enjoyed a boom in war subjects, depicted the Japanese soldiers as courageous and the Chinese as cowards, but they further depicted the Chinese in garishly coloured traditional clothing and with jutting cheekbones, broad noses, gaping mouths, slanting eyes and pigtails, all symbolic of primitive taste and barbarism. In contrast, the prints represented Japanese as dignified with their military moustaches and trim Western-style haircuts and uniforms, standing tall with European facial features.

Soldiers' letters and diaries suggest that it was not only elite artists who viewed the Chinese and Koreans as uncivilized 'Others'. Sergeant Hamamoto concluded upon arriving in Korea that:

… though we belong to the same East Asian race, the only thing in common is our yellow faces.… [The Koreans are] very mild but they are lazy and have no spirit for progress.[5]

Consequently, ordinary Japanese as well as Japanese government leaders felt great resentment over the Triple Intervention.

These bitter feelings underlay Japan's eagerness to have its share when the imperialist powers carved up the 'melon' China into spheres of influence during the last years of the 19th century. This culminated in the entry of Japanese and Western military forces into the Chinese capital, Beijing, to protect their legations during the Boxer Rebellion in 1900. During the crisis Russia also sent many troops to protect its interests in Manchuria. Some Japanese leaders believed that if Russia remained there indefinitely, that would threaten the independence of Korea and affect Japanese interests adversely. The negotiation of the Anglo-Japanese Alliance in 1902 was therefore intended to show British support for Japan's emerging sphere of influence in Korea as well as to open up commercial advantages in British colonies. It was effective, for Russia agreed to withdraw its forces from Manchuria. Since Britain was the most powerful nation in the world at the time, the alliance also provided recognition of Japan as a member of the club of imperialist powers.

## The Russo-Japanese War: The Start of Japanese Imperialism

Victory in the Sino-Japanese War had made Japan a regional power; victory in the Russo-Japanese War (1904–05) made Japan an international power. Japan had declared war when Russia delayed withdrawal of its troops from Manchuria without any explanation. After the Japanese navy won control of the seas around the Liaodong Peninsula, the army moved into Manchuria, waging a year-long campaign that succeeded in capturing Port Arthur. While the army advanced against Mukden, the navy won an astounding victory over Russia's Baltic fleet, which had sailed half-way around the world, only to lose thirty-eight of its forty-two warships during a battle in the Tsushima Straits. Nevertheless, the land war bogged down, incurring heavy casualties and unsustainable expenditures for Japan, and a small anti-war movement arose at home. Russia also wished to avoid further war costs and humiliating losses while revolution was being fomented at home. Consequently, both sides welcomed the US President Theodore Roosevelt's offer to mediate a peace treaty. The treaty did not include an indemnity to pay for the war, a fact that aroused mass protests in Japan, but Japanese leaders were pleased with the war's other outcomes.

Taking a longer-term perspective, historians such as Peter Duus have argued that the Russo-Japanese War marked a turning point in Japanese foreign policy and was the take-off point for the spread of Japanese imperialism: it was 'the historical moment when a position on the Asian mainland and hegemony in East Asia becomes a fundamental national commitment'.[6] The war inflated, rather than reduced, a sense of Japan's strategic military needs and increased the military's influence in domestic politics because of its role in defending the imperial perimeter.

Moreover, the Russo-Japanese War was even more significant than the Sino-Japanese War in bringing Japanese military power to world attention. The defeat of China had had an enormous psychological impact on the Japanese people because they had looked up to China as the source of advanced civilization for a thousand years. Nevertheless, China was an Asian nation, whereas Russia was a Western, and white, nation. That is why this second victory, rather more than the first, provoked fears of the Yellow Peril in Western countries, while it evoked great admiration among anti-colonial nationalists in Asia. The conflict also reinforced growing anti-Japanese sentiment on the west coast of the United States, which had been sparked off by Japanese immigrants' success in agriculture. Sensationalist journalism and other writings painted a picture of an invasion by Japanese hordes.

In terms of the growth of Japan's empire itself, Korea did not immediately become a colony, but the war secured control over the country. In addition, in establishing Manchuria as part of Japan's sphere of influence, the victory laid the foundation for international friction and further imperialist expansion during the following decades. Through war Japan gained Russia's recognition of Japan's pre-eminence in Korea, and with British and American acquiescence, Korea soon after became a Japanese protectorate. Within five years Korea was formally annexed, though against strong resistance from the Koreans themselves. In addition, Japan obtained the southern half of Sakhalin Island (Karafuto) and railway rights and concessions in southern Manchuria.

Marxist historians have attributed Japan's colonial expansion to a capitalist desire for markets and raw materials, but political and security considerations may have been more important than economic interests. In fact, one historian points out that Japanese business interests were concerned that war with Russia would increase taxes and hurt commerce and industry. Some businessmen even thought a Russian occupation of Manchuria might bring about stability and better communications that would foster Japan's trade.[7] However, once colonies were acquired, Japanese businessmen and settlers in the colonies generated interests that had to be protected. Consequently, although control over Korea for the defence of Japan had been the Japanese leaders' primary objective until the Russo-Japanese War, enhancement as well as preservation of the sphere of influence in Korea and south Manchuria became the primary goal of Japanese foreign policy during the subsequent four decades.

This escalation in Japan's imperialist ambitions and willingness to resort to war to accomplish them during the 1930s and 1940s replicates traits in what has been called the 'imperial syndrome'. In other words, the enlargement of territory or influence was required to confirm the new political order, which then needed to defend the new, contested boundaries.[8] This is what happened after Japan acquired spheres of influence in Korea and Manchuria. Unlike Korea, which became an outright colony, Manchuria remained part of China. So although Japan stabilized its interests in Manchuria by defeating Russia, its success was only temporary. The fall of the Qing dynasty in 1911 and the rise of Chinese nationalism undermined the treaty port and sphere of influence system that supported Japan's economic and strategic interests, that is, its informal empire, on the mainland. Thereafter, for approximately two decades until 1931 Japan pursued peaceful expansion, based on a cooperative relationship with Western powers, and focused on governing and containing resistance to Japanese rule within its formal empire.

## Japan's Colonial Project in Taiwan and Korea

As a small island of minor strategic importance, Taiwan was little more than an 'imperial accessory',[9] which Japan had occupied after defeating China in 1895. However, Taiwan gave Japan a chance to create a model colony that could be shown off to other world powers. Colonial administrators, led by Goto Shinpei, took a 'scientific' approach to colonial governance, based on research into Western models of colonial administration. Goto viewed Taiwan as a 'laboratory' for Japan's experiment in colonial modernization. Policies introduced there demonstrated the pattern of governance and underlying attitudes and assumptions towards their colonial subjects that would be replicated, but with different results, in Korea. Repression, assimilation policies and discriminatory treatment of colonial subjects, as well as modernizing policies, characterized Japanese rule in both Taiwan and Korea and provoked anti-colonial movements. Nevertheless, by the end of their rule in 1945 Japanese had won considerable good will among Taiwanese of all classes, in stark contrast to the situation in Korea.

Japan won its colonies through war, and in administering them also encountered resistance, but whereas Taiwan was brought under control after two years, Korea remained difficult. In Taiwan, systematic extermination campaigns reduced the aborigine population to less than 2 per cent of the total population, and offering Chinese settlers from the mainland a chance to return to China meant that those who remained were prepared to make some accommodation to life under the new rulers. This helps to explain why the anti-colonial movement there did not gain much momentum. Korea, in contrast, was not only much larger in population and area, but also had a long history of cultural accomplishment. Even more significantly, Japan colonized Korea just when Koreans were developing a national consciousness. Their new sense of national identity therefore became directed against Japan, and harsh Japanese rule and cultural assimilation policies reinforced, rather than pacified, Korean resistance. In contrast to Western colonizers, Japanese colonial rule in theory stressed racial and cultural affinities with their subjects, but in practice their policies revealed assumptions of superiority that contradicted any claims of benefits and inclusiveness that might have justified their rule. Japan's powerful, highly authoritarian colonial governments, supported both by pervasive police and military power, aroused the continuing mistrust of their subjects.

The contradictions in their colonial programme are evident in the economic policies introduced first in Taiwan and later Korea. From the beginning, Japan not only sought to make its colonies self-sufficient, but also wanted the colonies to support the home islands. Through the 1920s colonial investment focused on agricultural production. In Taiwan, the colonial government built up a successful sugar industry. In Korea, there were efforts to turn the colony into a supplier of rice to overcome the home islands' domestic food problems. The hardships suffered by Koreans from the colonial land policies of the 1910s caused many Korean farmers to lose their land to Japanese settlers. Encouraged by Japanese recruiters seeking cheap labour, many of these peasants made up a flow of emigrants to Japan, which increased during the 1920s and 1930s despite discriminatory treatment in both employment and living conditions there.

Education policies also exemplify the subordinate role Taiwanese and Koreans played in relation to the Japanese. Theoretically, Taiwanese and Koreans might be capable of becoming Japanese through Japanese tutelage (though in some unspecified future) because of their racial and cultural affinities. However, as Goto Shinpei pronounced, 'You do not turn a flounder into a sea bream overnight'.[10] The educational system set up for the Taiwanese consequently provided only basic skills training and a large dose of moral and political education to mould the colonized into hard-working, loyal subjects. In contrast, and to reinforce the superiority of the colonizers, schools for Japanese in the colony possessed beautiful facilities and had a more rigorous academic curriculum. The only secondary schooling available to Taiwanese was to train indigenous teachers and doctors for the colony. Taiwanese seeking higher education had to go to

Japan, where they might also acquire anti-colonial ideas. Some did in the 1920s and, on returning to Taiwan, began to criticize the two-track education system. Nevertheless, it has been noted that their Japanese education was apparently successful, in that the criticisms were directed at lack of access to the superior Japanese track, rather than at the system itself.[11]

The colonial government in Korea attempted to implement the same kind of educational policies as in Taiwan, but with striking lack of success. The Japanese takeover had occurred after the Korean government had begun a campaign of 'education for the nation' that was contributing to the creation of a sense of national unity as well as basic literacy. The colonial Japanese government also found a diversity of well-developed school systems in Korea that had not existed in Taiwan. These included schools for training gentry children for entry into the Chinese-style higher civil service. After colonization, attendance at these schools did not decline quickly, since the schools set up for Koreans by the Japanese did not offer appealing programmes for the elite, nor secondary level education. Another alternative in Korea that did not exist in Taiwan were Christian missionary schools. The colonial government tolerated them partly because it did not want to offend the Western powers and partly because it supported the modernizing skills and scientific knowledge that they taught.

Until the 1920s the colonial government in Korea did not heed liberal calls from political reformers at home for a softer approach to the colony. Draconian military rule continued to suppress Korean resistance, epitomized by the words of the first governor-general, General Terauchi Masatake: 'I will whip you with scorpions'.[12] Terauchi had quickly closed down many private schools that he believed were fostering Korean nationalism, and he made clear that opposition to Japanese rule would be ruthlessly suppressed:

Among the private schools, there are schools that teach songs and use other materials which encourage independence and incite rebellion against the Japanese empire. This is forbidden, and utmost care must be exercised to ensure that the prohibition of these activities is enforced. Koreans themselves should deeply reflect upon the consequences of fostering this type of thought. For instance, the cry for independence will eventually lead Koreans to rebel against Japan. Will this promote the happiness of Koreans? Japan will just suppress such rebellion with force. This will not hurt Japan; only Koreans will suffer.[13]

Despite the warning, harsh military rule and educational policies that attempted to keep Koreans in their 'proper', inferior place had the opposite effect. Resistance to Japanese rule peaked on 1 March 1919 with a demonstration calling for independence that spread to all parts of the colony. The colonial government responded with a systematic ruthlessness that horrified liberals like Yoshino Sakuzo at home, radicalized Korean students in Japan and prompted criticism in the West. The massive size of the protests stimulated a serious rethinking of colonial policy that resulted in the 'cultural policy' of the 1920s. The number of schools for Koreans increased greatly, and the colonial government tried to win over Koreans by allowing them to study Korean history and geography as well as the Japanese language. But while school attendances increased, education failed to turn Koreans into loyal Japanese subjects. Student strikes erupted periodically, often protesting against the attitudes of superiority displayed by Japanese teachers and students. Even more than in Taiwan, the inequality of opportunities for Koreans compared to Japanese fuelled resentment against Japan.

Moreover, another aspect of the cultural policy that aimed at coopting nationalists proved to nurture Korean nationalism instead. The cultural policy introduced some relaxation of publication controls. Censorship continued (as it did in the home islands), and blatantly radical political and anti-Japanese publications were suppressed, but the colonial government hoped that allowing moderate and non-political newspapers and magazines to publish would act as a safety valve for discontent. The policy failed, in that the resurgence in Korean publishing stimulated nationalism, undermined Japan's efforts at linguistic assimilation by spreading the use of the Korean language and laid the foundation for a modern Korean literature. At the same time, the policy of tolerating moderate cultural nationalism and commercialization of publications, while repressing leftist publications, was effective in keeping nationalist activities under control.[14]

## The Informal Empire in China and the Road to War

Governing its formal empire in Korea and Taiwan did not take all of Japan's attention in overseas matters during the 1910s and 1920s. Japan pursued its interests in China, but primarily through peaceful means and in cooperation with the Western powers within the framework of the unequal treaty system. Japanese interests in China, unlike those in Korea, were more commercially than strategically motivated, and because of the Western powers' interest there, Japanese expansion was contingent on their assent. Until the late 1920s Japanese prospered in the collective informal empire, enabling enterprises such as Japanese-owned cotton mills and the South Manchuria Railway to be very profitable. During World War I Japanese industry at home boomed as the Western powers' temporary withdrawal from China opened opportunities for expanded markets. Japan failed to extract more influence in China, but it occupied German concessions and territories in China and the Pacific and gained the islands of Micronesia as a trust territory in the peace settlement. However, China's disintegration into warlord territories following the 1911 revolution and Chinese nationalist attacks on the unequal treaty system created anxieties among Japanese leaders and businessmen. From the late 1920s, Japanese military leaders in Manchuria feared that these developments would threaten Japanese security, making its formal empire vulnerable, as well as threatening economic assets in the territory.

Many Japanese poured into China during the 1910s and 1920s. They included writers, artists and intellectuals as well as businessmen. As participants in the unequal treaty system, Japanese enjoyed a privileged status in the foreign concessions of Shanghai and other treaty ports and did not integrate with the Chinese. Despite respect for China's past accomplishments and Japan's acknowledgement of its cultural debt to China, the easy defeat of China in 1895 had engendered contempt for China's present weakness and the idea that Japan should take up 'the yellow man's burden' and lead China towards 'civilization'. The notion of a special relationship with China based on a common culture and race, and now economic interests, fed a sense of vulnerability and insecurity when Chiang Kai-shek's Nationalist (Kuomintang) armies threatened to include Manchuria in a reunited China in the late 1920s.

In response to this threat, the Japanese field army commanders in Manchuria took matters into their own hands in 1931. They created a pretext for invasion by bombing a section of the South Manchuria Railway and blaming Chinese saboteurs. The Japanese government backed up the field commanders, which led to the occupation of Manchuria and the establishment of the puppet state of Manchukuo in 1932. Japanese historians see this so-called Manchurian Incident as the beginning of the Fifteen Year War. Most Japanese did not consider their country to be at war yet, but the Manchurian Incident did end the policies of peaceful internationalism that had characterized the 1920s. It created friction with the Western powers, and when the League of Nations condemned Japan's actions in Manchuria, Japan withdrew from the League in anger.

The large role played by field commanders in the Manchurian Incident is indicative of the increasing influence the military wielded in Japanese politics during the 1930s. The actions of young military officers and the field army in South Manchuria should be seen in the context of the transformation of urban Japanese society, centred on a new middle class of white-collar salaried workers seeking a Westernized lifestyle. This modern lifestyle and the materialistic, individualistic values that it represented emphasized a growing gap with the standard of living and values of the countryside. As the Agriculturalists' Self-Rule Society declared:

The cities grow more luxurious day by day…while the villagers have to live on mouldy salted fish and wear shopworn clothes…the cities are living off the sweat of the farmers.[15]

With the world depression, the plight of the countryside became a national issue, and many civilian critics blamed the suffering of rural families and breakdown of traditional communal values on party governments, big business and the imitation of Western societies.

Such ideas and various right-wing reformist and revolutionary theorists inspired what is known as the Young Officers' Movement to carry out assassinations and coup attempts during the first half of the 1930s in the hope that higher military officers would take over leadership in constructing a new society. The Young Officers' Movement reflected intense factional rivalries in the army and wider military services that finally ended with suppression of a nearly successful rebellion of First Division army elements in February 1936. The rivalries were complicated but, in simple terms, they represented different views of how to protect Japan's empire. All factions, however, believed that resorting to war was a rational and legitimate way to ensure Japan's national security and autonomy. Rather than accepting the passing of the old imperialist world order in the face of Chinese nationalism and the West's disillusionment with war after World War I, Japanese army leaders argued for increasing preparations for war with the Soviet Union on the continent while the navy promoted preparations for war with the United States in the Pacific.

## Total War and the Greater East Asia Co-Prosperity Sphere

Suppression of the 1936 rebellion ended domestic terrorism by military officers so that military leaders could focus on mobilizing national resources to create a 'national defence state'. This does not mean that the war with China was being planned in a concrete way at this stage, and even less so war with the United States. However, there was a general willingness among Japanese elites to see war as a means to protect Japanese interests.

During the 1930s political and military leaders increasingly felt that the Western powers were working to isolate Japan and saw the creation of economic blocs as a threat to strangle Japan, a 'have-not' nation, by the 'haves'. In 1937 Japan joined other 'have-not' nations, Italy and Germany, in what became the Tripartite Pact of 1940. North China became the new frontier for more frequent military incursions, and in 1937 a minor skirmish near Beijing, known merely as the 'China Incident', escalated into total war.

The war in China was never won, despite Japan's occupying ports and cities, including Beijing, in the north, then Shanghai and major centres along the Yangzi River and in the south. In what became known as the 'Rape of Nanjing', Japanese forces captured Chiang Kai-shek's capital in December 1937 and committed large-scale atrocities including an estimated 200,000 killings. However, the Nationalist government never surrendered and instead retreated inland to Chungking, while the Communists waged guerrilla warfare in the countryside from their base in north-western China. The protracted war drained Japan's colonies as well as the home islands of men and materials. Since the beginning of the 1930s the focus on agricultural production and the cultural policy in Korea had given way to industrialization and intensified assimilation policies in the name of 'imperialization'. For example, Japanese was made the language of instruction in schools and Japanese history and culture were compulsory subjects in the curriculum. In addition, Koreans were forced to change their names to Japanese ones, worship at Shinto shrines and give up other manifestations of their cultural identity, which was resented even more than in Taiwan. With war, Korea became a logistical base and supplier for military operations in China in addition to continuing to send rice to the home islands. As colonial subjects, Koreans became liable for both military and labour conscription, and Korean women were sometimes forcibly recruited as so-called 'comfort women' for brothels throughout the war zones in Asia. Although the industrial infrastructure built by the Japanese laid the foundation for Korea's postwar economic growth, Korean nationalism remained strongly based on anti-Japanese sentiments.

Meanwhile, after the establishment of the puppet state of Manchukuo in 1932, Japan utilized racial ideas as well as financial incentives to recruit poor peasants as settlers in a 'Millions to Manchuria' colonization programme. As members of the 'leading race', settlers who had been social inferiors at home became socially superior to the Chinese and Koreans whom they displaced. They have been described as 'grassroots agents of empire' or 'subimperialists', who viewed superior Japanese levels of technology and standards of personal hygiene as a reflection of racial differences between Japanese and other Asians.[16]

Racialized attitudes of superiority and exploitative policies also characterized Japan's treatment of South-East Asian peoples who came under Japanese rule in 1942. Japanese forces blitzed through South-East Asia, driving out the Western colonial powers in a matter of months. This included taking the supposedly impregnable Singapore in five days. The Japanese empire now reached its height, dominating all of South-East Asia up to India's border in the west and the middle of the Pacific in the east. South-East Asians initially welcomed the Japanese, who proclaimed 'Asia for the Asians' and established the Greater East Asia Co-Prosperity Sphere. An Indian member of the Malayan civil service declared that, although his 'reason utterly rebelled against it', his sympathies 'instinctively ranged themselves with the Japanese in their fight against Anglo-America'.[17]

However, Japan's pan-Asianism proved to be an extension of those ideas and policies of a 'natural' hierarchy of race and power deployed in Taiwan, Korea and China. Based on its success as the first non-Western modernizer and its 'bright and strong'[18] moral superiority and purity, Japan would uplift the less fortunate peoples of Asia. Some Japanese military leaders, intellectuals and political leaders sincerely believed in Japan's 'mission' to free Asia, but the arrogance and brutality of many Japanese officers, military police and colonial administrators soon turned the joyful welcome of South-East Asians into fear, dislike and hostility. The region's rich natural resources were commandeered for the Japanese war effort, and hundreds of thousands of men and women were rounded up for forced labour. Numerous other policies also made clear that Japanese imperialism was simply replacing European imperialism – use of Tokyo time, the Japanese calendar, Japanese occupation money and the Japanese flag. Censorship of all media was enforced, and schools taught Japanese language and 'superior' Japanese modes of thought and behaviour.

## Defeat in War and the End of Empire

Asians suffered greatly as victims of Japanese expansionism, and by 1945 so did the Japanese people at home as well as at the front. However, when the war first began with China in 1937, and later with the attack on Pearl Harbor in December 1941, most Japanese were thrilled by the victories. Defending the empire had become a national commitment since the Russo-Japanese War, and Western economic sanctions since the invasion of Manchuria seemed to threaten Japan's lifelines to raw materials. Moreover, government propaganda aimed to liberate Japanese as well as other Asians from Anglo-American cultural imperialism, that is, the despised values of materialism, selfish individualism, hedonism and liberalism. State Shinto and school textbooks promoted self-sacrifice for the nation and Japan's unique kokutai (national polity), derived from its divinely descended imperial family. Popular songs as well as government rhetoric emphasized Japanese purity and spiritual superiority. In addition, the government enforced strict censorship and repressed any anti-government views. Consequently, although material hardships and destruction by B-29 bombing raids eventually became even greater in the home islands than elsewhere in the empire, most Japanese were resigned to fighting to the bitter end.

There was such a shortage of resources by the last months of the war that volunteer corps trained with bamboo spears, and the navy turned to pitting spiritual power against the materially superior enemy in the form of *kamikaze* suicide squadrons. Criticism of the government increased, even at grass roots level, but the cabinet could not agree on surrender because the Potsdam Declaration issued by the Allies required unconditional surrender. This left the fate of the emperor and imperial institution in jeopardy. It was finally the atomic bombings of Hiroshima and Nagasaki and the entry of the Soviet Union into the war that moved the emperor to break the deadlock.

Unlike the Western empires in Asia, Japan's empire evaporated in 1945, and decolonization was complete. The repatriation of Japan's abruptly abandoned colonial settlers was chaotic and traumatic. Thousands died as they fled Manchuria and Korea, and many met rejection by relatives when they finally returned to occupied Japan. Moreover, although many historians say that the atomic bombings and privations of war created a sense of victimhood and 'war amnesia', they also created a strong sense of pacifism at grass-roots level that continues to the present. Japanese governments as well as the majority of Japanese people gave up the objective of a 'strong military' and cooperated in pursuing the goal of the 'rich country' and accepting a new democratic constitution that turned the emperor into a constitutional monarch. At the same time, issues of war responsibility continue to be raised even in the 21st century, and denials of aggression by politicians, bureaucrats and nationalist historians have inflamed anti-Japanese sentiments in China and Korea, and to a lesser extent in South-East Asia. Consequently, the legacy of Japan's imperial ambitions runs deep. Even as the number of people who actually experienced Japanese imperialism as perpetrators, collaborators or victims declines with the decades, memories of Japanese imperialism both in Japan and other parts of Asia remain highly contested, emotive terrain.

# The End of Empire

JIM MASSELOS

It is difficult to avoid hyperbole when speaking of the empires presented in these chapters. Superlatives come easily when describing the size of their territories and populations, the beauty of their monuments, the magnificence of their palaces and the extent of their wealth – and that is before we have considered the calibre of their administration, the piety of their religion, and the peaks of their intellectual and cultural attainments. Epithets such as 'biggest', 'greatest', 'grandest', 'most magnificent' and 'most advanced' fit quite naturally into discussions of most of these empires. Clearly, paeans to their grandeur, size and achievement were rooted in reality: almost all of these empires were, indeed, grand affairs. At their height, they achieved levels of magnificence that – more often than not – lived up to the rhetoric and grandiloquence heaped upon them at the time, and afterwards.

However, a different kind of hyperbole also attaches to empire, in hostile descriptions around such terms as 'barbaric', 'cruel' and 'destructive'. For conquered populations, as well as for neighbours living in fear of conquest and of the killing, looting and destruction that went with it, an empire could be a ferocious and fearsome presence. As Christopher Marlowe, the English Elizabethan playwright, put it in the Prologue to *Tamburlaine the Great*, the Mongol warlord Timur was:

Threatening the world with high astounding terms,
And scourging kingdoms with his conquering sword.[1]

Later, in Part II of the play, Timur's intentions are clear in the advice he gives one of his sons:

Be thou the scourge and terror of the world.[2]

This is the hyperbole of terror and unrestrained force – naked power manifest. And this, too, reflects a reality of empire, especially in its early stages, when territory was being conquered and rulership established. It applies as much to the Mongols, as they sped across the steppes into distant parts of Asia and Europe, as it does to later Japanese invasions into China, Manchuria and Korea, with their deployment of modern, European military technologies of killing. The intention, of course, was conquest. For the victors, this was a matter of celebration and self-congratulation: when Ismail became the first Safavid monarch of Persia he wore, in Khwandamir's description, 'the crown of the caliphate and world conquest on his head'.[3] The conquerors took pride in their achievements, whatever the feelings of the vanquished.

Such hyperbole incorporates the ambiguity and duality inherent in empire. It also captures the formation of long-lasting attitudes towards empire, from both inside and outside. Loyalties were created over time within the empires, loyalties that survived even regal decline and overthrow. A good example is the lingering aura of power that clung to the Mughal emperor in India. This was so strong and entrenched a notion that, long after the Mughal leader had become merely the king of Delhi, a puppet of other rulers, he remained emperor in name. The Mughals still conjured such strong and potent images of power that the British rulers who succeeded them deployed Mughal regal symbolism, and used Mughal monuments, to reinforce their own position.

## The Occidental's Orient

Outsiders, viewing these empires from their own vantage points, developed a complex mix of views and attitudes. A fear of the Mongol hordes permeated European consciousness, as (later on) did the threatening sensation of the Turkish Ottomans gnawing at the edges of a beleaguered Europe. Conversely, thanks initially to Marco Polo, there was also admiration for the great Mongol ruler of China, Qubilai Khan. The narrative of Polo's travels, *Description of the World* (*c.* 1300) recorded, as Colin Thubron has put it:

> A land of such fabulous difference that to enter it was like passing through a mirror, and it is this passage – from a still-provincial Europe to an empire of brilliant strangeness – which gives the tale even now a dream-like quality.[4]

The Ming Empire also attracted admiration from later Western travellers. The sense of a romanticized exoticism surfaced again, when Samuel Taylor Coleridge voiced a similar wonderment at distant empires and their picturesque strangeness:

> In Xanadu did Kubla Khan
> A stately pleasure-dome decree: Where Alph, the sacred river, ran
> Through caverns measureless to man
>     Down to a sunless sea.
> So twice five miles of fertile ground
> With walls and towers were girdled round:
> And there were gardens bright with sinuous rills,
> Where blossomed many an incense-bearing tree;
> And here were forests ancient as the hills,
> Enfolding sunny spots of greenery.[5]

From the time of the Mongols right through into the late 18th and even the 19th century – the very time when these Asian empires were either spent forces, or were entering into deep and terminal decline – they featured in the European imagination. The imagined Orient was the opposite of mundane European realities. European Orientalism[6] deployed stereotypes of a fantasy Asia, stereotypes of exoticism, luxurious wealth, languorous sexuality, harem plenitude and sybaritic indulgence. The femininity of Orientalist Asia and the seductiveness of its imagined persona were starkly contrasted with qualities considered European: masculinity, intellectual rigour, a protestant ethos and the scientific and technological attainments of a Europe entering into the industrial revolution and the world of the Enlightenment. The difference justified assertions of national and ethnic superiorities, racist privileging and separation. What had been admired became devalued and debased. After all, Asia was, as Karl Marx contended, the place for Oriental despotisms and all the tyrannies that went with them.

So, as the 19th century advanced, European progressiveness was increasingly contrasted with Asiatic backwardness, and European Christianity with what were seen as heathen or idolatrous religions. Europeans, Britons in particular, entered a century of self-confidence and assertiveness, a century in which they loudly affirmed their superiority and moral worth. They turned from what had been, in earlier years, a largely admiring contact with Asia and moved into a time of hostile encounters and, finally, of conquest. The elements that had once been so attractive – Asia's grand buildings and its artefacts, textiles and ceramics – were less and less appreciated as their rarity was overtaken by mass-produced European copies for European markets. There was another consequence: instead of being the production house for exports to Europe, Asia became the market for imports from Europe. Empire and trade went hand in hand. European naval power ate at the rim territories, the littoral of Asia, and either took them over, as part of the new empires, or dominated them (just as effectively) in indirect ways. Orientalist stereotypes of difference accompanied the new spatial alignments, maintaining markers of distinctiveness and separation between the new rulers and their alien subject populations. Attitudes tracked changed realities. Asia and its empires, which through much of the last thousand years had been a, if not the, core element in world history, moved into a position of inferiority and subordination. The great cities, the prosperity, the favourable trade and the creativity in arts and sciences all diminished in the changing circumstances presented by aggressive European expansion. The weaponry and military machinery produced by an industrialized West overcame indigenous defence, no matter how spirited and determined it might be.

Most of the Asian empires in the early stages of their expansion had created or progressively adapted to new technologies of warfare – muskets, rifles and cannon – and had, in consequence, been able to maintain their domains by military means. In later centuries, some had even come to employ European military men and adventurers to advise on discipline and tactics. However, by the 19th century these adaptations proved insufficient to counter the military hardware and warships produced by Europe's Industrial Revolution. Only Japan undertook an extensive modernization, which gave it a Western-style army and navy and the wherewithal to contend with European military might. Japan was able to destroy Russia's navy early in the 20th century and to acquire, through conquest, the makings of an empire in coastal east Asia. All the force of the Allies in World War II – and two nuclear bombs – would be needed to effect Japan's surrender.

By then, the other Asian empires covered here had long gone. The Mongol Empire had disintegrated centuries earlier; the Safavids had been replaced by another great dynasty, the Qajar; the Ming had lost out to the Qing (a dynastic title, meaning 'clear' or 'pure', taken by the Manchus); the Mughals had finally been overthrown by the British; and the Khmer had disintegrated. The Ottomans had struggled during the 19th century, when nationalist movements seceded from the empire and set up independent nation-states. Nevertheless, much of the Ottoman Empire hung together till the 1920s, when internal revolution led to the establishment of a republic under Mustafa Kemal Ataturk. So ended the great Asian empires.

## The End of Empires

Still, there remains a final issue – why did such great state formations finally dissipate? A biological analogy is useful in describing a process of rise and growth, followed by decline and dissolution, but this is a description rather than an explanation. Some features are shared by most of these empires. A common element is the centrality of the emperor and the procedures by which emperors succeeded to their thrones. Originating as warrior leaders, who brought together kith and clan in ethnic military coalitions unstoppable in the first stages of conquest, the emperors became heads of sedentary states encompassing multi-layered ethnic populations. In such states it was the centralized monarchy that provided the crucial binding element. When successive emperors were capable in their governance, they were able to expand or at least cope with all the pressures and challenges of empire. When they were inadequate, then the empire was eventually affected. Moreover, given that the succession from one emperor to another was not clear cut (primogeniture did not strictly apply), the death of an emperor could have unsettling consequences. Sons and relatives vied for advantage in succession disputes that could escalate into civil war, and result in a consequent weakening of the empire as a whole. Whatever the impact of succession rivalries, military capabilities and administrative competence could become routinized and therefore less effective in managing the empire or protecting it from lean and hungry enemies on the borders. An ability to keep up to date with military advances was equally critical.

No single factor, then, seems enough to end a dynasty and its empire. Rather, it was a combination of elements that brought about decline or overthrow. By its late stages, an empire was typically no longer what it had been at its most vital. It had ceased to be that grand artefact, a great piece of social engineering, a unique civilization in and of itself.

## New Empires and Rulers

The rivals who immediately replaced the great Asian empires, in a repetition of customary empire-making patterns, were themselves mainly Asian.

However, the Europeans who came by sea were important in changing the equilibrium from around the 1600s. When the first Europeans knocked at the doors of the imperial courts, seeking diplomatic recognition and permission to trade, it was not apparent straight away that they were potential rivals to the established Asian order. Nor was it immediately obvious when the European traders, organized as multi-national profit-making trading companies, set up enclaves, trading posts or 'factories' in key locations around the Asian coastline. However, it did become clear when they won control first of adjacent lands and then of more distant and extended territories. The result was that, by the late 19th century, virtually all of Asia was under European control. For a time, a different style of empire held sway.

Like their predecessors, the new empires were centralized. However, they did not focus on an absolutist emperor but, via a figurehead constitutional monarch, on (partly) democratic parliaments. The new administrations drew on both Asian precedents and trading company structures: the result was that land organization and land control were modified, but not overturned. European legal codes introduced new notions of civil society, crime and punishment. New taxes were also introduced. Along with European law went new science and technology, which linked the Asian colonies and dependencies to Europe, while Europe's worldwide economic interests brought Asian parts of the new empires into global configurations that had little concern for the benefit of Asian subjects.

An amazingly small number of foreigners ruled vast territories and populations. For instance, during the period of British Crown rule over India from 1858 to 1947, there were only ever around 1,000–1,200 members of the 'Iron Frame', the Indian Civil Service, and most, though not all, were British. On the other hand, the lower ranks of clerks were mainly Indian. Similarly, though the Indian defence forces numbered about 310,000 in 1914 before World War I expansion, only 80,000 were British, though the officer cadres were predominantly Britons.[7] The new rulers retained differentiation between themselves and the ruled. This is hardly surprising, considering that they were overwhelmed numerically by the immense size of their subject populations. The division was reinforced by the fact that the European rulers did not turn their Asian territories into colonies for European settlement, as happened in Australia, Canada and elsewhere. European rulers, unlike their Asian predecessors in the days of the great kingdoms, remained foreigners and separate, and returned 'home' to Europe when their terms of service were over.

European empires developed their own style and culture but were, of course, affected by what had been achieved before them. Out of the intersection emerged new imperial cultures, even if the European ruling classes remained temporary imports who never became localized within their Asian context. In their time of empire that separateness was only rarely bridged.

## Memory of Empire

In our own time, as the once mighty European empires rapidly recede into the past, it has become easier to appreciate and re-interpret the lasting impact of the empires that went before them. As the successive chapters of this book demonstrate, what stands out is the vitality of their founders in carving out the space of empire and in developing innovative political structures to control their conquests. They were protean figures, these founding emperors, the stuff of myth and legend. They and their successors presided over the development of unique societies and cultures, which wielded extended influence and which have renewed relevance nowadays. Contemporary nation-states in Asia mine these pasts to formulate national collective memories and to shape national identities. History and the use of the past thus become part of modern nation-building, as do archaeological discoveries and the conversions of old buildings and city environments into protected, treasured national monuments. Many become UN World Heritage sites, reinforcing a sense of their special significance. While memories of past indigenous empires have utility for modern Asian states, a corollary of the idea of an extended past is that the period of European domination is reduced to a mere blip, a temporary break in an otherwise continuous lineage of activity, creativity, art and culture. The notion of a great Asian past is pervasive, and so is what it suggests for the future: if much of the last thousand years was the time for Asian achievement, why should not most of the coming millennium be again Asia's time?

# NOTES

## Chapter one Central Asia: The Mongols 1206–1405

1 Igor de Rachewiltz, 'The Title Cinggis Qan/Qaghan Re-examined', in *Gedanke und Wirkung: Festschrift zum 90. Geburtstag von Nicholaus Poppe*, ed. W. Heissig and K. Sagaster (Wiesbaden, 1989), 281–98. Previously it was assumed that Chinggis Khan meant 'Oceanic Ruler', based on early 20th-century attempts to link the name to the Turkic word tenggis, which translates as 'sea' or 'ocean'.

2 The incorrect version 'Genghis' was adopted from the 18th century, when a Western scholar transliterated an Arabic spelling of Chinggis. Arabic does not have a 'Ch' sound, so the name had been written in the Egyptian dialect with a 'G'. The first known use of 'Genghis' was in the French author Petis de La Croix's *Histoire du Gran Genghizcan* in 1710. However, because of the French pronunciation, it sounded more like 'Zhengiz Khan'. A 1722 English translation followed, and slowly the 'ZH' sound transformed into a soft 'G' as in 'gaol' or 'germ' and into a hard 'G' as in 'good'.

3 The Jin Empire was founded in 1125 when the Manchurian Jurchen tribes invaded and conquered the Liao dynasty (916–1125). The Jurchen, a semi-nomadic people, took the dynastic name of Jin (Golden) and ruled northern China until the Mongols conquered them in 1234.

4 The Khwarazmian Empire came into existence in the 12th century. After the Seljuq Empire, which had dominated much of the Middle East in the 11th and 12th centuries, collapsed, the governors of Khwarazm, located south of the Aral Sea, around the modern city of Khiva, became independent. Sultan Muhammad II (1200–1220) expanded the empire to its greatest extent. The dynasty was Turkic in origins and had strong marital ties to the Qangli Turks in Central Asia.

5 Ata Malik Juvaini, *Genghis Khan: The History of the World Conqueror*, trans. J. A. Boyle (Seattle, WA, 1997), 105.

6 Igor de Rachewiltz, ed., *The Secret History of the Mongols*, Brill's Inner Asian Library, 7/1 (Leiden, 2004), 196–200.

7 Marco Polo, *The Travels of Marco Polo*, trans. Henry Yule (New York, 1993), 263.

8 The split between Sunni (90 per cent of the world's Muslims) and Shia (10 per cent) occurred in the 7th century. The primary difference centres on who should lead the Islamic community. Shia believe that the Prophet Muhammad wanted his cousin and son-in-law Ali to be the leader and that the leadership should come from the offspring of Ali and Fatima (Muhammad's daughter). Ali was not selected as Caliph (successor) until 656 when he became the Fourth Caliph. After his death in 661, the Umayyad dynasty took over the Caliphate. The Shia (Partisans), so called because they were the Shiat Ali or Partisans of Ali's candidacy, became a religious group after the death of Ali's grandson Husayn at the battle of Karbala in 680, when he and a few dozen supporters were slaughtered by the Umayyads. The emphasis on martyrdom and a source of authority through the family of Ali (known as Imams) has made Shia Islam noticeably different. Also, it has a more hierarchical clergy than Sunni Islam, with the highest authorities known as Ayatollahs.

9 Ata Malik Juvaini, *Genghis Khan*, 725 (see note 5 above).

10 Rashid al-Din, *Jami'u't Tawarikhi: Compendium of Chronicles: A History of the Mongols*, vol. 2, trans. W. M. Thackston (Cambridge, MA: Harvard University Dept of Near Eastern Languages and Civilizations, 1998), 295.

11 Valentin A. Riasanovsky, *Fundamental Principles of Mongol Law*, Uralic and Altaic Series vol. 43 (Bloomington, IN, 1965), 88.

12 Ata Malik Juvaini, *Genghis Khan*, 248.

13 Nicholas Wade, 'A Prolific Genghis Khan, It Seems, Helped People the World', *New York Times*, 11 February 2003, D3.

14 William of Rubruck in 'The Mission of Friar William of Rubruck to the Court of the Khan' in Christopher Dawson, ed., *The Mongol Mission: Narratives and Letters of the Franciscan Missionaries in Mongolia and China in the Thirteenth and Fourteenth Centuries*, trans. a nun of Stanbrook Abbey (London, 1955), 195.

15 Ata Malik Juvaini, *Genghis Khan*, 67 (see note 5 above).

16 Valentin A. Riasanovsky, *Fundamental Principles of Mongol Law*, 74 (see note 11 above).

## Chapter two China: The Ming 1368–1644

*Spelling, Transliteration and Personal Names*
Chinese personal names and geographical terms have been transliterated into pinyin, the official system of romanization. For the most part pinyin spelling approximates to the phonetic values of English, with the following notable exceptions:
c is pronounced 'ts' as in Tsar;
i is pronounced 'ee', except when it follows c, ch, r, s, sh, z and zh, in which case it is pronounced approximately 'er';
ian is pronounced 'ien';
q is pronounced 'ch' as in cheap;
r is similar to the English 'r' but is pronounced with the tongue behind the front teeth;
x is pronounced 'sh' as in sham;
z is pronounced 'ds' as in hands;
zh is pronounced 'j' as in jasmine.

When citing Chinese names, the family name is given first, followed by the given name. Following the usual practice, Chinese emperors are designated by their reign titles, not by their personal names.

1 Edwin O. Reischauer and John K. Fairbank, *East Asia: The Great Tradition* (Boston, MA, 1960), 290.

2 Edwin O. Reischauer and John K. Fairbank, *East Asia: The Great Tradition*, 312.

3 Timothy Brook, *The Chinese State in Ming Society* (London, 2005), 182.

4 Timothy Brook, *The Chinese State in Ming Society*, 182–90.

5 Frances Wood, *The Forbidden City* (London, 2005), 10–16.

6 J.V.G. Mills, trans. and ed., *Ma Huan, Ying-yai Sheng-lan: 'The Overall Survey of the Ocean's Shores'* [1433] (Cambridge, UK, 1970), 174.

7 Louise Leviathes, *When China Ruled the Seas: The Treasure Fleet of the Dragon Throne 1405–1433* (New York and Oxford, 1994), 17.

8 J.V.G. Mills, *Ma Huan, Ying-yai Sheng-lan*, 174; Louise Leviathes, *When China Ruled the Seas*, 17.

9 Denis Twitchett and Tilemann Grimm, 'The Ch'eng-t'ung, Ch'ing-t'ai, and T'ien-shun reigns, 1436–1464', in Frederick W. Mote and Denis Twitchett, eds, *The Cambridge History of China*, vol. 7 (Cambridge, UK, 1988), 323.

10 Denis Twitchett and Tilemann Grimm, 'The Ch'eng-t'ung, Ch'ing-t'ai, and T'ien-shun reigns', 305–42.

11 Arthur Waldron, *The Great Wall of China: From History to Myth*

(Cambridge, UK, 1992), 55–164.

12  Albert Chan, *The Glory and Fall of the Ming Dynasty* (Norman, OK, 1982), 18, 32.

13  Shih-shan Henry Tsai, *The Eunuchs of the Ming Dynasty* (New York, 1996), 221–30.

14  Shih-shan Henry Tsai, *The Eunuchs of the Ming Dynasty*, 223.

15  Mark Elvin, *The Pattern of the Chinese Past* (London, 1973), 285.

16  Francesca Bray, *Technology and Society in Ming China* (1368–1644) (Washington, DC, (2000), 4.

17  See note 16.

18  Francesca Bray, *Technology and Society in Ming China*, 7–17.

19  Victoria Cass, *Dangerous Women: Warriors, Grannies, and Geishas of the Ming* (Lanham, MD, 1999), 3.

20  Ping-ti Ho, *The Ladder of Success in Imperial China: Aspects of Social Mobility, 1368–1911* (New York, 1967).

21  Ping-ti Ho, *The Ladder of Success*, 92–105.

22  Edwin O. Reischauer and John K. Fairbank, *East Asia: The Great Tradition*, 312 (see note 1 above).

23  Sarah Schneewind, *Community Schools and the State in Ming China* (Stanford, CA, 2006), 2–3.

24  Sarah Schneewind, *Community Schools and the State in Ming China*, 1–5.

25  Obituary for Shen Zhou (1427–1509). Craig Clunas, *Empire of Great Brightness: Visual and Material Cultures of Ming China*, 1368–1644 (Honolulu, HI, 2007), 147.

26  Craig Clunas, *Pictures and Visuality in Early Modern China* (London, 1997).

27  Pat Barr, *Westerners in the Far East: The Sixteenth Century to the Present Day* (Harmondsworth, 1970), 20–25.

28  Wang Wenlu (fl. 1551) on the low morals of government officials. Albert Chan, *The Glory and Fall of the Ming Dynasty* (Norman, IL, 1982), 297.

29  Timothy Brook, *Praying for Power: Buddhism and the Formation of Gentry Society in Late-Ming China* (Cambridge, MA, 1993).

30  Timothy Brook, *Praying for Power*, 311–21.

31  John W. Dardess, *Blood and History in China: The Donglin Faction and Its Suppression, 1620–1627* (Honolulu, HI, 2002).

32  Richard Von Glahn, *Fountain of Fortune: Money and Monetary Policy in China, 1000–1700* (Berkeley, CA, 1996).

33  James W. Tong, *Disorder under Heaven: Collective Violence in the Ming Dynasty* (Stanford, CA, 1991), 192–203.

34  James W. Tong, *Disorder under Heaven*, 192–203. Tong's argument has been challenged on the grounds that disorder was evident as early as the beginning of the 15th century and this was occurring near Beijing, not in a remote region. See David Robinson, *Bandits, Eunuchs, and the Son of Heaven* (Honolulu, HI, 2001).

## Chapter three  South-East Asia: The Khmer 802–1566

1  'Angkor' derives from the Sanskrit *negara*, meaning city, or city-state; in Khmer it becomes *nokor*.

2  The envoys were Kang Tai and Zhu Ying. The original records were lost but the facts were preserved, and indeed embellished, in dynastic records of the 5th century and later. One unprovable theory about 'Funan' holds that it is a transliteration of the Khmer *phnom* (mountain), a word associated with the home of the gods and hence with power.

3  Like 'Funan', 'Zhenla' is a name used only by the Chinese. In the absence of any known Khmer word for their own country, these terms have continued to be used by historians.

4   The inscription is K 53 from Ba Phnom in the classification established by George Coedès in *Inscriptions du Cambodge*, 8 vols (Paris 1937–66); see Michael Vickery, *Society, Economics, and Politics in Pre-Angkor Cambodia* (Tokyo, 1998), 109. Mahendravarman was the name used during his reign by Chitrasena, the same warrior mentioned by the Sui of China as the conqueror of Funan.

5   Both statues (Ka 1641 and Ka 1593 respectively) are on display in the National Museum of Cambodia in Phnom Penh. Clearly the sculpting mastery they embody could not have sprung into existence at a stroke: the prototypes were in all likelihood of wood that has disintegrated under assault from both tropical climate and pests.

6   Most of the octagonal temples are in the South group.

7   Both words mean 'city of Indra', the god who is king of the Brahmanistic pantheon and lord of storms. Suggestions for its location include the south, near Angkor Borei; the Tonle Sap region where Angkor would later evolve; and Banteay Prei Nokor in modern Kompong Cham province. The most valuable information about the historical information to be gleaned from inscriptions, particularly those in Khmer, is in the 1998 Vickery volume cited in note 4 above.

8   They are listed in the inscription K 124 dated 803 and written by the last of the three queens. See George Coedès, *Inscriptions du Cambodge* Vol. 3 (Paris, 1951) 170–74. Of the total of 140 pre-Angkorian inscriptions, only 16 date from the 8th century. This essay uses CE dates throughout, but in the inscriptions the dates were expressed according to the Shaka system, to which 78 must be added to express the CE equivalent.

9   Similar influences had spread to Champa, and to Indonesia, where early 5th-century epigraphic records in Kalimantan and West Java mention kings with Sanskritized names.

10  Ignorance of the South-East Asian custom was possibly what led Chinese historians, who adhered to the principle of primogeniture, to interpret such successions as usurpation.

11  See Ang Choulean, 'In the beginning was the Bayon', in Joyce Clark, ed., *Bayon, New Perspectives* (Bangkok, 2007), 362–79. The Bayon, a late 12th to early 13th century temple in Angkor Thom, will be discussed later.

12  One statue from the region, the so-called Lady of Koh Krieng, is perhaps the first portrait in Khmer art and may well be a representation of a Mekong queen, although it may predate the sovereigns mentioned in the inscription. The sculpture (Ka 1621) can be seen in the National Museum, Phnom Penh.

13  The inscription, K 235, is on four faces of a stele (now in the National Museum in Bangkok). Two faces are in Sanskrit (194 lines), two in Khmer (146 lines); see R.C. Majumdar, *Inscriptions of Kambuja* (Calcutta, 1953), 362–82.

14  Sdok Kak Thom temple, Face C, stanzas 56–58.

15  *Kamraten jagat ta raja* (Lord who is ruler of the world) is the Khmer phrase that translates into Sanskrit as *devaraja*. The Sdok Kak Thom text informs us that the *devaraja* always moved with the ruler, and that the rites of its guardianship were taught by a Brahman, Hiranyadama, to Shivakaivalya, the first of the family to hold the office of its priest, in 802. These rites ensured the sanctity of the proclamation of

Jayavarman II as *chakravartin* (universal monarch) at that time. The identity of this entity has provoked widely differing theories, none of which can be proved. K 235 states that the *devaraja* resided '…in all the capitals where successive kings took him as their protector'. Some consider it a royal linga. Others think it may have been a statue. It has been interpreted to mean that the king was a god ('god-king' is the literal translation of *devaraja*). Another theory proposes that the *devaraja* was the sacred flame that was kept alight perpetually, was housed in a special shrine, and accompanied the monarch in public processions. The inscription also says that Jayavarman returned 'from Java to reign in Indrapura'; later there is a reference to 'Kambujadesa no longer being dependent on Java' ('Kambujadesa' means 'the land of the Kambus'). Historians long accepted this implied domination by Java without challenge, but there is no historical basis for the theory. The long misapprehension springs from the probable mistranslation of the word interpreted as 'Java'. It is more likely to be chvea, a word applied by the Khmer to some parts of Champa. This neighbouring country, a frequent rival of Cambodia, is the likeliest place from which Jayavarman may have 'returned'.

16 Mahendraparvata, today's Phnom [Mount] Kulen, is the ridge to the north east of Angkor where the rivers providing water for Siem Reap rise. This rocky prominence is the source of the sandstone used in the construction of Cambodia's temples.

17 Recorded in K 134 of 781 CE; see Michael Vickery, *Society, Economics, and Politics in Pre-Angkor Cambodia*, 398.

18 The temple thought to be the site of the consecration of Jayavarman II as *chakravartin* is known today as Krus Preah Aram Rong Chen. Almost nothing remains except a large mound surrounded by enclosure walls, but in form and dimensions it resembles the ruins of the 8th-century Ak Yum and this suggests that it may have been Jayavarman's temple mountain, the state temple of his realm, which until now has not been identified. Like Ak Yum, it measured 100 m (328 ft) at the base.

19 Two of these are in the National Museum in Phnom Penh: Ka 883 and Ka 1620. Prasat Krabei Krap is sometimes called Damrei Krap.

20 Sdok Kak Thom temple, Face D, stanza 5.

21 Preah Ko stele, K 713, stanza 7. Preah Ko must have been started early in 877 as it was dedicated two years later. The same must have been the case for the enormous Bakong as its stele is dated 881 CE.

22 Preah Ko stele, K 713, stanzas 8 to 27.

23 Christophe Pottier, 'De brique à grès: précisions sur les tours du Prah Ko', *BEFEO* 92, 2007 [2005], 447–95. The second face of the stele appears to have been repolished and it seems that Yashovarman's inscription has replaced the original text of his father's time. Convincing evidence for the temple's modification was discovered during excavations conducted in conjunction with conservation of the temple carried out between 1993 and 1996 and later from 1999 until the present.

24 Bakong stele, K 826, stanza 25.

25 Christophe Pottier, 'Prei Monti: rapport de fouille de la campagne 2007: À la recherche du Palais Royal de Hariharalaya', 2007, unpublished, 49 pages.

26 K 694 from Ban Bung Ke.

27 Later examples are East Mebon, West Mebon and Neak Pean (see below).

28 Texts from three Yashodharashrama can be found in Majumdar, *Inscriptions of Kambuja*,119–37 (see note 13 above).

29 The subsidiary towers are placed at the sub-cardinal corners and complete the reference to Mount Meru, which had four surrounding peaks.

30 Sdok Kak Thom temple, Face D, stanza 31.

31 Baksei Chamkrong temple, K 286, stanza 24.

32 This is one of the very rare instances in Khmer history of an architect's identity being known.

33 K 262 of 968 CE (Khmer) and K 263 of at least 984 (Sanskrit and Khmer).

34 K 197 of Bakan (Preah Khan of Kompong Svay), stanza 7.

35 Sdok Kak Thom temple, Face D, stanzas 43–6.

36 K 235, stanzas 43–46.

37 The dispute between Thailand and Cambodia about sovereignty of the land surrounding this temple, a recent addition to the World Heritage Sites, is unfortunately still unresolved.

38 Bakan is sometimes called Preah Khan of Kompong Svay; the word is the Khmer equivalent of Preah Khan, meaning sacred sword.

39 Suryavarman I may have been Cambodia's first Buddhist king, a fact suggested by his posthumous name, Nirvanapada.

40 Found in a well in the West Mebon temple, the fragment that remains is 2.22 m (over 7 ft) long and of surpassing nobility. It is displayed in the National Museum of Cambodia, Ga 5387.

41 The so-called Prakhon Chai hoard was discovered in 1964 in Khao Plai Bat temples in Buriram province and was quickly distributed in mysterious circumstances. Examples now grace many museums. Among the finest is the Maitreya from the Rockefeller collection in the Asia Society and Museum. See Emma Bunker, 'The Prakhon Chai Story: Facts and Fiction', *Arts of Asia*, 32/2, (March–April 2002) 106–25.

42 K 364 from Ban Theat.

43 Much of the information about these wars comes from Cham inscriptions.

44 Ma Touan-lin, *Éthnographie des peoples étrangers à la Chine II: Méridionaux*, trans. Le Marquis d'Hervey de Saint-Denys (Geneva, 1883).

45 Eleanor Mannikka, *Angkor Wat. Time, Space and Kingship* (Hawaii, HI, 1996).

46 K 368, stanza 13.

47 Angkor Thom means 'Great City'.

48 Olivier Cunin, 'The Bayon: An Archaeological and Architectural Study', in Joyce Clark, ed., Bayon, *New Perspectives* (Bangkok, 2007), 136–229.

49 A study by George Groslier estimates that Banteay Chmar's construction would have required a minimum of 25,000 builders (including sculptors) working for 60 years to complete the temple if the area had a supporting population of at least 200,000 people. Since this was not the case, Groslier proposes that it must have taken more like a century or more, and that a reference by the Zhou Daguan, the Chinese envoy to Angkor in 1296, to newly completed constructions far from the capital may relate to Banteay Chmar. See George Groslier, 'Étude sur le temps passé à la construction d'un grand temple Khmèr (Bantay Chmar)', *BEFEO* 35, 1935, 159–76.

50 Zhou Daguan, *A Record of Cambodia: the Land and its People*, trans. Peter Harris (Chiang Mai, 2007). This important recent translation is the first

in English to derive directly from the Chinese original; previous versions were translations from the publication in French by Paul Pelliot in 1902. The new text is lively and enriched by footnotes giving invaluable information about Zhou's sources and background.

51  Michael Vickery, *Cambodia after Angkor: the Chronicular Evidence for the Fourteenth to Sixteenth Centuries* (Ann Arbor, MI, 1977).

52  David Chandler, *A History of Cambodia* (Boulder, CO and Oxford, 1992) provides a cogent and comprehensive account of this complex period.

## Chapter four  Asia Minor and Beyond: The Ottomans 1281–1922

1  The Abbasid caliphate (750–1258) that traced its origins to Abbas (d. 653), the uncle of the prophet Muhammad (570–632), replaced the Umayyad Caliphate (661–750) that had ruled the Islamic Empire from Damascus, following the death of Ali, the Fourth Caliph or successor of the prophet, in 661. The Abbasids ruled from Baghdad, but by the 11th century had lost control over most of their realms to local Muslim dynasties. In 1258 the invading Mongols killed the last reigning Abbasid caliph and destroyed Baghdad. However, a surviving member of the dynasty managed to escape to Egypt and his descendants lived in Mamluk Egypt until the Ottomans conquered Egypt in 1517. According to a 17th-century Ottoman chronicle, the last Abbasid caliph in Egypt, al-Mutawakkil, supposedly handed over his power to the conquering Ottoman Sultan Selim I. Though the event has been disputed since then, the Ottomans used this to legitimize their power in the Sunni Muslim world.

2  Reported by De Noailles, French ambassador in Constantinople to Charles IX on 8 May 1572. Quoted in English in Kenneth M. Setton, *The Papacy and the Levant (1204–1571)* vol. 4. *The Sixteenth Century from Julius III to Pius V* (Philadelphia, PA, 1984), 1075.

3  Guillaume Postel, quoted in Colin Imber, *The Ottoman Empire 1300–1650: The Structure of Power* (London, 2002), 157.

4  Lord Charlemont, who visited the Grand Vizier's office, then known as the Sublime Porte or the Ottoman government, in 1749. Quoted in English in Philip Mansel, *Constantinople: City of the World's Desire* (London, 1997), 135.

5  Established in 1881, the Public Debt Administration was a financial control administration which consisted of seven representatives of British, Dutch, German, Austro-Hungarian, Italian and Ottoman bondholders of Ottoman debt. It had the right to collect taxes directly from revenues allocated to the administration in order to repay the debt of the Ottoman state to the lenders.

6  See, among others, Godfrey Goodwin, *A History of Ottoman Architecture* (London, 1971); Gülru Necıpoglu, *The Age of Sinan. Architectural Culture in the Ottoman Empire* (Princeton, NJ, 2005); Nurhan Atasoy, Julian Raby and Yanni Petsopoulos, *Iznik, the Pottery of Ottoman Turkey* (London, 1994); M. Ugur Derman, *Letters in Gold: Ottoman Calligraphy from the Sakip Sabanci Collection, Istanbul* (New York: Metropolitan Museum of Art, 1998).

## Chapter five  Persia: The Safavids 1501–1722

1  For an historical overview, see Hans R. Roemer, 'The Safavid Period' in Peter J. Jackson and Laurence Lockhart, eds, *The Cambridge History of Iran*,

vol. 6, *The Timurid and Safavid Periods* (Cambridge, 1986), 189–350; for a more recent synthesis of Safavid history, see Andrew J. Newman, *Safavid Iran: Rebirth of a Persian Empire* (London and New York, 2006). For a general introduction to Safavid art and architecture, see Sheila R. Canby, *The Golden Age of Persian Art: 1501–1722* (New York, 2000).

2  The name Iran, and the idea of 'Iranzamin', or the land of the Aryans, has been used locally and regionally since antiquity and with reference to a vast cultural landscape. In the West, Persia (the Greek appellation for the empire of Cyrus the Great) remained widely in use until 1935. Persia, derived from the name of the province of Fars (Parsa) in southern Iran, is considered by some to be inadequate, but it remains in use interchangeably with Iran.

3  Mir Ghiyas al-Din Muhammad Hussayni, Khwandamir, *Habibu's-Siyar*, vol. 3: *The Reign of the Mongol and the Turk*, trans. and ed. W.M. Thackston (Cambridge, MA, 1994), 576.

4  Mir Ghiyas al-Din Muhammad Hussayni, *Khwandamir*, 576.

5  For the historical background of Shiism and its Safavid adaptations, see Said Amir Arjomand, *The Shadow of God and the Hidden Imam: Religion, Political Order, and Societal Change in Shi'ite Iran from the Beginning to 1890* (Chicago, IL, 1984), 27–31 and especially 105–210.

6  An excellent source on the Aqquyunlu period is the collection of chronicles by Italian merchants: *A Narrative of Italian Travels in Persia, in the Fifteenth and Sixteenth Centuries,* trans. and ed. by Charles Grey (New York, 1960); see page 73 on Ismail's grandmother.

7  From 'The Travels of a Merchant in Persia', in Charles Grey, ed., *A Narrative of Italian Travels in Persia*, 206.

8  Mir Ghiyas al-Din Muhammad Hussayni, *Khwandamir*, 576 (see note 3 above).

9  The quotation comes from one of Ismail's own poems. Translated by Andrew J. Newman (see note 10 below).

10  The poems are translated in Andrew J. Newman, *Safavid Iran: Rebirth of a Persian Empire* (London & New York, 2006), 13; the translation is slightly adjusted by the author for clarity. Ismail's poetry in Turkmen Turkish and an illustrated manuscript copy of it are discussed by Wheeler M. Thackston, 'The *Diwan* of Khata'i: Pictures for the Poetry of Shah Isma'il I' in *Asian Art*, vol. 1, no. 4 (Fall 1998), 37–63.

11  For Abu Muslim legends, see Kathryn Babayan, *Mystics, Monarchs and Messiahs: Cultural Landscapes of Early Modern Iran* (Cambridge, MA, 2003), 82–83 and passim.

12  For the development of this literary taste, see Paul Losensky, *Welcoming Fighani: Imitation and Poetic Individuality in the Safavid-Mughal Ghazal* (Costa Mesa, CA, 1998).

13  The dismantling of this manuscript and dispersal of its pages makes it difficult to fully appreciate its magnitude as a work of art; for a facsimile and discussions of the workshops and artists, see Martin Dickson and Stuart Cary Welch, eds, *The Houghton Shahname*, 2 vols. (Cambridge, MA, 1981). Several recent studies analyse the place of the *Shahnama* in the formation of a Persianate ethos; see, for example, Robert Hillenbrand, ed., *Shahnama: The Visual Language of the Persian Book of Kings* (Edinburgh, 2004) and Kathryn Babayan, *Mystics, Monarchs and Messiahs.*

14  To appreciate the psychological impact of Ismail's fall, one need only read about

how his Qizilbash followers held him as a divine protector and thus charged into battle without armour; see 'The Travels of a Merchant in Persia' in Charles Grey, ed., *A Narrative of Italian Travels*, 206 (see note 6 above).

15  For an introduction to Safavid *ghulams*, as well as more focused studies of their role as patrons and members of the royal household, see Sussan Babaie, Kathryn Babayan, Ina Baghdiantz-McCabe and Massumeh Farhad, *Slaves of the Shah: New Elites of Safavid Iran* (London and New York, 2004), especially 1–19.

16  The transfer of the capital is discussed in M. Mazzaoui, 'From Tabriz to Qazvin to Isfahan: Three Phases of Safavid History', *Zeitschrift der deutschen morgenlaendischen Gesellschaft* (1977), 514–22, esp. 517–19. For a history of the development of the royal precinct in Qazvin, see Maria Szuppe, 'Palais et Jardin: le complexe royal des premiers safavides à Qazvin, milieu XVIe–début XVIIe siècles' in R. Gyselen, ed., *Sites et monuments disparus d'après les témoignages de voyageurs, Res Orientales* 8 (Bures-sur-Yvette, 1996), 143–77. For a recent analysis of the development of Qazvin as a capital, see Sussan Babaie, *Isfahan and Its Palaces; Statecraft, Shi'ism and the Architecture of Conviviality in Early Modern Iran* (Edinburgh, 2008), 47–58.

17  Qazi Ahmad Qomi's history, Kholasat al-tavarikh, is among the most important sources on Safavid Qazvin; for the translation of the full passage and a discussion of its significance, see Sussan Babaie, *Isfahan and Its Palaces*, 50.

18  Mariana Shreve Simpson with Massumeh Farhad, Sultan Ibrahim Mirza's Haft Awrang: *A Princely Manuscript from Sixteenth-Century Iran* (Washington, DC, 1997). The migration of artists from court to court is discussed by Abolala Soudavar, 'Between the Safavids and the Mughals: Art and Artists in Transition,' *Iran* 37 (1999), 49–66.

19  These two carpets are now in the Victoria & Albert Museum, London, and the Los Angeles County Museum of Art.

20  Lâle Uluç, 'Selling to the Court: Late Sixteenth-Century Manuscript Production in Shiraz', *Muqarnas* 17 (2000), 73–96.

21  After its arrival in the Ottoman library, the *Shahnama* of Shah Tahmasb seems to have made its way back to Iran in the 19th century before it was sold on the European market into the collection of Baron Edmond de Rothschild in 1903 and then into the possession of Arthur A. Houghton Jr. in 1959, only to be dismantled and given or sold into various collections since the late 1970s. For the tracing of the travels and travails of this manuscript and the intriguing suggestion of a return 'home', see Abolala Soudavar, 'The Early Safavids and their Cultural Interactions with Surrounding States', in Nikki Keddie and Rudi Matthee, eds, *Iran and the Surrounding World, Interactions in Culture and Cultural Politics* (Seattle, WA, 2002), 89–120, figs 1–8.

22  For the Second Civil War, see Andrew J. Newman, *Safavid Iran*, 41–45; for the Safavid women, see Kathryn Babayan, 'The Safavid Household Reconfigured: Concubines, Eunuchs and Military Slaves' in Babaie, Babayan, Baghdiantz-McCabe, and Farhad, *Slaves of the Shah*, 20–48.

23  Some of the most significant Safavid sources on the inception of Isfahan as the capital are translated and discussed in Robert McChesney, 'Four Sources on Shah Abbas's Building of Isfahan',

*Muqarnas* 5 (1988), 103–34. Important preliminary studies on various socio-cultural facets of the history of the city are gathered in Renata Holod, ed., *Studies on Isfahan*, special issue of *Iranian Studies VII*, nos 1–2 (1974). Sussan Babaie, Isfahan and Its Palaces, 65–112, reviews the history of the city and repositions it as the imperial capital of Shiism as much as of the Safavids.

24 Thomas Herbert, *Travels in Persia 1627–1629*, abridged and ed. by W. Foster (London, 1928), 127.

25 The Islamic calendar is lunar (unlike the solar Western calendar) and the beginning of Islamic history is fixed on the formation in Medina of the first community of Muslims (umma) at the time of the Prophet's hijra (emigration) to that city in 622 CE.

26 The Nuqtavi movement (or heresy) is studied by several scholars; see, for example, Said Amir Arjomand, *The Shadow of God*, 198–99 (see note 5 above) and Sussan Babayan, *Mystics, Monarchs and Messiahs*, 3–7 (see note 11 above).

27 For the imported Shia scholars and their role, see Rula Jurdi Abisaab, *Converting Persia: Religion and Power in the Safavid Empire* (London, 2004), especially the introduction.

28 Rudolph P. Matthee, *The Politics of Trade in Safavid Iran: Silk for Silver 1600–1730* (Cambridge, UK, 1999).

29 European and world contacts and conflicts with Persia constitute one of the most active fields within Safavid studies: Nikki Keddie and Rudi Matthee, eds, *Iran and the Surrounding World: Interactions in Culture and Cultural Politics* (Seattle, WA, 2002). Two publications expand on these studies: Willem Floor and Edmund Herzig, eds, *Iran and the World in the Safavid*
*Age* (forthcoming: London, 2010); and a special issue of the *Journal of Early Modern History* 13 (Leiden, 2009) devoted to the study of contacts between European travellers and Safavid society.

30 For the houses of the Armenians, see John Carswell, *New Julfa: the Armenian Churches and Other Buildings* (Oxford, 1968); for the visual implications of cultural encounters in mural decoration, see Sussan Babaie, 'Shah Abbas II, the Conquest of Qandahar, the Chihil Sutun, and its Wall Paintings', *Muqarnas* 11 (1994), 125–42. Equally fascinating but never studied for their visual significance are the Europeans depicted in the murals at the entrance into the bazaar of Isfahan; for a study of the bazaar entrance, see Markus Ritter, 'Das königliche Portal und die Nordseite des Maid ns von Schah 'Abbas I. im Safawidischen Isfahān,' in Markus Ritter, Ralph Kauz and Brigitt Hoffmann, eds, *Iran und iranisch geprägte Kulturen* (Wiesbaden, 2008), 357–76 and Tafel 3b–5.

31 Sussan Babaie, 'Launching from Isfahan: Slaves and the Construction of the Empire' in Babaie, Babayan, Baghdiantz-McCabe and Farhad, *Slaves of the Shah*, 80–113, especially 94–97.

32 Rudi Matthee, 'The East India Company Trade in Kerman Wool, 1658–1730' in Jean Calmard, ed., *Etudes Safavides* (Paris and Tehran, 1993), 343–83. Lisa Golombek's extensive studies on the Safavid ceramic production and trade will be forthcoming in a book; with regards to Kerman, see her article, 'The Safavid Ceramic Industry at Kirman', *Iran* 41 (2003), 253–69.

33 Although cosmopolitanism in Isfahan remains to be addressed as a subject by itself, the vast bibliography on various aspects of contact may be found in

note 29 above. European chronicles of travel in Persia are especially rich sources; for a couple of examples, see Francis Richard, *Raphaël du Mans, missionaire en Perse au XVIIe siècle*, 2 vols (Paris, 1995) and Ronald W. Ferrier, trans. and ed., *A Journey to Persia: Jean Chardin's Portrait of Seventeenth-Century Empire* (London and New York, 1996).

34 For the mercantile ties and other networks of cultural exchange between Safavid Persia and India, see Sanjay Subrahmanyam, ed., *Merchant Networks in the Early Modern World* (Aldershot, UK, 1996); and Muzaffar Alam and Sanjay Subrahmanyam, *Indo-Persian Travels in the Age of Discoveries 1400–1800* (Cambridge, UK, 2007). See also Soudavar, 'Between the Safavids and the Mughals' (1999) (see note 18 above) and Losensky, *Welcoming Fighani* (1998) (see note 12 above) for Safavid–Mughal artistic and literary cross-fertilization.

35 Jean Chardin quoted in Ronald W. Ferrier, trans. and ed., *A Journey to Persia: Jean Chardin's Portrait of Seventeenth-Century Empire* (London and New York, 1996). For Chardin's famous travel accounts, see L. Langlès, ed., *Voyages du Chavalier Chardin, en Perse, et autres lieux de l'Orient* (Paris: Le Normant, 1811).

36 Babaie, *Isfahan and Its Palaces*, 157–266.

37 The administrative structure of the Safavid empire is outlined in *Tadhkirat al-muluk: A Manual of Safavid Administration*, trans. and explained by V. Minorsky (London, 1980, reprint edn). See also Willem Floor, *Safavid Government Institutions* (Costa Mesa, CA, 2001).

38 Andrew J. Newman, *Safavid Iran*, 1–12 addresses the 'decline' narrative in Safavid studies.

39 Heinz Luschey, 'The Pul-i Khwāju in Isfahan: a Combination of Bridge, Dam and Water Art', *Iran* 23 (1985), 143–51. Evidence of a vibrant scene of artistic production in this later period abounds; see for example, Massumeh Farhad, '"Searching for the New": Later Safavid Painting and the Suz u Gawdaz (Burning and Melting) by Nau'i Khabushani', *The Journal of the Walters Art Museum* 59 (2001), 115–29.

40 For the Hasht Behesht palace, see Sussan Babaie, *Isfahan and Its Palaces*, 198–206. For its extensive decoration, see Ingeborg Luschey-Schmeisser, *The Pictorial Tile Cycle of Hašt Bihišt in Isfahan and its Iconographic Tradition* (Rome, 1978). Other important artistic developments of the late Safavid period may be exemplified by a few focused studies: Massumeh Farhad, 'An Artist's Impression: Mu'in Musavvir's "Tiger Attacking a Youth"', *Muqarnas* 9 (1992), 116–23; the magnificent examples of late Safavid painting and calligraphy in Oleg F. Akimushkine, Anatole Ivanov and Francesca von Habsburg, *The St. Petersburg Muraqqa. Album of Indian and Persian Miniatures from the 16th through the 18th Century and Specimens of Persian Calligraphy by 'Imad Al-Hasani*, 2 vols (Lugano and Milan, 1996), and for the textiles, especially voided velvet, Carol Bier, *Woven from the Soul, Spun from the Heart, Textile Arts of Safavid and Qajar Iran* (Washington, DC, 1987).

41 The Chahar Bagh Madrasa remains to be studied in full; see Robert Hillenbrand, 'Safavid Architecture', in Peter J. Jackson and Laurence Lockhart, eds, *The Cambridge History of Iran*, vol. 6, 808–11. The fine metalwork of the late Safavid period, including the doors of the Chahar Bagh Madrasa, are studied by

James W. Allen, 'Silver Door Facings of the Safavid Period', *Iran* 33 (1995), 123–37 and pls XIV–XXII.

42 Willem Floor, *The Afghan Occupation of Safavid Persia, 1721–1729* (Paris, 1998).

43 On Nader Shah, see, for example, Ernest Tucker, *Nadir Shah's Quest for Legitimacy in Post-Safavid Iran* (Gainesville, FL, 2006).

## Chapter six  India: The Mughals 1526–1858

1 Babur, Zahir al-Din Muhammad, *The Baburnama: Memoirs of Babur, Prince and Emperor*, trans. and ed. Wheeler M. Thackston (Washington, DC: Freer Gallery of Art, Smithsonian Institution, 1995), 330.

2 Adb al-Qadir ibn Muluk Shah Al-Badauni, *Muntakhab al-Tawarikh*, 3 vols, trans. W. Haig (Delhi, 1973, reprint edn), II, 378; 415.

3 Muzaffar Alam, The *Languages of Political Islam* (Delhi, 2004), 122–40.

4 Abu al-Fazl ibn Mubarak, *Aʿin-i Akbari*, trans. H. Blockmann (Osnabruck, 1983 [1868–94], reprint edn), vol. 1.3.

5 Abu al-Fazl ibn Mubarak, *Akbar Nama*, 3 vols, trans. Henry Beveridge (Delhi, 1977 [1902–1939], 2nd reprint edn) II: 223–35.

6 Nur al-Din Muhammad Jahangir, *The Jahangirnama: Memoirs of Jahangir, Emperor of India*, trans. and ed. Wheeler M. Thackston (Washington, DC and New York, 1999), 219.

7 Nur al-Din Muhammad Jahangir, *The Jahangirnama*, 268.

8 Nur al-Din Muhammad Jahangir, *The Jahangirnama*, 133.

9 Nur al-Din Muhammad Jahangir, *The Jahangirnama*, 383.

10 The inscription is found in Nur al-Din Muhammad Jahangir, *The Jahangirnama*, 477.

11 The inscription is found in Nur al-Din Muhammad Jahangir, *The Jahangirnama*, 477–78.

12 Ebba Koch, *Mughal Art and Imperial Ideology* (New Delhi, 2001), 138.

13 Ebbsa Koch, *The Complete Taj Mahal and the Riverfront Gardens of Agra* (London, 2006).

## Chapter seven  Japan: The Meiji Restoration 1868–1945

1 Howard Martin, writing in the *North American Review*, quoted in William Newmann, *America Encounters Japan, from Perry to MacArthur* (Baltimore, MD, 1963), 105.

2 Quoted in Marius Jansen, 'Modernization and Foreign Policy in Meiji Japan', in Robert E. Ward, ed., *Political Development in Modern Japan* (Princeton, NJ, 1968), 175.

3 A view from *The Spectator* in Britain, quoted in Donald Keene, 'The Sino-Japanese War of 1894–1895 and Its Cultural Effects in Japan', in Donald Shively, ed., *Tradition and Modernization in Japanese Culture* (Princeton, NJ, 1971), 132.

4 Quoted in Donald Keene, 'The Sino-Japanese War of 1894–1895 and Its Cultural Effects in Japan', in Donald Shively, ed., *Tradition and Modernization in Japanese Culture* (Princeton, NJ, 1971), 132.

5 Stewart Lone, *Japan's First Modern War* (London, 1994), 60.

6 Peter Duus, 'The Takeoff Point of Japanese Imperialism', in Harry Wray and Hilary Conroy, eds, *Japan Examined: Perspectives on Modern Japanese History* (Honolulu, HI, 1983), 154.

7 See chapters by Peter Duus, Mark Peattie and others in Ramon H. Myers and Mark R. Peattie, eds, *The Japanese Colonial Empire, 1895–1945* (Princeton,

NJ, 1984); W.G. Beasley, *Japanese Imperialism, 1894–1945* (Oxford, 1987), 79.

8  Charles Maier, 'America Among Empires? Imperial Analogues and Imperial Syndrome', *Bulletin of the German Historical Institute* Issue 41 (Fall 2007), 24–25.

9  Mark Peattie's description in his 'Introduction', in Ramon H. Myers and Mark R. Peattie, *The Japanese Colonial Empire*, 16.

10  E. Patricia Tsurumi, 'Colonial Education in Korea and Taiwan', in Ramon H. Myers and Mark R. Peattie, *The Japanese Colonial Empire*, 288.

11  E. Patricia Tsurumi, 'Colonial Education in Korea and Taiwan', in Ramon H. Myers and Mark R. Peattie, *The Japanese Colonial Empire*, 291.

12  The alleged statement is quoted in Mark Peattie, 'Introduction', in Ramon H. Myers and Mark R. Peattie, *The Japanese Colonial Empire*, 18.

13  Translation of quote in E. Patricia Tsurumi, 'Colonial Education in Korea and Taiwan', in Ramon H. Myers and Mark R. Peattie, *The Japanese Colonial Empire*, 288.

14  Michael Robinson, 'Colonial Publication Policy and the Korean Nationalist Movement', in Ramon H. Myers and Mark R. Peattie, *The Japanese Colonial Empire*, 312–43.

15  Quoted in Mikiso Hane, *Peasants, Rebels, and Outcastes: The Underside of Modern Japan* (New York, 1982), 36.

16  Louise Young, *Japan's Total Empire: Manchuria and the Culture of Wartime Imperialism* (Berkeley, CA, 1998), 364–82; Louise Young, 'Imagined Empire: The Cultural Construction of Manchukuo', in Peter Duus, Ramon H. Myers and Mark R. Peattie, eds, *The Japanese Wartime Empire, 1931–1945* (Princeton, NJ, 1996), 71–96. For a memoir of a Japanese colonist, the daughter of a minor government official, see Kazuko Kuramoto, *Manchurian Legacy: Memoirs of a Japanese Colonist* (East Lansing, MI, 2004).

17  Quoted in Joyce Lebra, ed., *Japan's Greater East Asia Co-Prosperity Sphere in World War II, Selected Readings and Documents* (Kuala Lumpur, 1975), 159.

18  Quote from the January 1942 issue of *Bungei Shunju*, but this was a common characterization and justification for Japan's claim to be 'the leading race'. John Dower, *War without Mercy: Race and Power in the Pacific War* (London and Boston, MA, 1986), 211.

## Conclusion  The End of Empire

1  'The Prologue', 'The First Part of Tamburlaine the Great', in Christopher Marlowe, *Plays*, Everyman's Library (London, 1950), 1.

2  Act I, Scene III, ibid., 68.

3  See Sussan Babaie's chapter in this volume, pages 139–40, and her note 4.

4  Colin Thubron, 'Marco Polo Goes to Gorgeous Xanadu' in *New York Review of Books* (9 October 2008), 36.

5  'Kubla Khan' in Ernest Hartley Coleridge, ed., *The Poems of Samuel Taylor Coleridge* (London, 1954), 297.

6  The term Orientalism as used in the sense presented here of course derives from Edward W. Said's highly influential *Orientalism* (London, 1995).

7  B.R. Tomlinson, *The Political Economy of the Raj 1914–1947. The Economics of Decolonisation in India* (London, 1979), 106.

# FURTHER READING

## Introduction  The Distinctiveness of Asian Empires

Beckwith, Christopher I., *Empires of the Silk Road. A History of Central Eurasia from the Bronze Age to the Present* (Princeton and Oxford, 2009)

Brown, Cynthia Stokes, *Big History. From the Big Bang to the Present* (New York and London, 2007)

Darwin, John, *After Tamerlane. The Global History of Empire since 1405* (London, 2007)

Ferguson, Niall, *Empire: How Britain Made the Modern World* (Camberwell, Australia, 2008).

Frankopan, Peter, *The Silk Roads: A New History of the World* (London, 2015)

Gordon, Stewart, *When Asia was the World* (Philadelphia, PA, 2009)

Jackson, Anna and Amin Jaffa, eds, *Encounters. The Meeting of Asia and Europe 1500–1800* (London, 2004)

Said, Edward W., *Orientalism* (London, 1995)

## Chapter one  Central Asia: The Mongols 1206–1405

Allsen, Thomas T., *Culture and Conquest in Mongol Eurasia*, Cambridge Studies in Islamic Civilization (Cambridge, UK, 2001)

Amitai-Preiss, Reuven, *Mongols and Mamluks: The Mamluk-Ilkhanid War, 1260–81* (Cambridge, UK and New York, 1995)

Biran, Michal, Chinggis Khan, *Makers of the Muslim World* (Oxford, 2007)

al-Din, Rashid, *Jami'u't Tawarikhi: Compendium of Chronicles: A History of the Mongols*, vol. 2, trans. W.M. Thackston (Cambridge, MA, 1998)

Halperin, Charles, *Russia and the Golden Horde: The Mongol Impact on Medieval Russian History* (Bloomington, IN, 1987)

Jackson, Peter, *The Mongols and the West* (London, 2005)

Juvaini, Ata Malik, *Genghis Khan: The History of the World Conqueror*, trans. J.A. Boyle (Seattle, WA, 1997)

Lane, George, *Genghis Khan and Mongol Rule*, Greenwood Guides to Historic Events of the Medieval World, ed. Jane Chance (Westport, CT, 2004)

May, Timothy, *The Mongol Art of War: Chinggis Khan and the Mongol Military System* (Barnsley, UK, 2007)

Morgan, David, *The Mongols, The Peoples of Europe* (Oxford, 2007, 2nd edn)

Rachewiltz, Igor de, 'The Title Cinggis Qan/Qaghan Re-examined', in *Gedanke und Wirkung: Festschrift zum 90. Geburtstag von Nicholaus Poppe*, ed. W. Heissig and K. Sagaster (Wiesbaden, 1989), 281–98.

Rachewiltz, Igor de, ed., *The Secret History of the Mongols, Brill's Inner Asian Library*, vol. 7/1 (Leiden, 2004)

Ratchnevsky, Paul, *Genghis Khan: His Life and Legacy* (1983). English edn trans. Thomas Haining (Cambridge, MA, 1991)

Rossabi, Morris, *Khubilai Khan: His Life and Times* (Berkeley, CA, 1988)

William of Rubruck, 'The Mission of Friar William of Rubruck to the Court of the Khan', in Dawson, Christopher, ed., *The Mongol Mission: Narratives and Letters of the Franciscan Missionaries in Mongolia and China in the Thirteenth and Fourteenth Centuries*, trans. a nun of Stanbrook Abbey (London, 1955)

## Chapter two  China: The Ming 1368–1644

Beattie, Hilary J., *Land and Lineage in China: A Study of T'ung-ch'eng County, Anhwei, in the Ming and Ch'ing Dynasties* (Cambridge, UK, 1979)

Bray, Francesca, *Technology and Society in Ming China (1368–1644)* (Washington, DC, 2000)

Birch, Cyril, *Stories from a Ming Collection: Translations of Chinese Short Stories Published in the Seventeenth Century* (London, 1958)

Brook, Timothy, *The Chinese State in Ming Society* (London, 2005)

Brook, Timothy, *Praying for Power: Buddhism and the Formation of Gentry Society in Late-Ming China* (Cambridge, MA, 1993)

Cass, Victoria, *Dangerous Women: Warriors, Grannies, and Geishas of the Ming* (Lanham, MD, 1999).

Clunas, Craig, *Fruitful Sites: Garden Culture in the Ming Dynasty* (London, 1996)

Clunas, Craig, *Pictures and Visuality in Early Modern China* (London, 1997)

Dardess, John W., *A Ming Society: T'ai-ho County, Kiangsi, Fourteenth to Seventeenth Centuries* (Berkeley, CA, 1996).

Dardess, John W., *Blood and History in China: The Donglin Faction and Its Suppression, 1620–1627* (Honolulu, HI, 2002)

Dreyer, Edward, *Early Ming China: A Political History, 1355–1435* (Stanford, CA, 1982)

Huang, Ray, *Taxation and Governmental Finance in Sixteenth-Century Ming China* (Cambridge, UK, 1974)

Huang, Ray, *1587: A Year of No Significance – The Ming Dynasty in Decline* (New Haven, CT, 1981)

Hucker, Charles O., *The Ming Dynasty: Its Origins and Evolving Institutions* (Ann Arbor, MI, 1978)

Mills, J.V.G., trans. and ed., *Ma Huan, Ying-yai Sheng-lan: 'The Overall Survey of the Ocean's Shores' [1433]* (Cambridge, UK, 1970)

Mote, Frederick W. and Denis Twitchett, eds, *The Cambridge History of China*, vol. 7 *The Ming Dynasty, 1368–1644*, Part I, (Cambridge, 1988) and vol. 8 *The Ming Dynasty, 1368–1644*, Part II, (Cambridge, UK, 1998)

Shen, Grant Guangren, *Elite Theatre in Ming China, 1368–1644* (London, 2005)

Tong, James W., *Disorder under Heaven: Collective Violence in the Ming Dynasty* (Stanford, CA, 1991)

Waldron, Arthur, *The Great Wall of China: From History to Myth* (Cambridge, UK, 1992)

Wood, Frances, *The Forbidden City* (London, 2005)

## Chapter three South-East Asia: The Khmer 802–1566

*Abbreviations*

*BEFEO*: Bulletin de l'École française d'Extrême-Orient

*EFEO*: École française d'Extrême-Orient

Ang, Choulean, 'In the beginning was the Bayon', in Joyce Clark, ed., Bayon, *New Perspectives* (Bangkok, 2007), 362–79

Barth, A. and A. Bergaigne, *Inscriptions sanskrites de Campæ et du Cambodge* (Paris, 1885–93)

Bénisti, M., *Rapports entre le premier art khmer et l'art indien*, 2 vols, *Mémoires archéologiques V*, EFEO (Paris, 1970)

Bhattacharya, K., *Les Religions brahmaniques dans l'ancien Cambodge, d'après l'épigraphie et l'iconographie*, EFEO 49 (Paris, 1961)

Boisselier, J., *La Statuaire khmère et son evolution*, EFEO 37 (Saigon, 1955)

Boisselier, J., *Le Cambodge* (Paris, 1966)

Briggs, Lawrence Palmer, *The Ancient Khmer Empire* (Philadelphia, PA, 1951)

Bunker, Emma, 'The Prakhon Chai Story: Facts and Fiction', *Arts of Asia* 32/2 (March–April 2002), 106–25

Chandler, David, *A History of Cambodia* (Boulder, CO, and Oxford, 1992)

Coe, Michael J., *Angkor and the Khmer Civilization* (London, 2003)

Coedès, George, *Inscriptions du Cambodge*, 8 vols (Hanoi then Paris, 1937–66)

Cunin, Olivier, 'The Bayon: an archaeological and architectural study', in Joyce Clark, ed., *Bayon, New Perspectives* (Bangkok, 2007), 136–229

Freeman, Michael and Claude Jacques, *Ancient Angkor* (Bangkok, 1999)

Glaize, M., *Les monuments du groupe d'Angkor* (Paris, 1963, reprinted 1994 and Saigon 1944)

Groslier, George, *Arts et archéologie khmers* 1/3 (Paris, 1921–23)

Groslier, George, 'Étude sur le temps passé à la construction d'un grand temple Khmèr (Bantay Chmar)', *BEFEO* 35, 1935, 159–76

Hall, K.R. and J.K. Whitmore, eds, *Explorations in Early South-East Asian History: The Origins of South-East Asian Statecraft* (Ann Arbor, MI, 1976)

Jessup, Helen Ibbitson, *Art and Architecture of Cambodia* (London, 2004)

Jessup, Helen Ibbitson and Thierry Zéphir, *Sculpture of Angkor and Ancient Cambodia: Millennium of Glory* (Washington, DC, and Paris, 1997)

Kulke, H., *The Devaraja Cult*, Data Paper 108, Southeast Asia Program (Ithaca, NY, 1978)

Ma, Touan-lin, *Éthnographie des peoples étrangers à la Chine II: Méridionaux*, trans. Le Marquis d'Hervey de Saint-Denys (Geneva, 1883)

Lunet de Lajonquière, E., *Inventaire descriptif des Monuments du Cambodge*, 3 vols, EFEO 4, 8, 9 (Paris, 1902–11)

Mabbett, I.W., 'Devaraja', *Journal of Southeast Asian History* 10/2 (September 1969), 202–23.

Majumdar, R.C., *Inscriptions of Kambuja* (Calcutta, 1953)

Marr, D.G. and A.C. Milner, eds, *Southeast Asia in the 9th to 14th Centuries* (Singapore, 1986)

Mannikka, Eleanor, *Angkor Wat. Time, Space, and Kingship* (Hawaii, HI, 1996)

Parmentier, Henri, *L'Art khmer primitif*, 2 vols, EFEO 21, 22 (Paris, 1927)

Parmentier, Henri, *L'Art khmer classique. Monuments du quadrant nord-est*, 2 vols, EFEO 29 b (Paris, 1939)

Pottier, Christophe and R. Lujàn-Lunsford, 'De brique à grès: précisions sur les tours de Prah Ko', *BEFEO* 92, 2007 [2005]

Pottier, Christophe, 'Prei Monti: rapport de fouille de la campagne 2007: À la recherche du Palais Royal de Hariharalaya', unpublished report, 2007, 49 pages.

Smith, R. B. and W. Watson, eds, *Early South East Asia, essays in Archaeology, History, and Historical Geography* (New York and Kuala Lumpur, 1979)

Stern, Philippe, 'Le temple-montagne khmèr, le culte du linga et le devaraja', *BEFEO* 34, 1934, 611–16.

Vickery, Michael, *Cambodia after Angkor: The Chronicular Evidence for the Fourteenth to Sixteenth Centuries* (Ann Arbor, MI, 1977)

Vickery, Michael, *Society, Economics, and Politics in Pre-Angkor Cambodia* (Tokyo, 1998)

Zhou Daguan, *A Record of Cambodia: The Land and its People*, trans. Peter Harris (Chiang Mai, 2007)

## Chapter four   Asia Minor and Beyond: The Ottomans 1281–1922

Ágoston, Gábor and Bruce Masters, eds, *Encyclopedia of the Ottoman Empire* (New York, 2009)

Faroqhi, Suraiya, Kate Fleet, and Res at Kasaba, eds, *The Cambridge History of Turkey*, 4 vols (Cambridge, UK, 2009–13)

Faroqhi, Suraiya, *Subjects of the Sultan. Culture and Daily Life in the Ottoman Empire* (London and New York, 2000)

Finkel, Caroline, *Osman's Dream: The Story of the Ottoman Empire, 1300–1923* (New York, 2006)

Goffman, Daniel, *The Ottoman Empire and Early Modern Europe* (Cambridge, UK, 1992)

Hanioglu, M. Sükrü, *A Brief History of the Late Ottoman Empire* (Princeton, NJ, 2008)

Ihsanoglu, Ekmeleddin, ed., *History of the Ottoman State, Society and Civilisation*, 2 vols (Istanbul, 2002)

Imber, Colin, *The Ottoman Empire 1300–1650: The Structure of Power* (London, 2002)

Inalcık, Halil, *The Ottoman Empire: The Classical Age, 1300–1600*, trans. Norman Itzkowitz and Colin Imber (London, 1973)

Inalcık, Halil and Günsel Renda, *Ottoman Civilization*, 2 vols (Istanbul, 2004)

McCarthy, Justin, *The Ottoman Peoples and the End of Empire* (London, 2001)

Quataert, Donald, *The Ottoman Empire, 1700–1922* (New York, 2000)

### Chapter five  Persia: The Safavids 1501–1722

Amir Arjomand, Said, ed., *Authority and Political Culture in Shi'ism* (Albany, NY, 1988)

Babaie, Sussan, *Isfahan and Its Palaces: Statecraft, Shi'ism and the Architecture of Conviviality in Early Modern Iran* (Edinburgh, 2008)

Babaie, Sussan, Kathryn Babayan, Ina Baghdiantz-McCabe and Massumeh Farhad, *Slaves of the Shah: New Elites of Safavid Iran* (London and New York, 2004)

Babayan, Kathryn, *Mystics, Monarchs and Messiahs: Cultural Landscapes of Early Modern Iran* (Cambridge, MA, 2003)

Canby, Sheila R., *The Golden Age of Persian Art: 1501–1722* (New York, 2000)

Haneda, Masashi, 'The Character of the Urbanization of Isfahan in the Later Safavid Period', in Charles Melville, ed., *Safavid Persia: The History and Politics of an Islamic Society* (London, 1996), 369–88

Holod, Renata, ed., *Studies on Isfahan*, special issue of *Iranian Studies* 7, nos. 1–2 (Boston, MA, 1974)

Jackson, Peter J. and Laurence Lockhart, eds, *The Cambridge History of Iran*, vol. 6, *The Timurid and Safavid Periods* (Cambridge, UK, 1986)

Matthee, Rudolph P., *The Politics of Trade in Safavid Iran: Silk for Silver 1600–1730*, (Cambridge, UK, 1999)

McChesney, Robert, 'Four Sources on Shah Abbas's Building of Isfahan', *Muqarnas* 5 (1988), 103–34

Newman, Andrew J., *Safavid Iran: Rebirth of a Persian Empire*, (London and New York, 2006)

Newman, Andrew J., ed., *Society and Culture in the Early Modern Middle East. Studies on Iran in the Safavid Period* (Leiden, 2003)

Szuppe, Maria, 'Palais et Jardin: le complexe royal des premiers safavides à Qazvin, milieu XVIe–début XVIIe siècles', in R. Gyselen, ed., *Sites et monuments disparus d'après les témoignages de voyageurs, Res Orientales* 8 (Bures-sur-Yvette, 1996), 143–77

Thompson, Jon and Sheila Canby, eds, *Hunt for Paradise: Court Arts of Safavid Iran, 1501–1576* (New York and Milan, 2003)

### Chapter six  India: The Mughals 1526–1858

Abu al-Fazl ibn Mubarak, *Akbar Nama*, trans. *Henry Beveridge* (Delhi, 1977 [1902–1939], reprint edn)

Abu al-Fazl ibn Mubarak, *A'in-i Akbari*, trans. H. Blockmann (Osnabruck, 1983 [1868–94], reprint edn)

Alam, Muzaffar and Sanjay Subrahmanyam, eds, *The Mughal State, 1526–1750* (Delhi, 1998)

Asher, Catherine B., *The Architecture of Mughal India* (Cambridge, UK, 2001)

Asher, Catherine B., and Cynthia Talbot, *India before Europe* (Cambridge, UK, 2006)

Babur, Zahir al-Din Muhammad, *The Baburnama: Memoirs of Babur, Prince and Emperor*, trans. and ed. Wheeler M. Thackston (Washington, DC, 1995)

Beach, Milo Cleveland, *Mughal and Rajput Painting* (Cambridge, UK, 1992)

Brand, Michael and Glenn Lowry, *Akbar's India: Art from the Mughal City of Victory* (New York, 1985)

Jahangir, Nur al-Din Muhammad, *The Jahangirnama: Memoirs of Jahangir, Emperor of India*, trans. and ed. Wheeler M. Thackston (Washington, DC, and New York, 1999)

Richards, John F., 'The Formulation of Imperial Authority under Akbar and Jahangir', in J.F. Richards, ed., *Authority and Kingship in South Asia* (New Delhi, 1998 [1978], reprint edn), 285–326

Richards, John F., *The Mughal Empire* (Cambridge, UK, 1993)

## Chapter seven  Japan: The Meiji Restoration 1868–1945

Beasley, W.G., *Japanese Imperialism, 1894–1945* (Oxford, 1987)

Dower, John, *War without Mercy: Race and Power in the Pacific War* (London and Boston, 1986)

Duus, Peter, 'The Takeoff Point of Japanese Imperialism', in Harry Wray and Hilary Conroy, eds, *Japan Examined: Perspectives on Modern Japanese History* (Honolulu, HI, 1983), 153–57

Duus, Peter, Ramon H. Myers and Mark R. Peattie, eds, *The Japanese Informal Empire in China, 1895–1937* (Princeton, NJ, 1989)

Duus, Peter, Ramon H. Myers and Mark R. Peattie, eds, *The Japanese Wartime Empire, 1931–1945* (Princeton, NJ, 1996)

Han, Jung-Sun N., 'Envisioning a Liberal Empire in East Asia: Yoshino Sakuzô in Taisho Japan', *Journal of Japanese Studies*, 33/2 (Summer 2003), 357–82

Hane, Mikiso, Peasants, *Rebels, and Outcastes: The Underside of Modern Japan* (New York, 1982)

Jansen, Marius, 'Modernization and Foreign Policy in Meiji Japan', in Robert E. Ward, ed., *Political Development in Modern Japan* (Princeton, NJ, 1968), 149–88

Keene, Donald, 'The Sino-Japanese War of 1894–1895 and Its Cultural Effects in Japan', in Donald Shively, ed., *Tradition and Modernization in Japanese Culture* (Princeton, NJ, 1971), 121–75

Kuramoto, Kazuko, *Manchurian Legacy: Memoirs of a Japanese Colonist* (East Lansing, MI, 2004)

Lebra, Joyce, ed., *Japan's Greater East Asia Co-Prosperity Sphere in World War II, Selected Readings and Documents* (Kuala Lumpur, 1975)

Liao, Ping-hui and David Der-Wei Wang, *Taiwan Under Japanese Colonial Rule, 1895–1945* (New York, 2006)

Lone, Stewart, *Japan's First Modern War* (London, 1994)

Myers, Ramon H. and Mark R. Peattie, eds, *The Japanese Colonial Empire, 1895–1945* (Princeton, NJ, 1984)

Newmann, William, *America Encounters Japan, From Perry to MacArthur* (Baltimore, MD, 1963)

Robinson, Michael Edson, *Cultural Nationalism in Colonial Korea, 1920–1925* (Seattle, WA, 1988)

Saaler, Sven and J. Victor Koschmann, eds, *Pan-Asianism in Modern Japanese History: Colonialism, Regionalism and Borders* (London, 2007)

Shin, Gi-Wook and Michael Robinson, eds, *Colonial Modernity in Korea* (Cambridge, MA, 1999)

Tamanoi, Mariko Asano, ed., *Crossed Histories: Manchuria in the Age of Empire* (Honolulu, HI, 2005)

Young, Louise, *Japan's Total Empire: Manchuria and the Culture of Wartime Imperialism* (Berkeley, CA, 1998), 364–82

## ILLUSTRATION SOURCES

Maps drawn by Drazen Tomic, © Thames & Hudson Ltd, London.

*First plates section (after page 96)*
I British Museum, London
II Staatsbibliothek, Berlin
III Davids Samling, Copenhagen
IV National Palace Museum, Taiwan
V iStockphoto.com
VI National Palace Museum, Taiwan
VII Luciano Mortula/iStockphoto.com
VIII Helen Ibbitson Jessup
IX Thomas Bradford/iStockphoto.com
X Luciano Mortula/iStockphoto.com
XI Topkapi Sarayi Museum, Istanbul
XII Topkapi Sarayi Museum, Istanbul
XIII Murat Sen/iStockphoto.com
XIV Library of Congress, Washington, DC

*Second plates section (after page 160)*
XV Freer Gallery of Art and Arthur M. Sackler Gallery, Smithsonian Institution, Washington, DC
XVI Serdar Yagci/ iStockphoto.com
XVII Department of Islamic Art, Musée du Louvre, Paris
XVIII British Museum, London
XIX Seniz Yoruk/ iStockphoto.com
XX Victoria & Albert Museum, London
XXI iStockphoto.com
XXII Victoria & Albert Museum, London
XXIII Royal Asiatic Society, London
XXIV The Nour Foundation, New York
XXV Hiroshige Utagawa/Library of Congress, Washington, DC
XXVI Felice Beato
XXVII Hayakawa Hiroshi

# CONTRIBUTORS

## The Editor

**Jim Masselos** is an Honorary Reader in the History Department of the University of Sydney and a founding member of both the Asian Arts Society of Australia and the South Asian Studies Association of Australia. His broad-ranging research on the social history and visual culture of India includes modern South Asian history and historiography, Indian art and religion, and the city of Mumbai. His publications include *The City in Action: Bombay Struggles for Power* (2007) and (as co-author) *Dancing to the Flute: Music and Dance in Indian Art* (1997).

## The Contributors

**Gábor Ágoston** was born and educated in Hungary. He is currently Associate Professor at the University of Georgetown, where he teaches courses on Ottoman and Middle Eastern history, the Balkans and the Black Sea. In 2003 he was Gastprofessor at the University of Vienna. He published *Guns of the Sultan: Military Power and the Weapons Industry in the Ottoman Empire* in 2005. He is also co-author and co-editor of the first English-language *Encyclopedia of the Ottoman Empire*, published in 2009.

**Catherine Asher** of the Department of Art History at the University of Minnesota is a specialist in Islamic and Indian art from 1200 to the present. She has written *Architecture of Mughal India* (1992) and co-authored *India before Europe* (2006).

**Sussan Babaie**, who is herself Iranian, is Dr Andrew W. Mellon Reader in the Arts of Iran and Islam at the Courtauld Institute of Art, London. She was previously Visiting Scholar at the Getty Research Institute and Fulbright Regional Scholar, Egypt and Syria. Her publications include *Isfahan and Its Palaces* (2008) and, as co-editor, *The Mercantile Effect: Art and Exchange in the Islamicate World During the 17th and 18th Centuries* (2018).

**Helen Ibbitson Jessup** is a scholar and curator specializing in the art and architecture of South East Asia. She curated and co-authored *Sculpture of Angkor and Ancient Cambodia* (1997) and wrote *Art and Architecture of Cambodia* (2005). She is also the author of *Masterpieces of the National Museum of Cambodia* (2006).

**Timothy May**, a leading expert on the Mongol empire, is Associate Dean and Professor of Middle Eastern and Central Asian History at the University of North Georgia. In 2006, May was honoured by the Mongolian Academy of Sciences for his contributions to the writing of Mongolian history. His publications include *The Mongol Art of War* (2007), *Cultures and Customs of Mongolia* (2009) and *The Mongol Conquests in World History* (2012).

**J.A.G. Roberts** is Principal Lecturer at the University of Huddersfield, specializing in the history of China and Japan. His publications include *China to Chinatown: Chinese Food in the West* (2002), *A History of China* (2nd edn, 2006) and *Life in Early China* (2008).

**Elise Kurashige Tipton** is Honorary Associate Professor of Japanese Studies in the School of Languages and Cultures of the University of Sydney. Her publications include *Modern Japan: A Social and Political History* (2nd edn, 2008).

# INDEX